Recognising Symptoms

GEDDES & GROSSET

© 1996 Geddes & Grosset
David Dale House, New Lanark Scotland, ML11 9DJ

First published 1996
Published in this edition 2000
Reprinted 2001

All rights reserved. No part of this publication may be reproduced, stored in a retrieval system, or transmitted, in any form or by any means, electronic, mechanical, photocopying, recording or otherwise, without the prior permission of the copyright holder

ISBN 1 85534 943 4

Printed and bound in the UK

Typeset by Palimpsest Book Production Ltd.
Polmont, Stirlingshire

Contents

Symptoms and Self-Diagnosis: 5
A Word of Warning

Quick Reference to Symptoms   7

A–Z of Illnesses and Disorders   23

Symptoms and Self-Diagnosis:

A Word of Warning

From even a brief study of the contents of this book, it will be apparent that most illnesses and disorders produce a range of symptoms. For any given illness or condition, certain symptoms may be more pronounced in one individual than in another. Diagnosis is a skilled undertaking, which must always be carried out by a doctor and not from the pages of a book. Also, it is overwhelmingly the case that early diagnosis and treatment produce the best results and outlook for the patient. If you are experiencing any symptoms, however slight, that are causing you concern, you should always consult your doctor and not attempt to diagnose and treat yourself.

Given the variable nature of the symptoms of many illnesses and disorders, the latter may be listed under more than one heading in the Quick Reference to Symptoms on page 7.

Quick Reference to Symptoms

HEAD AND NECK

headache that may be accompanied by other symptoms, e.g. numbness or weakness, nausea and vomiting, confusion, vision disturbance

Possible cause:
aneurysm	33
brain abscess	48
brain tumour	49
Caisson disease	58
carbon monoxide poisoning	59
concussion	72
encephalitis	92
glaucoma	110
head injury	123
heatstroke	125
hypertension	135
meningitis	166
migraine	169
phaeochromocytoma	198
polycythaemia	206
polymyalgia rheumatica	206
sinusitis	244
subarachnoid haemorrhage	253
subdural haemorrhage	255

dizziness, loss of balance, fainting, convulsions, paralysis and loss of consciousness *see* **general symptoms**

eyes and eyelids – inflammation, itching, pain, discharge, swelling, protrusion

Possible cause:
blepharitis	44
conjunctivitis	73
corneal foreign bodies	75

Recognising Symptoms

entropion	93
exophthalmos	97
iritis	141
keratitis	145
ptosis	213
scleritis	238
stye	253
subconjunctival haemorrhage	254
trichinosis	274

eyes – visual disturbance, loss of vision

Possible cause:

brain abscess	48
brain tumour	49
cataract	62
glaucoma	110
Graves' disease	116
head injury	123
hydrocephalus	133
iritis	141
migraine	169
phaeochromocytoma	198
polycythaemia	206
ptosis	213
retinal detachment	226
senile macular degeneration	240
stroke	252
tapeworms	258
thromboembolism	265
toxoplasmosis	271
transient ischaemic attack	273
trichinosis	274

ears – discharge, pain, ringing noise, nausea, vomiting, deafness, dizziness

Possible cause:

deafness	81
labyrinthitis	149
Ménières disease	165
otitis externa	188
otitis media	188
otosclerosis	188
ruptured eardrum	234

nose – abnormal, profuse discharge or sudden bleeding

Possible cause:

leishmaniasis	153
leptospirosis	153
leukaemia	154
sinusitis	244
thrombocytopaenia	264
typhoid fever	277

mouth – soreness, ulceration, dryness, bleeding

Possible cause:

agranulocytosis	26
botulism	48
candidiasis	59
cold sores	70
hand, foot and mouth disease	121
pemphigus	194
sprue	249
systemic lupus erythematosus	257
tetanus	261
thrombocytopaenia	264
tooth abscess	268

mouth – paralysis or difficulty with speech

Bell's palsy	42
Friedreich's ataxia	102
Parkinson's disease	193
stroke	252

neck – swelling, redness or rash, possibly with swollen glands

Possible cause:

Cushing's syndrome	79
diphtheria	85
German measles	108
glandular fever	109
goitre	112
hyperthyroidism	136
Kawasaki disease	145
laryngeal cancer	149
Lassa fever	151
lupus erythematosus	159
lymphoma	161

Recognising Symptoms

oesophageal cancer	183
salivary gland enlargement	234
scarlet fever	236
systemic lupus erythematosus	257
thyroid gland tumour	267
tonsillitis	268

neck – sudden, spontaneous stiffness
Possible cause:

encephalitis	92
meningitis	166
polymyalgia rheumatica	206
subarachnoid haemorrhage	253

throat – soreness, coughing, hoarseness
Possible cause:

agranulocytosis	26
bronchitis	53
candidiasis	59
chicken pox	66
croup	78
diphtheria	85
German measles	108
glandular fever	109
hand, foot and mouth disease	121
hay fever	121
influenza	140
laryngeal cancer	149
laryngitis	150
pharyngitis	198
tonsillitis	268
typhoid fever	277

CHEST

chest pain
Possible cause:

aneurysm	33
angina pectoris	34
aortic valve disease	35
atherosclerosis	40
atrial fibrillation	41

coronary artery disease	76
coronary thrombosis	77
heartburn	124
hiatus hernia	130
neuralgia (ribs)	179
pericarditis	195
pleurisy	200
pulmonary embolism	214
pulmonary hypertension	215
pulmonary valve stenosis	216
Wolf-Parkinson White syndrome	285

chest pain with other symptoms, e.g. breathing difficulty, cough, fever, chills

Possible cause:

angina pectoris	34
aortic valve disease	35
asbestosis	37
atrial fibrillation	41
bronchiectasis	52
bronchiolitis	52
bronchitis (acute and chronic)	53
cardiomyopathy	60
emphysema	91
legionnaire's disease	152
lung abscess	158
lung cancer	158
mesothelioma	167
pericarditis	195
pleurisy	200
pneumoconiosis	201
pneumonia	202
pneumothorax	203
silicosis	243
tapeworms (in children)	258
tuberculosis	275

breathlessness, wheezing, difficulty in breathing, cyanosis (blue tinge to the skin), anxiety *see also* **chest pain with other symptoms**

Possible cause:

adult respiratory distress sydrome	25
allergy	28

Recognising Symptoms

anaphylactic shock	32
asthma (severe)	39
croup (in children)	78
cystic fibrosis (in children)	80
diphtheria	85
epiglottitis (usually children)	93
hay fever	121
hyperventilation	136
mitral incompetence	169
mitral stenosis	170
pulmonary oedema	215
roundworms	233
shock	241
whooping cough (in children)	283

breast – tenderness or pain with swelling or mass, possibly including swelling of lymph nodes in armpit etc

Possible cause:

breast abscess	50
breast cancer	50
mastitis	163

ABDOMEN

abdominal pain, sudden or severe

Possible cause:

abruptio placentae (in pregnancy)	23
appendicitis	36
cholecystitis	67
colic	70
colitis	71
Crohn's disease	78
ectopic pregnancy (in women)	90
gallstones	104
hernia	128
ileitis	139
intestinal obstruction	140
liver abscess	156
ovarian cyst (ruptured–in women)	189
ovarian tumours (in women)	190
pancreatic cancer	191

pancreatitis	192
peritonitis	196
porphyria	208
stomach ulcer	251
threadworms (in children)	263

gastrointestinal symptoms – diarrhoea, nausea, vomiting, abdominal swelling, abdominal pain, indigestion, constipation, weight loss, abnormal faeces

Possible cause:

appendicitis	36
cholecystitis	67
cholera	67
coeliac disease (in children)	69
constipation	73
Crohn's disease	78
diverticular disease	86
dysentery	88
fascioliasis	97
food poisoning	101
gallstones	104
gastritis	106
gastroenteritis	107
giardiasis	109
hepatitis	126
hiatus hernia	130
hookworm disease	132
irritable bowel syndrome	142
roundworms (in children)	233
sprue (pale fatty stools)	249
stomach cancer	250
Wilm's tumour (in children)	284

profuse vomiting and vomiting of blood

Possible cause:

gastric erosion	106
hyperemesis gravidarum (in pregnancy)	134
oesophageal stricture	183
pyloric stenosis (in children)	217
stomach cancer	250
yellow fever	286

Recognising Symptoms

BACK, LIMBS AND JOINTS AND MUSCLES

back – lower back pain, sudden or severe

Possible cause:

ankylosing spondylitis	35
endometriosis (in women)	92
kidney stones	148
osteoporosis	186
pancreatic cancer	191
polycystic disease of the kidney	205
prolapsed intervertebral disc	210
pyelitis	216
sciatica	238
spondylosis	247

joints and limbs – pain with general stiffness and weakness and other symptoms such as swelling, inflammation and pain

Possible cause:

anaphylactic shock	32
atherosclerosis	40
bursitis	57
carpal tunnel syndrome	61
dislocation	85
Ewing's sarcoma	97
frozen shoulder	103
glomerulonephritis	111
gout	114
Legg-Calvé Perthes' disease	151
nephrotic syndrome	178
Osgood-Schlatter's disease	184
osteoarthritis	184
osteomyelitis	186
osteosarcoma	187
Paget's disease of the bone	190
polymyalgia rheumatica	206
psoriasis	212
rheumatic fever	228
rheumatoid arthritis	229
spinal cord tumour	247
Still's disease (in children)	250
systemic lupus erythematosus	257
tendinitis	260

limb weakness and fatigue with restriction of movement and mobility or paralysis

Possible cause:

multiple sclerosis	171
muscular dystrophy	173
myalgic encephalomyelitis	174
myasthenia gravis	175
neuritis	180
osteogenesis imperfecta	185
polymyositis	207
Raynaud's disease (in fingers)	221
scleroderma (in fingers)	239

leg – pain and tenderness

Possible cause:

atherosclerosis	40
Buerger's disease	55
fibrositis	100
thromboembolism	265
thrombophlebitis	265
thrombosis	266
varicose veins	281

general muscular weakness, twitches or spasms – abnormal and involuntary

Possible cause:

cerebral palsy	64
convulsions	74
epilepsy	94
Guillain–Barré syndrome	117
Huntingdon's chorea	132
multiple sclerosis	171
Parkinson's disease	193
tetanus (including face)	261

RECTUM AND ANUS

rectum – bleeding, pain and blood in faeces

Possible cause:

anal fissure	32
cirrhosis of the liver	68
colitis	71

Recognising Symptoms

constipation	73
dysentery	88
gastric erosion	106
haemorrhoids	120
hepatoma	127
polyarteritis nodosa	204
rectal abscess	222
rectal prolapse	222
rectal tumour	223
small intestine tumours	246
stomach cancer	250
stomach ulcer	251
thrombocytopaenia	264

REPRODUCTIVE SYSTEM

vagina – abnormal bleeding from

Possible cause:

abruptio placentae (in pregnancy)	23
cervical cancer	65
ectopic pregnancy	90
endometriosis	92
fibroid	99
placenta praevia (in pregnancy)	200
thrombocytopaenia (post surgical)	264
uterine cancer	279
vaginal cancer	279

vagina – abnormal discharge from

Possible cause:

candidiasis	59
cervical cancer	65
fibroid	99
gonorrhoea	113
non-specific urethritis	181
pelvic inflammatory disease	194
threadworms (in chidren)	263
vaginitis	280

penis – abnormal discharge, pain or ulceration (*see also* **frequency of urine with pain or burning sensation on passing,**

possibly with other symptoms, e.g. discharge of bleeding or discharge)

Possible cause:
gonorrhoea	113
non-specific urethritis	181
Reiter's syndrome	223
syphilis	256

testicles – swelling and pain

Possible cause:
testicular cancer	261
tortion of a testis	269

SKIN

lesions, pustules, ulcers or swelling with possible accompanying symptoms of illness, e.g. fever, malaise, aches and pains, headaches, itching and tenderness

Possible cause:
acne	23
agranulocytosis	26
AIDS	26
athlete's foot	41
boil	46
Buerger's disease	55
candidiasis	59
chilblain	66
cold sores	70
corns and bunions	75
dermatitis	83
diabetes mellitus	84
eczema	90
erythema	95
erythroderma	96
erythromelalgia	96
frostbite	103
granuloma annulare	115
hand, foot and mouth disease	121
herpes simplex infection	129
icthyosis	138
impetigo	139
Kaposi's sarcoma	144

Recognising Symptoms

keratosis	146
lipoma	155
lupus erythematosus	159
melanoma	164
pemphigus	194
psoriasis	212
Raynaud's disease	221
Reiter's syndrome	223
ringworm	230
rodent ulcer	231
scabies	236
scleroderma	239
shingles	240
skin cancer	245
sporotrichosis	248
syphilis	256
thalassaemia	262
varicose veins	281
warts	282
yaws	285

skin – rash with accompanying symptoms of fever, aches and pains, and chills

Possible cause:

allergy	28
anaphylactic shock	32
chicken pox	66
German measles	108
Lassa fever	151
lupus erythematosus	159
Rocky Mountain spotted fever	230
rosacea	232
roseola infantum	232
scarlet fever	236
sleeping sickness	245
systemic lupus erythematosus	257
thrombocytopaenia	264

skin – yellow, jaundiced appearance or discoloration

Possible cause:

cholecystitis	67
cirrhosis of the liver	68
fascioliasis	97

favism	98
gallstones	104
gangrene	105
haemolytic disease of the newborn	117
hepatitis	126
hepatoma	127
jaundice	143
leptospirosis	153
lymphoma	161
methahaemoglobinaemia	168
myxoedema	177
pancreatic cancer	191
pancreatitis	192
relapsing fever	224
sickle-cell anaemia	242
thalassaemia	262
toxoplasmosis	271
yellow fever	286

URINARY SYSTEM

urine – frequency of, pain or burning sensation on passing, possibly with other symptoms, e.g. blood in urine or urethral discharge or bleeding

Possible cause:

bladder stones	43
bladder tumour	44
cystitis	81
glomerulonephritis (in children)	111
gonorrhoea	113
hypernephroma	134
non-specific urethritis	181
ovarian cyst	189
prostate gland cancer	210
prostate gland enlargement	211
pyelitis	216
schistosomiasis (tropical disease)	237
thrombocytopaenia	264
urethra, stricture of	278
vaginal cancer	279
Wilm's tumour (in children)	284

Recognising Symptoms

urine – retention of or significant reduction in amount passed

Possible cause:

botulism	48
kidney failure (acute)	147
nephrotic syndrome	178
polyarteritis nodosa	204
prostate gland enlargement	211
yellow fever	286

urine – dark or discoloured and/or strong-smelling

Possible cause:

cirrhosis of the liver	68
cystitis	81
jaundice	143
porphyria	208
tuberculosis	275

urine – passing large amounts, possible pale coloured

Possible cause:

diabetes insipidus	84
diabetes mellitus	84
glomerulonephritis (acute–in children)	111

PSYCHOLOGICAL DISTURBANCE

behavioural changes – confusion, loss of memory, abnormal fatigue, aggression, etc

Possible cause:

alcoholism	27
Alzheimer's disease	30
brain tumour	49
catalepsy	61
catatonia	63
concussion	72
delirium	82
dementia	83
drug abuse	87
head injury	123
Huntingdon's chorea	132
hypothermia	137
myxoedema	177
narcolepsy	178

porphyria	208
rabies	219
Reye's syndrome (in children)	227
stroke	252
syphilis	256

GENERAL SYMPTOMS

sudden fever, fatigue and weakness, dizziness, chills, aches and pains, with possible other symptoms, e.g. weight loss, fainting, rapid pulse, vomiting and nausea

Possible cause:

Addison's disease	24
AIDS	26
anaemia	30
atrial fibrillation	41
blood poisoning	45
botulism	48
brain abscess	48
brucellosis	55
cat scratch fever	63
dengue	83
diabetes insipidus	84
diabetes mellitus	84
encephalitis	92
fever	98
heat exhaustion	125
heatstroke	125
Hodgkin's disease	131
influenza	140
Lassa fever	151
listeriosis	156
malaria	161
myalgic encephalomyelitis	174
psittacosis	212
Q fever	218
rat bite fever	220
relapsing fever	224
renal carbuncle	225
renal tuberculosis	226
sandfly fever	235

Recognising Symptoms

    sinus node disease   244
    toxic shock syndrome   270
    toxoplasmosis   271
    typhoid fever   277

loss of balance, dizziness, fainting, convulsions, paralysis and loss of consciousness

    Possible cause:
    brain compression   49
    epilepsy   94
    labyrinthitis   149
    stroke   252
    transient ischaemic attack   273
    vasovagal attack   282

bleeding or bruising – spontaneous or abnormal

    Possible cause:
    AIDS   26
    anaemia   30
    haemophilia   118
    haemorrhage   119
    Lassa fever   151
    leukaemia   154
    polycythaemia   206
    thrombocytopaenia   264

A–Z of Illnesses and Disorders

A

abruptio placentae
Description: bleeding from the placenta after the 28th week of pregnancy, which may result in the placenta becoming completely or partially separated from the wall of the uterus (womb).
Persons affected: females during pregnancy.
Organ or part of body involved: uterus.
Symptoms and indications: these depend upon the degree of separation of the placenta and so range from slight to severe but include bleeding from the vagina, pain in the abdomen and abdominal hardness. In very serious untreated cases: maternal shock and foetal distress with possible fatal outcome for both mother and baby.
Always tell your doctor if you experience bleeding at any time during pregnancy.
Treatment: Admittance to hospital for rest and observation. An ultrasound examination is usually carried out to establish the diagnosis of abruptio placentae as the symptoms are very similar to those of PLACENTA PRAEVIA. If the bleeding is slight, the foetus is in good health and the pregnancy is not near to term, continued bed rest is required until the bleeding stops. If the bleeding worsens, delivery of the foetus by Caesarian section is usually required. (Delivery may sometimes be vaginal if labour has already started.)
Causes and risk factors: the cause is unknown, but abruptio placentae is more likely to occur in women who already have children, who are aged over 35 and who smoke. Also it may result from an accidental blow in the abdominal region.

acne or **acne vulgaris**
Description: a disorder of the skin, especially common in adolescents, characterised by the presence of pustules and blackheads on the face, upper back, chest and shoulders. It is associated with the sebaceous (oil-secreting) glands in the skin.
Persons most commonly affected: adolescents, especially boys.

acne rosacea

Organ or part of body involved: skin.
Symptoms and indications: presence on the skin of blackheads, pustules and whiteheads. The surrounding skin may be inflamed, red and sore, especially with scratching.
Treatment: the skin should be carefully and thoroughly washed and dried, and the spots should not be scratched or squeezed to avoid scarring of the skin. Sunlight is helpful, and acne is often worse in the winter months than during the summer. The use of a topical preparation containing benzoyl peroxide, tretinoin (retinoic acid), salicylic acid, vitamin A and/or clindamycin may be recommended by your doctor. Some cosmetics aggravate acne and should be avoided. Also, it is possible that certain foods make the condition worse in some people. Acne in adolescence usually clears up with time.
Causes and risk factors: increased production of androgen hormones at puberty, blockage of sebaceous glands and the breakdown of sebum (the secretion of the glands by bacteria (propionibacterium acnes) seem to be responsible for the inflammation that causes acne.

acne rosacea *see* ROSACEA

Addison's disease

Description: a disease caused by the destruction or failure of the cortex of the adrenal glands, so that there is insufficient secretion of the adrenocortical hormones (cortisol, aldosterol and androgens).
Persons most commonly affected: all age groups and both sexes.
Organ or part of body involved: adrenal glands situated above the kidneys.
Symptoms and indications: weakness, fatigue, wasting, anorexia and weight loss, which may be accompanied by gastrointestinal upset including diarrhoea and sickness; low blood pressure with symptoms of dizziness, fainting and feeling cold; dark pigmentation of the skin and loss of underarm hair in women; mood changes, depression.
Treatment: hormone replacement therapy to restore adrenocortical hormones, which effects a complete cure.
Causes and risk factors: in the past, Addison's disease often occurred in patients with tuberculosis, which caused damage to or destruction of the adrenal gland cortex. Today this damage is more commonly caused by disturbances in the immune system (autoimmune damage) and, more rarely, secondary cancerous growths. Damage to the adrenal glands through accidental injury, diabetes mellitus and stress are conditions that may increase the risk of developing Addison's disease.

adult respiratory distress syndrome (ARDS)

Description: severe respiratory failure, which is often fatal, brought about by a number of different disorders. In newborn babies, a similar condition is known as hyaline membrane disease.

Persons most commonly affected: adults and children (except newborn) of both sexes and all ages.

Symptoms and indications: a lack of oxygen in the blood, which is indicated by a blueness (cyanosis) of the skin, an abnormally rapid rate of breathing (tachypnoea) and a raised heartbeat rate (tachycardia). There is pulmonary oedema (a collection of fluid in the lungs) and the substance known as surfactant, which prevents the lungs' sacs (alveoli) from collapsing and allows oxygen to pass in and carbon dioxide to pass out, is lost. These conditions lead to the lungs becoming stiff and ineffective; death follows without emergency medical intervention. A person with signs of this disorder requires urgent medical treatment.

Treatment: intensive care treatment, including mechanical ventilation of the lungs and management of the patient's fluid balance to reduce pulmonary oedema. Also, the underlying cause of the respiratory failure is treated if this is possible. Surfactant may be given by means of a nebuliser or aerosol.

Causes and risk factors: there are a variety of different causes of this disorder, which may be broadly divided into four categories:
- Physical causes, including injury to the lungs, inhalation of water as in drowning, vomit or other foreign substance.
- Bacterial, viral or fungal infection of the lungs or other part of the body, as in various diseases including PNEUMONIA, sepsis, poliomyelitis.
- As a response by the patient's immune system following blood transfusion or cardiopulmonary bypass surgery.
- Accidental inhalation of poisonous fumes and smoke, ingestion of certain chemicals and drugs.
- As a complication of various other diseases and disorders, including ASTHMA, EMPHYSEMA, MUSCULAR DYSTROPHY, PANCREATITIS, GUILLAIN-BARRÉ SYNDROME, uraemia, MYASTHENIA GRAVIS.

Patients who receive mechanical ventilation for a long period may develop complications in the form of secondary infections and PNEUMOTHORAX, which require additional treatment. The survival rate for patients with this condition is about 50%, and those who respond well suffer little lung damage. There is a greater likelihood of lung damage in those patients needing prolonged mechanical ventilation.

African trypansomiasis

African trypansomiasis *see* SLEEPING SICKNESS

agranulocytosis
Description: an abnormality of the blood involving white blood cells, called granulocytes or neutrophils, which are a vital part of the body's defence or immune system.
Persons most commonly affected: all age groups and both sexes.
Organ or part of body involved: blood and bone marrow.
Symptoms and indications: fever, aches and pains, sore throat, with ulcers in mouth and throat. Ulcers may also occur in the rectum and vagina. A person with this condition requires prompt medical treatment.
Treatment: admittance to hospital for intensive treatment with antibiotics and, possibly, transfusion of white blood cells. Patient requires to be isolated to avoid or lessen the possibility of acquiring infections. Once the condition is improving, strict attention should be paid to cleanliness and hygiene (particularly oral hygiene) until cured. The condition is usually curable but can be rapidly fatal if a severe and dangerous infection develops.
Causes and risk factors: agranulocytosis is caused by an abnormal fall in or even absence of granulocytes because of destruction of these cells or failure of the bone marrow to produce them. This itself usually results from an adverse reaction to certain drugs, including immunosuppressants and anticancer drugs, sulphonamides, chloramphenicol and others. Certain chemicals may also produce the disease. A person who has recovered from agranulocytosis should avoid drugs or chemicals that were suspected of causing the condition.

AIDS
Description: acquired immune deficiency syndrome, first recognised in Los Angeles, USA, in 1981, which affects the body's natural defence or immune system. The person slowly and progressively succumbs to various infections and tumours that eventually prove to be fatal.
Persons most commonly affected: all age groups and both sexes but affected infants acquire the condition at birth from mothers who have AIDS.
Organ or part or body involved: the immune system, especially cells known as T-lymphocytes and lymph glands, bone marrow, liver and spleen.
Symptoms and indications: early symptoms include enlargement of lymph glands and spleen, fever, fatigue, bruising and bleeding easily, THRUSH-type infections, diarrhoea and weight loss, DERMATITIS and

respiratory illnesses. Later, a person develops further serious infections or cancers. These include herpes infections, PNEUMONIA, MENINGITIS, serious gastrointestinal disorders (e.g. salmonella infections), KAPOSI'S SARCOMA and NON-HODGKIN'S LYMPHOMA. A number of illnesses may occur, some of which are particularly associated with AIDS and are known as 'AIDS indicator conditions'.

Treatment: the symptoms of AIDS-related infections can be alleviated with appropriate drug treatments, if not entirely cured. Other drugs, such as dideoxyinosine and zidovudine, may be useful, and many other preparations are helpful depending on the nature of the symptoms.

Causes and risk factors: AIDS is caused by a virus called human immunodeficiency virus (HIV), a ribonucleic (RNA) retrovirus. The presence of the virus can be established by a blood test, and it is generally accepted that a person infected with HIV will eventually develop AIDS, although there may be a period of many years without signs of illness. HIV is transmitted in blood and body fluids. Those generally accepted to be at risk are sexually active persons who have sexual intercourse with partners infected with HIV. (The use of barrier methods of contraception lessens the risk of infection.) Also, intravenous drug users who share needles that may be contaminated and babies born to mothers who have the HIV virus or AIDS. Hospital, dental and medical staff need to follow strict procedures to guard against the possibility of infection. Ordinary social or family contact with a person who has HIV or AIDS is generally accepted to pose no risk of the infection being passed on.

alcoholism

Description: a physical and psychological need, and dependence on alcohol to such an extent that deprivation may result in withdrawal symptoms. The continued and long-term overconsumption (abuse) of alcoholic drink leads to both physical and mental illness. The person's behaviour may become so disordered and disruptive that he or she loses employment, family, friends and home unless counselling and medical help are sought and accepted.

Persons most commonly affected: both sexes and all age groups after adolescence, although more common in males.

Organ or part of body involved: brain, liver, heart.

Symptoms and indications: early indications include the need for an alcoholic drink first thing in the morning before the person does anything else, and it being noticed by others that the person is drinking too much. Also, disturbance of sleep, irritability, attempts to conceal amount being drunk and irritation when overconsumption

is suggested. In addition, the person may need to take time off work because of the effects of drinking and may become sexually impotent. Later on, an alcoholic person may become unconscious because of drink, or die from respiratory failure. He or she may suffer from withdrawal symptoms (including hallucinations, fear and imagined persecution, delirium tremens) if drink is withdrawn and experience loss of memory. The person may develop CIRRHOSIS OF THE LIVER, inflammation and ulceration of the gastrointestinal tract and PANCREATITIS. There may be inflammation of peripheral nerves, causing numbness and tingling sensations in hands and feet, and congestive heart failure. A form of DEMENTIA may eventually develop. The physical diseases that result from alcoholism are liable to cause premature death. The unborn child of an alcoholic mother is likely to suffer lasting damage.
Treatment: the success or otherwise of treatment depends on a recognition by the alcoholic person that a problem exists, and a willingness to overcome it. Treatment includes detoxification ('drying out'), counselling and joining a support group such as Alcoholics Anonymous. Physical diseases associated with alcoholism may require appropriate medical and drug therapy and are likely to improve once drinking stops.
Causes and risk factors: the causes are not entirely clear, but some researchers believe that a genetic element exists and some people are more inclined to alcoholism than others. Personality and the environment in which a person lives (e.g. a young person in a family or social group in which alcohol is important) and stress related to work and family and personal relationships are all significant contributory factors. Many people are successfully cured.

allergy
Description: a state of hypersensitivity (or heightened or oversensitivity) in an affected individual to a particular substance, called the 'allergen'. This produces a characteristic response whenever the person is exposed to the allergen.
Persons most commonly affected: both sexes and all age groups.
Organ or part of body involved: various parts of the body depending on the nature of the allergy but including skin, respiratory system, joints and gastrointestinal system.
Symptoms and indications: symptoms usually develop rapidly, within a few minutes, and depend on the nature of the allergy (*see also* ANAPHYLACTIC SHOCK, ASTHMA, DERMATITIS, ECZEMA, HAY FEVER). Common symptoms include nettle rash and skin reactions, swellings and puffiness, e.g. around eyes, wheezing and breathing difficulties,

headaches, stomach pains, sickness and diarrhoea. Medical advice should be sought.

Treatment: this depends upon the nature of the reaction but commonly involves the taking of antihistamine drugs. If the allergic response is more serious, as in an asthma attack, hospital treatment may be required, with the administration of bronchodilator and corticosteroid drugs by inhalation. If the allergic response is in the rare form of anaphylactic shock, prompt emergency treatment is necessary with the administration of adrenaline by means of an injection. This condition is fatal unless emergency treatment is promptly received.

Causes and risk factors: in a nonallergic, unaffected person, antibodies present in the bloodstream destroy their particular allergens (antigens). However, in an allergic, affected person this reaction causes some cell damage and there is a release of substances such as histamine and bradykinin, which cause the reaction. Many substances, usually of a protein nature, can be allergens. The list includes many common foods, such as eggs, strawberries and shellfish, colourings and additives used in foods, plants and pollen, mites or dust from animals such as cats, dogs, horses and the feathers of birds. If the allergen is known then it may be possible for the individual to avoid exposure to it. Sometimes it is possible to decrease sensitivity to a particular allergen by gradually increasing exposure under careful medical supervision. However, a person may be allergic to a range of substances. In many people there may be a genetic element, with a family history of allergy.

altitude sickness

Description: also known as mountain sickness, this condition affects individuals (usually mountaineers) who are exposed to high altitudes to which they are unaccustomed.

Persons most commonly affected: both sexes and all age groups (normally adults).

Organ or part of body involved: lungs, respiratory system, blood, brain.

Symptoms and indications: rapid, deep breathing (hyperventilation), nausea, headache, exhaustion, anxiety. In severe cases, there may be breathing difficulties due to PULMONARY OEDEMA, caused by fluid collecting in the lungs, and this is a dangerous condition that may prove fatal.

Treatment: the person must be brought down to a lower altitude for rest and further acclimatisation. An individual with pulmonary oedema requires urgent medical treatment in hospital.

Alzheimer's disease

Causes and risk factors: the cause is climbing to a high altitude (above 3000 metres) too quickly without giving the body time to adjust to lower oxygen levels and reduced atmospheric pressure. This causes the person to breathe more deeply and rapidly (hyperventilate) with a consequent lowering of CO_2 levels in the blood. It is essential to allow the body to adjust by spending time at a particular altitude and attaining height gradually. Usually, the symptoms are relatively mild, but if they prove to be disabling the climber must return to a lower altitude.

Alzheimer's disease

Description: the commonest cause of DEMENTIA, being a degenerative disease of the cerebral cortex, characterised by gradual and progressive loss of mental faculties.

Persons most commonly affected: both sexes affecting people in middle and old age (over 40).

Organ or part of body involved: brain.

Symptoms and indications: the early indications are forgetfulness and increased difficulty in performing simple, normal tasks to which the person is well accustomed. There may be changes in personality out of character with the person's normal behaviour. There is a progressive deterioration in the person's mental and physical abilities and memory. In the very late stages of the disease, the person is incapable of any task, may be doubly incontinent, may have lost the power of speech, suffer from some paralysis and have total loss of memory. If symptoms are noticed, medical help should be sought.

Treatment: there is no cure or medication to halt the progress of the disease. In the early stages, as much mental activity as possible should be encouraged and carried out. Support and help is needed for the family of a person with Alzheimer's disease. It is usually desirable for the person to be placed in a nursing home in the later stages of the disease when home care becomes too difficult.

Causes and risk factors: the cause is not known but is the subject of ongoing, intensive research. Some researchers believe that there is a connection with the deposition of aluminium in brain cells. It is advisable to avoid cooking acidic fruits in aluminium pans to avoid contamination with aluminium.

amoebic dysentery *see* DYSENTERY

anaemia

Description: a decrease in the ability of the blood to carry oxygen because of a reduction in the number of red blood cells and/or the amount of haemoglobin that they contain. Haemoglobin is the

pigment within the red blood cells that binds to oxygen. There are a number of different kinds of anaemia, which may be usefully grouped into four main types:
- microcytic hypochromic anaemia;
- megaloblastic hyperchromic anaemia (see pernicious anaemia);
- aplastic anaemia;
- haemolytic anaemia.

In Britain, the great majority of cases of anaemia (90%) belong to the first group, about 7% to the second group, with the remaining 3% being of the aplastic or haemolytic type.

Persons most commonly affected: all age groups and both sexes but more common in females than in males.

Organ or part of body involved: blood, bone marrow.

Symptoms and indications: the symptoms of anaemia depend to a certain extent on the cause but more especially whether the onset is sudden or gradual. If it is sudden, as in the case of serious haemorrhage, the patient becomes weak and dizzy, may be unable to stand and may lose consciousness. Blood pressure drops, the breathing is fast and laboured, and there is a rapid pulse. In all cases of anaemia, the skin is pale and there is an absence of (or poor) colour inside the inner lower eyelid, if this is gently pulled down. The nails may be concave and brittle, the voice may be husky, and the tongue may be inflamed (glossitis) with accompanying difficulty in swallowing. The person often feels tired and generally weak, and not as well as usual. However, because the changes are sometimes gradual, the person may adapt and not be aware of them until the anaemia has become quite severe. If a person shows signs of anaemia, medical advice should be sought.

Treatment: this depends on the type of anaemia and the cause, but the aim of all treatment is to restore and maintain haemoglobin at normal levels in the blood. A person with serious haemorrhaging will require emergency medical treatment in hospital to stop the bleeding. Hospital treatment may also be required for patients with other forms of anaemia. In severe cases blood transfusions may be needed, but usually iron preparations (in the form of ferrous sulphate) are required until haemoglobin levels and red blood cell counts are normal.

Causes and risk factors: anaemia is caused by a fall in the number of red blood cells and haemoglobin in the blood, so that the oxygen-carrying capacity is reduced. As outlined above, the reasons for this are varied and depend on the type of anaemia. Causes include bleeding caused by injury or illness, menstruation, childbirth, haemophilia, gastrointestinal bleeding, haemorrhoids or piles, iron deficiency in the diet, or malabsorption of iron in the intestine because of disease. Also, some infections, toxins (especially those produced in certain kidney diseases), drugs (anticancer and immunosuppressives, nonsteroidal anti-inflammatory drugs, aspirin and chloramphenicol), and chemicals of the benzene type, are causes of anaemia.

anal fissure
Description: an abnormal break or tear in the skin and lining tissue surrounding the anus.
Persons most commonly affected: all age groups and both sexes, but it most often occurs in young children and infants and elderly people aged over 60 years. Also, more common in females than in males.
Organ or part of body involved: anus.
Symptoms and indications: sharp, stabbing pain and bleeding on passing stool with the pain possibly persisting for some time and then subsiding. A person with symptoms of anal fissure should seek medical advice.
Treatment: treatment involves the taking of certain preparations that soften the stool or act as laxatives, and the use of lubricating suppositories to ease stretching and protect the anal tissues. Healing usually occurs naturally after a certain period of time, but occasionally hospital treatment and surgery may be needed. Warm sitz baths (containing salt solution or plain water) are helpful in easing pain.
Causes and risk factors: the cause is thought to be overstretching of the anus from the passage of a hard, large stool, usually caused by constipation. To prevent constipation, plenty of fluids should be drunk and the diet should be high in fibre. An active lifestyle also helps to prevent constipation.

anaphylactic shock
Description: anaphylaxis is a response exhibited by a hypersensitive (highly sensitive) person when confronted with a particular substance or antigen. It results from the release of histamine in body tissues following the antigen-antibody reaction within cells. An allergic reaction is an example of mild anaphylaxis (*see* ALLERGY). Anaphylactic shock is a much rarer and more serious condition that can follow the injection of drugs or vaccines, or a bee sting, to which the person is hypersensitive. Its onset is immediate and results from a widespread release of histamine in the body.
Persons most commonly affected: all age groups and both sexes.
Organ or part of body involved: respiratory and circulatory system, skin and heart.

Symptoms and indications: the symptoms appear rapidly in the form of severe breathing difficulties, swelling (oedema), acute itching and rash (urticaria), a fall in blood pressure leading to fainting, and loss of consciousness. Heart failure leading to shock, cardiac arrest and death. Anaphylactic shock is a medical emergency and requires immediate prompt treatment.
Treatment: the only effective treatment is an intramuscular injection of adrenaline (epinephrine) that should be given as soon as possible. A person receiving prompt treatment usually makes a full recovery.
Causes and risk factors: there are a variety of causes for this condition, including vaccines, drugs and medications, especially if injected, wasp or bee stings and insect bites, and some foods such as peanuts, beans, shellfish, eggs and certain types of fruit. A person with a history of allergy in the form of ECZEMA, ASTHMA or HAY FEVER, or who has had a previous mild reaction to a particular substance, is likely to be at greater risk.

ancyclostomiasis *see* HOOKWORM DISEASE

aneurysm
Description: a balloon-like swelling of the wall of an artery that occurs when it becomes weakened or damaged in some way.
Persons most commonly affected: adult persons of both sexes, especially in older age.
Organ or part of body involved: arteries in any part but especially in the brain (circle of Willis), aorta or leg arteries.
Symptoms and indications: these vary a great deal depending on the site and size of the aneurysm. Pain may be present if the aneurysm compresses nerves, and also bulging, which may throb and contract and expand. A thoracic aneurysm may press on the windpipe and cause a hoarseness of the voice and a cough. A brain aneurysm may cause a throbbing headache and changes in the eyes (pupils of different sizes) or disturbances of vision. If the aneurysm affects the heart there may be disturbances of heartbeat rhythm and other symptoms of cardiac failure. Oedema also occurs, causing swelling of the skin because of interference with the circulation. An aneurysm is a medical emergency, and the doctor should be called immediately.
Treatment: hospital treatment and surgery to remove or isolate the aneurysm and restore the circulation by means of a graft or anastomosis (artificial joining of sections of the arteries involved). Anticoagulant drugs may be needed after surgery and penicillin if the aneurysm was caused by SYPHILIS.
Causes and risk factors: aneurysms occur because of a weakness in

the walls of the arteries, which is usually caused by atheroma or ATHEROSCLEROSIS (a degenerative disease of the arterial walls with scarring and a buildup of fatty deposits). Syphilis is another cause, especially affecting the aorta in the thorax. More rarely, there may be a congenital weakness affecting the arteries, especially in the case of aneurysms in the circle of Willis (a circle of arteries supplying, and sited beneath, the brain). The danger with aneurysm is that of rupture causing haemorrhage and death, and also the risk of stroke. Some changes in the arteries tend to occur naturally in older people. Atheroma or atherosclerosis is more likely to be a problem in people eating a diet rich in saturated fat. Smoking, obesity, high blood pressure and a sedentary lifestyle are additional contributory factors.

angina pectoris
Description: a pain and feeling of choking felt in the chest, brought on by exercise or exertion and relieved by rest. It occurs when the blood supply to the heart muscle is inadequate.
Persons most commonly affected: more common in men in middle and older age; postmenopausal women.
Organ or part of body involved: coronary arteries.
Symptoms and indications: the main symptom is pain behind the breastbone, brought on by exertion and relieved by rest. The pain may be more or less severe and often passes to the left arm and face. There may be a numbness or feeling of heaviness and tingling in the whole or part of the left arm. Also, there may be a feeling of choking and breathlessness and tightness across the chest. A person with symptoms of angina should always seek medical advice.
Treatment: diagnosis is usually confirmed in hospital by means of an electrocardiogram. Treatment involves rest and avoidance of the exertion that caused the angina attack. The patient needs to keep warm, especially in severe winter weather, and may need to adjust the diet and lose weight. Changes in lifestyle may be necessary to avoid tiredness and stress. Medication in the form of glyceryl trinitrate tablets (or amyl nitrite for inhalation) are used to bring immediate relief during an angina attack. It may be necessary for the patient to undergo coronary-artery bypass surgery or angioplasty.
Causes and risk factors: angina pectoris is caused by an inadequate blood supply to the heart muscle. During exercise, the demand for blood supplied by the coronary arteries is increased and if the supply is insufficient because the arteries are damaged, chest pain results. The most common reason for this damage is ATHEROSCLEROSIS or atheroma, along with spasm of the coronary arteries. Less commonly, aortic valve disease or disease in the aorta itself may be a cause of

angina pectoris. Factors thought to contribute to the development of this condition include inadequate exercise, a diet rich in saturated fats and salt, high blood pressure (HYPERTENSION), stress, obesity, smoking and DIABETES MELLITUS. Also, genetic factors, i.e. a family history of CORONARY-ARTERY DISEASE.

ankylosing spondylitis
Description: a progressive, inflammatory rheumatic disease affecting the spine and hip joints, characterised by stiffening and pain.
Persons most commonly affected: young males, the condition usually beginning between the ages of 10 and 40. It is rare in females.
Organ or part of body involved: sacroiliac region, hips and spine, sometimes affecting joints in the hand, arm and shoulder.
Symptoms and indications: in the early stages there is lower back pain in the lumbar region and stiffness, especially on rising in the morning. Later the disease progresses to involve the whole spine, and fibrous tissue replaces and fuses spinal discs and ligaments. Eventually, the whole spine may become rigid, and the patient's body may be bent forward. This is called a 'bamboo' or 'poker' spine. A person with back pain should seek medical advice.
Treatment: this involves taking non-steroidal anti-inflammatory drugs and physiotherapy, with special exercises designed to maintain the flexibility of the spine. At the present time there is no known cure, and the disease progresses slowly over a number of years. However, symptoms can be alleviated, and it is desirable for an affected person to stay as active as possible. Activities that may stress the back should be avoided, but exercise, especially swimming, is helpful. There is a possibility of other conditions developing in a patient with ankylosing spondylitis.
Causes and risk factors: the cause is unknown, but there is a genetic link and a tendency for the condition to run in families.

anorectal abscess *see* RECTAL ABSCESS

aortic valve disease
Description: disease of the aortic valve of the heart, which occurs in two forms – either a narrowing (stenosis) or a widening and scarring causing leaking (incompetence) of the valve. As a result, the left ventricle has to work harder in order to maintain the blood flow into the aorta and become thicker (hypertrophy). In the case of a leaking aortic valve, there is a backflow of blood into the ventricle, causing dilation.
Persons most commonly affected: both sexes and all age groups but more common in older people.

Organ or part of body involved: heart.
Symptoms and indications: these vary in severity according to the extent of damage to the valve. They commonly include breathlessness, ANGINA PECTORIS, dizziness and fainting, and heart murmur. A person with symptoms of heart disease should always seek medical attention.
Treatment: the usual form of treatment in severe cases is surgical, in the form of an operation to replace the defective valve. Also, drugs of various kinds are likely to be required, depending on the nature of the disease. These may include anti-arrhythmic drugs, antibiotics and other heart drugs. A change to a low-salt and low-fat diet may be advised.
Causes and risk factors: in the case of aortic stenosis, the usual cause is a degeneration and calcification that occurs with advancing age. However, the other causes include RHEUMATIC FEVER and a congenital, inherited defect in which the valve has two cusps instead of the normal three. Both of these cause scarring, calcification and narrowing. The causes of a leaking aortic valve include those listed above but, in addition, SYPHILIS, inflammation (ENDOCARDITIS) of the heart and aortic ANEURYSM. Also, HYPERTENSION (high blood pressure) and an inherited disease of connective tissue called Marfan's syndrome. A person who has had rheumatic fever in childhood is more likely to be at risk of heart valve disease in later life.

apoplexy *see* STROKE

appendicitis (acute)
Description: the vermiform appendix is a blind-ended tube, about 9 or 10 cm long, projecting from the caecum (a pouch), which is the first part of the large intestine. Appendicitis is inflammation of the vermiform appendix, which, in its acute form, is the most common abdominal emergency in the western world.
Persons most commonly affected: all age groups and both sexes, but it is rare in young children under the age of two. It is most common in young people up to the age of 25.
Organ or part of body involved: vermiform appendix.
Symptoms and indications: the symptoms include abdominal pain that often begins over the navel and then moves to low on the right ileac fossa, with pronounced local tenderness. The pain is severe and worse with movement e.g. coughing or deep breathing, etc. Also, there may be nausea and vomiting, diarrhoea, loss of appetite and fever. Eventually, there is abdominal swelling and tenderness. A person with symptoms of appendicitis should seek immediate medical attention, as it is an emergency condition.

Treatment: usually appendicitis occurs in the acute form, requiring hospital treatment or appendicectomy – the surgical removal of the appendix. The condition is normally completely cured with prompt surgery but is dangerous if left untreated.

Causes and risk factors: blockage and subsequent infection of the appendix are the causes of appendicitis, which can occur at any time. Danger arises if the condition is left untreated or misdiagnosed. In this instance, the appendix may become the site of an abscess or may become gangrenous and rupture, causing PERITONITIS. This arises because infected material from the burst appendix spreads into the peritoneal cavity, and it is often fatal. Rupture of the appendix is more likely to occur in older patients.

asbestosis

Description: a disease of the lungs that is a form of PNEUMOCONIOSIS, caused by the inhalation of asbestos dust.

Persons most commonly affected: men in middle or older age who have been exposed to asbestos dust over a number of years.

Organ or part of body involved: lungs.

Symptoms and indications: the early stages of the disease produce symptoms that include breathlessness, tiredness and persistent cough. Later, the person may suffer from severe breathing difficulties, cough up blood, experience disturbance of sleep and pain in the chest, and develop congestive heart failure. There is a serious risk of the development of MESOTHELIOMA or LUNG CANCER, which also produce these symptoms. A person with these symptoms should seek medical advice. The condition is not curable, but various drug treatments can help to alleviate the symptoms. These include bronchodilators, analgesics and antibiotics for infections. Also, bronchial drainage may be needed to remove excess fluid and the use of a humidifier to ease breathing.

Causes and risk factors: asbestos has been used in many industries in the past, although less widely today since the risks have been known. Anyone working with asbestos should keep to strict health and safety procedures, including the wearing of protective clothing and measures to suppress the dust. The particles of asbestos dust cause scarring of the lungs and risks of disease or cancer are greatly increased by smoking.

ascariasis *see* ROUNDWORMS

asphyxia

Description: this translates literally as an absence of pulse but is used in a wider sense to describe the state of suffocation. During

asphyxia

the course of this, breathing and heartbeat cease and oxygen fails to reach the tissues and organs. Brain cells are irreparably damaged if deprived of oxygen for more than about four minutes.

Persons most commonly affected: all age groups and both sexes.

Organ or part of body involved: lungs, heart, respiratory and circulatory systems.

Symptoms and indications: in most cases, the person fights and gasps for breath, has a rapid pulse rate, throbbing in the head as blood pressure rises and blueness of the skin. Eventually, there may be convulsions, followed by a state of paralysis, unconsciousness and death. However, in some instances, where the inhalation of toxic fumes such as carbon monoxide is responsible for the asphyxia, death may occur peacefully, without the struggles described above and during sleep. A person suffering from asphyxia requires urgent, prompt treatment if death is to be avoided.

Treatment: this depends on the cause of the asphyxia in the first instance. If the cause is choking because of a piece of food, or other foreign body, becoming lodged in the windpipe, this must be removed. A young child can be held upside down by the legs and struck firmly on the back, as this results in the object being dislodged more easily. In adults, blows on the back over the shoulder blades in time with coughing may help the object to be expelled. However, it may be necessary to perform the Heimlich's manoeuvre. The person carrying out the procedure encircles the patient from behind with his or her arms. A fist is made with one hand slightly above the patient's navel and below the ribs. With the free hand, the fist is thrust firmly into the abdomen with a rapid, upward push, which may need to be repeated several times. As a result of this, the foreign body is expelled through or into the patient's mouth. In the situation outlined above, the patient usually recovers rapidly and resumes normal breathing. If toxic fumes are the cause of asphyxia, the person must be removed into clean air (*see* CARBON MONOXIDE POISONING). In all cases of asphyxia, the essential aim of treatment is to increase the amount of oxygen in the blood. If respiration and heartbeat have stopped, emergency resuscitation methods (mouth-to-mouth breathing and external cardiac massage) must be used. Once respiration and heartbeat have started (or if still present), the person requires further intensive care treatment in hospital.

Causes and risk factors: as indicated above, there are a number of different causes of asphyxia, including drowning, strangulation, choking and inhalation of toxic fumes. Also, swelling leading to obstruction of breathing and asphyxia may occur in certain diseases and conditions, including DIPHTHERIA, ASTHMA, CROUP and infection of a wound.

asthma

Description: a chronic, hypersensitive condition characterised by recurrent bouts of illness or asthma attacks. The affected person has breathing difficulties caused by a narrowing of the airways (the bronchi and bronchioles) leading to the lungs.

Persons most commonly affected: all age groups except newborn babies, often beginning in early childhood. In childhood, more boys than girls suffer from asthma but in adult life both sexes are affected equally.

Organ or part of body involved: airways (bronchi and bronchioles) and lungs.

Symptoms and indications: the main symptoms are breathlessness and a wheezing cough that may be worse at night. The extent to which the bronchi are narrowed varies considerably and governs the severity of the attack. In a severe attack, the breathing rate increases considerably and is rapid and shallow. The pulse rate also increases. In a very severe attack, the person may be so breathless as to make speech impossible and may show signs of cyanosis, i.e. a bluish colour of the skin because of a lack of oxygen in the blood. A severe asthma attack or one that does not respond to the usual controlling medication taken by the patient is an emergency condition and medical help should be sought immediately. Prolonged and repeated attacks of asthma, with no break in between, are called *status asthmaticus*. This also is a serious emergency that can cause death due to exhaustion and respiratory failure.

Treatment: the day-to-day treatment of asthma is one of management to avoid the occurrence of an attack. This includes avoidance of the particular substance or allergen that triggers the asthma, if this is known and if it is possible to do so. Drugs used in the treatment of asthma are of two kinds. Bronchodilators are used to dilate the airways, and these include beta-adrenergic agonists such as salbutamol and anticholinergics such as theophyllines. The second group are anti-inflammatory drugs, which are inhaled corticosteroids and sodium cromoglycate. Most of the drugs used in the management of asthma are inhaled. Patients with severe asthma attacks or status asthmaticus require immediate admittance to hospital and treatment in intensive care.

Causes and risk factors: the cause of asthma is swelling and inflammation of the walls of the airways, and contraction of the muscles,

atherosclerosis

so that the openings are narrowed. This is triggered by a hypersensitive response to a number of different allergens. Common allergens include pollen, dust from mites, domestic pets, birds and farm animals and airborne pollutants from, e.g. car exhaust emissions. An asthma sufferer may have other hypersensitive conditions such as ECZEMA or HAY FEVER, and there may be a genetic element with prevalence within a family. Exercise and stress may also trigger an asthma attack, and the condition is exacerbated by exposure to tobacco smoke.

atherosclerosis and atheroma

Description: a degenerative disease of the arteries in which the inner and middle coats of the arterial walls become scarred and fatty deposits (cholesterol) are built up at these sites. The channel or lumen of the artery becomes progressively narrowed so that the blood circulation is impaired and may become completely blocked.

Persons most commonly affected: adults in middle and older age groups. Less common in women before the menopause than in men in the same age range. However, older (postmenopausal) women experience the same rates of disease as men.

Organ or part of body involved: arteries in any part of the body.

Symptoms and indications: the condition is often well advanced before any symptoms are noticed, and these depend on the arteries involved. If leg arteries are affected, there may be pains and cramps in the legs. If it is the coronary arteries the symptoms could be of ANGINA PECTORIS or CORONARY THROMBOSIS. If the disease involves the arteries in the brain, the person may suffer a STROKE. A person with symptoms of atherosclerosis or atheroma should seek immediate medical help.

Treatment: treatment is aimed at prevention as there is at present no cure for this condition. These measures include eating a low-fat diet that does not contain too much cholesterol or salt, not smoking, taking regular exercise, losing weight if obese and trying to avoid stress. Also, persons suffering from HYPERTENSION or DIABETES MELLITUS should keep strictly to their prescribed treatment. The serious complications that can arise as a result of atherosclerosis obviously require immediate treatment and are described elsewhere.

Causes and factors: the cause of atherosclerosis or atheroma is a buildup of fatty deposits on the inner walls of the arteries leading to reduced blood flow or blockage. The reasons why this occurs are not entirely clear, but there is an association with the western lifestyle, i.e. lack of exercise, smoking, obesity and too high an intake of animal fats. Older persons and those with high blood pressure or diabetes mellitus are also more at risk.

athlete's foot
Description: a fungal infection of the skin of the foot, particularly occurring between the toes and often due to RINGWORM.
Persons most commonly affected: older children and adults of both sexes and all age groups.
Organ or part of body involved: foot.
Symptoms and indications: the appearance of damp, white or greyish-coloured skin, red patches and dead skin on the soles of the feet and between the toes.
Treatment: involves paying special attention to hygiene, especially washing and drying the feet thoroughly at least once a day or more frequently if they become sweaty. An antifungal cream, ointment or dusting powder, which may be prescribed by a doctor but can also be bought over the counter, should be applied to affected skin. Socks should be of cotton or other natural fibres, and shoes worn that allow air to circulate as much as possible (ideally, sandals). The condition usually clears up in two or three weeks but may recur.
Causes and risk factors: the cause is a species of fungus (*see also* RINGWORM).

atrial fibrillation
Description: a serious form of arrhythmia affecting the atria (upper chambers) of the heart.
Persons most commonly affected: adults of both sexes in middle and older age, usually with some form of heart disease or damage.
Organ or part of body involved: heart.
Symptoms and indications: irregular, rapid heartbeat and pulse, which are felt as unpleasant palpitations and may cause chest pain, breathlessness, faintness and weakness. There may be symptoms of STROKE because of the formation of blood clots in the heart. In severe cases, this may lead to heart failure and death. Immediate medical help should be sought if a person has these symptoms.
Treatment: emergency medical treatment and intensive care in hospital will be required. This involves attempting to restore a normal heartbeat by means of electric shock and drug treatment. The drugs that may be used include digoxin, betablockers and calcium antagonists. Surgery and the fitting of a pacemaker is sometimes (but rarely) required. Underlying heart disease, responsible for the atrial fibrillation, is also treated, although this is rarely sufficient to restore the normal heartbeat on its own. An exception is if the cause is HYPERTHYROIDISM. Later, the patient may be prescribed blood-thinning drugs such as warfarin.
Causes and risk factors: in atrial fibrillation, the output of the heart

is maintained by the contraction of the ventricles (the lower, larger chambers) alone. It can arise spontaneously in persons with no apparent heart disease, but often an underlying disorder is present. These diseases include CORONARY ARTERY DISEASE, rheumatic heart disease, ATHEROSCLEROSIS, high blood pressure (HYPERTENSION) and overactive thyroid gland (hyperthyroidism). There is a risk of CORONARY THROMBOSIS because of the formation of blood clots in the heart.

B

bacillary dysentery *see* DYSENTERY

Bell's palsy
Description: a sudden paralysis of the facial muscles, usually on one side of the face but sometimes on both.
Persons most commonly affected: usually adults of both sexes and all age groups.
Organ or part of body involved: seventh cranial nerve – the facial nerve.
Symptoms and indications: paralysis on one or both sides of the face, resulting in an inability to move the eyelids and close or open the eyes, smile or close the mouth. The features on the affected side are flat and lacking expression. There may be pain, especially behind the ear, prior to the development of the paralysis. Some people experience loss of the sense of taste, and sounds may seem too loud if hearing is affected. A person affected by symptoms of Bell's palsy should seek medical advice so that the cause of the nerve disorder can be determined.
Treatment: recovery depends on the nature of the damage to the facial nerve, may or may not be complete and may take some time. Treatment includes the use of heat (lamps or compresses) if there is pain and facial massage and exercises for the affected muscles once recovery is under way. While the person is unable to blink, the eyes require additional protection to avoid trauma and injury. This usually involves the wearing of an eye patch or goggles and the use of drops containing methylcellulose. Oral corticosteroid drugs may be prescribed, and in severe cases, which do not recover after six to twelve months, surgery may be performed to improve the function of the facial muscles.

Causes and risk factors: the cause is thought to be inflammation of the facial nerve because of injury or infection or possibly a disorder of the immune system (an autoimmune disease).

bends, the see CAISSON DISEASE

benign prostatic hypertrophy see PROSTATE GLAND ENLARGEMENT

benign rectal growth see RECTAL GROWTH

bilharziasis see SCHISTOSOMIASIS

bladder stones or **calculi** (*singular* **calculus**)
Description: stones occurring in the urinary bladder, which may be of three different types: phosphatic, the most common type, associated with recurrent inflammation and decomposition of the urine contained in the bladder; uratic (particularly in persons suffering from gout); and oxalic. The stones are usually quite small but are too large to be passed with the urine. However, they may occasionally be of considerable size and weight.
Persons most commonly affected: adults of all age groups and both sexes.
Organ or part of body involved: urinary bladder.
Symptoms and indications: the symptoms are those of inflammation of the bladder, including pain on passing urine, feeling the need to urinate frequently although little or nothing is passed, and blood in the urine, or the urine may be cloudy and the person may experience abdominal pain or discomfort and feverishness. A person with symptoms of bladder inflammation should seek medical advice.
Treatment: prompt treatment of any bladder infection that arises, drinking plenty of fluids and adjustment in diet are measures that help to prevent the formation of stones in susceptible people. However, once the stones are formed, and if they are too large to be passed with the urine, the only treatment available is surgical removal. This may be performed in two ways. Lithoplaxy involves passing an instrument (lithotrite) into the bladder via the urethra, which breaks up the stones into small pieces that can pass to the outside. Lithotomy is the name given to direct removal of stones through an incision made in the bladder and is the method needed for larger stones. If infection has been present, antibiotics may be prescribed and possibly drugs to alter the acidity of the urine.
Causes and risk factors: stones grow for a variety of reasons but mainly because of the presence in the urine of an excess of salts or minerals from which they are formed. This may occur because of a

bladder tumour　　　　　　　　　　　　　　　　　　　　44

number of causes and disorders, including bladder infections, gout and thyroid disorders. Also, excess consumption of certain foods containing the minerals from which stones are formed in susceptible people and some hereditary conditions. Other risk factors include illness or injury to the bladder, and dehydration and inadequate drinking of fluids.

bladder tumour (cancer)
Description: an abnormal growth of cells and tissue in the bladder that is often malignant or cancerous.
Persons most commonly affected: adults of all age groups and both sexes but more common in males and people in middle or older age.
Organ or part of body involved: bladder.
Symptoms and indications: the early signs are those of bladder infection, including pain or burning sensation on passing urine, feeling the urge to urinate frequently but passing little or no urine, blood in the urine. Also, pain in the region of the bladder and eventual weight loss. A person with signs of bladder disorder or infection should seek immediate medical advice.
Treatment: the course of treatment depends upon the nature of the cancer, i.e. whether it is superficial or has invaded deeply into the muscular wall of the bladder. Treatments include radiation therapy and the use of radioactive isotopes, chemotherapy, including the placing of certain drugs into the bladder, and surgery. Also, photoradiation using a light-sensitive dye that releases chemicals that kill the cancer cells is used in some patients with a particular form of superficial malignancy. Preventative measures are directed towards certain industries whose workers are known to be more at risk. This involves following strict health and safety procedures and regular screening of the workforce.
Causes and risk factors: the precise cause remains unclear, but this is regarded as an occupational cancer, with workers in some industries being particularly at risk. These are the chemical and rubber industries, laboratory workers, pest control operators and engineering industries using lubricant oils. The chemicals involved include benzidine, and alpha and beta naphthylamine, and persons exposed to these must follow strict guidelines. Also, people who smoke are more at risk, and there may be a greater risk for those with a family history of the disease.

bleeding *see* HAEMORRHAGE

blepharitis
Description: inflammation of the outer edges of the eyelids.

Persons most commonly affected: adults of all age groups and both sexes.
Organ or part of body involved: eyelids and sometimes the cornea and conjunctiva of the eye.
Symptoms and indications: symptoms include reddening of the eyelids with the appearance of scales caught in the eyelashes. Ulcers may form on the edges of the eyelid and yellowish crusts form on top of these. The lashes become matted and project in various directions, or they may fall out. The conjunctiva and cornea may become reddened and inflamed. A person with symptoms of eye inflammation should seek medical attention.
Treatment: blepharitis is a stubborn condition that is somewhat resistant to treatment but usually clears in time, although it may recur. Treatment involves cleaning the eyes, bathing them with warm water containing sodium bicarbonate and removing the scales. Also, antibiotic eyedrops and solutions of artificial tears may be prescribed by the doctor.
Causes and risk factors: the cause is dry eyes because of lessened tear secretion, along with seborrhoeic dermatitis and infection by staphylococcal bacteria. The risk of developing blepharitis is greater in poor or overcrowded living conditions and possibly in older persons subject to dry eyes.

blood clot *see* EMBOLISM, THROMBOSIS

blood poisoning or **septicaemia**
Description: a serious and potentially life-threatening condition characterised by the presence of pathogenic microorganisms (especially bacteria) in the blood.
Persons most commonly affected: all age groups and both sexes.
Organ or part of body involved: blood circulation and all body systems.
Symptoms and indications: a temperature that rises rapidly to a high level along with shivering chills, flushing, copious sweating, pains and aches, and a fall in blood pressure. The person feels generally unwell and requires prompt medical attention as there is a risk of shock and death. This is especially the case in a vulnerable person who has an existing illness.
Treatment: involves admittance to hospital and antibiotic therapy. Antibiotics may be required in large amounts until the condition is brought under control. If blood poisoning has arisen as a result of infection in some other organ or part of the body (e.g. the gall bladder), surgery may be necessary to treat this.

boil

Causes and risk factors: blood poisoning may result from infection in a wound or operation site or a tooth abscess. Also as a result of an infection in the gall bladder, appendix, burns or abscesses. Elderly persons and babies are more at risk, and people with lessened immunity, e.g. those suffering from cancer. Preventative measures include seeking prompt medical attention for infections, wounds and injuries, and having regular dental checkups and treatment.

boil or furuncle

Description: a skin infection in a hair follicle or gland that produces inflammation and pus. A group of boils that are deeper and more spread are called a carbuncle.
Persons most commonly affected: all age groups and both sexes.
Organ or part of body involved: the skin and its hair follicles and glands.
Symptoms and indications: a painful red swelling or lump, which usually comes up quite quickly and may be fairly large. Also, there is swelling of lymph glands close to the site of the boil and the person may be feverish. The boil usually 'comes to a head' itself and bursts within several days but should be treated by a doctor before this occurs.
Treatment: usually the boil needs to be surgically lanced and the pus drained out. As this is performed by a doctor under clean, aseptic conditions, there is much less likelihood of the pus (which is infective) causing another boil to occur in an adjacent area of skin. Also the boil heals more quickly than if left untreated. Antibiotics may be prescribed to fight the infection that caused the boil.
Causes and risk factors: a boil is caused by a bacterial infection at the base of a hair and the organism involved is usually staphylococcus aureus, or the organism may enter through a small cut or nick in the skin. Occasionally, a boil may cause a more widespread infection, especially in people who are somewhat 'run-down' or with lowered immunity because of illness. Frequent recurrence of boils usually requires further medical investigation to ensure that the patient is not suffering from DIABETES MELLITUS.

bone cancer *see* OSTEOSARCOMA, EWING'S SARCOMA

bone fracture

Description: any break in a bone, which may be complete or incomplete. There are many different forms of fracture, and these are listed below:
- Simple fracture (or closed fracture). In this type, the skin remains more or less intact.

- Compound fracture (or open fracture). An open wound connects the bone with the surface. This type of fracture is more serious as it provides a greater risk of infection and more blood loss.
- Pathological fracture. A fracture in a diseased bone, which often occurs in people, especially women, with osteoporosis.
- Stress fracture. Occurs in a bone that suffers recurrent, persistent stress e.g. the march fracture sometimes seen in the second toe of soldiers after long marches.
- Greenstick fracture. This occurs only in young children, whose bones are still soft and tend to bend. The fracture occurs on the opposite side to the causal force.
- Complicated fracture. This involves damage to surrounding soft tissue including nerves and blood vessels.
- Depressed fracture. This refers only to the skull when a piece of bone is forced inwards and may damage the brain.
- Comminuted fracture. A serious injury to a bone in which more than one break occurs, accompanied by splintering and damage to the surrounding tissues. It usually results from a crushing force with damage to nerves, muscles and blood vessels, and the bone is difficult to set.

Persons most commonly affected: all age groups and both sexes.
Organ or part of body involved: bones.
Symptoms and indications: symptoms include pain, bruising, swelling and bleeding. Also, if nerves are damaged there may be numbness or even paralysis below the level of the injury. If a limb is fractured there is severe pain on movement and an inability to perform normal activities, and the affected limb may appear deformed or rotated. Occasionally there may be a loss of pulse below the fracture site, particularly in the region of the hands and wrists or feet and ankles. Immediate and often emergency medical attention is needed if a person has a fracture or suspected fracture.
Treatment: involves admittance to hospital where X-rays (radiography) are taken to determine the nature and extent of the injury. Surgery is often necessary to repair or set a fracture and the bone or body part is usually immobilised, generally by means of a plaster cast and splints. Sometimes traction is needed, which involves the use of weights and pulleys to apply a pulling force. This ensures that the bone is kept in correct alignment while healing takes place. Once recovery is well under way, physiotherapy is often needed to restore movement.
Causes and risk factors: with more serious and complex fractures particularly, healing may take a long time or be only partial. Also,

botulism

there may be shock and death because of HAEMORRHAGE if the injury is severe. There may be damage or obstruction of arteries causing problems in blood circulation or EMBOLISM. Fractures are caused by trauma to the bone through accident or injury or repeated stress.

botulism
Description: the most dangerous type of FOOD POISONING, caused by the anaerobic (living without oxygen) bacterium *Clostridium botulinum*.
Persons most commonly affected: all age groups and both sexes but less common in children.
Organ or part of body involved: central nervous system and muscles.
Symptoms and indications: symptoms may appear within a few hours of eating food contaminated by the bacteria and/or their toxin. These include a dry mouth, blurred vision, constipation, retention of urine and dilation of the pupils of the eye. This leads on to muscle weakness and paralysis and may be fatal. Death results from paralysis of the muscles involved in respiration. If botulism is suspected, emergency medical help should be summoned immediately.
Treatment: requires admittance to hospital for intensive care nursing, which may involve the need for a ventilator. Also, drugs that counter the effects of the bacterial toxin are given.
Causes and risk factors: the bacteria that cause botulism grow in tinned foods that have not been properly preserved, especially canned raw meats, fish, vegetables or fruit. Very rarely, infection may occur via an open wound or cut. During its growth the bacteria produce a toxin, one component of which attacks the nervous system and produces the symptoms. The toxin is destroyed by heat so it is a problem only in foods that have not been thoroughly cooked. The toxin has a very small lethal dose, hence it is a wise precaution never to taste suspect food but to discard it immediately.

brain abscess or epidural abscess
Description: a bacterial infection in the brain resulting in an accumulation of pus.
Persons most commonly affected: all age groups and both sexes.
Organ or part of body involved: brain and meninges (membranes) that cover the brain and spinal cord.
Symptoms and indications: early indications may be vague, but eventually the person develops a severe headache, nausea and vomiting, feverishness and often a disturbance of vision. This is a very serious condition, and a person with these symptoms requires emergency medical treatment.

Treatment: involves admittance to hospital and, usually, surgery to drain the abscess. Antibiotics may be needed to combat infection.
Causes and risk factors: common causes of a brain abscess include injury or wounds on the scalp, an infection that spreads to the brain e.g. from a discharging ear or sinus infection. Also, infection may spread via the blood circulation to the brain, from another infected organ elsewhere in the body. It is wise where possible to prevent the occurrence of a brain abscess. This means that scalp injuries, ear infections, etc, should always be taken seriously and treated properly by a doctor.

brain compression
Description: pressure or squeezing of the brain within the limited space of the skull, due to some form of trauma or injury.
Persons most commonly affected: all age groups and both sexes.
Organ or part of body involved: brain.
Symptoms and indications: symptoms include drowsiness, breathing difficulties, weak pulse, paralysis in one side of the body and unconsciousness. Emergency medical treatment is needed if a person shows signs of brain compression.
Treatment: involves admittance to hospital and a surgical operation (trepanning or trephining of the skull – removal of an area of bone) so that the cause of the compression can be dealt with.
Causes and risk factors: there are various reasons why compression of the brain occurs. These include injury and rupture of a blood vessel producing a clot, tumour and a collection of pus or blood from an infection. As with brain abscess, preventative measures include seeking prompt medical attention for any injury, wound or trauma involving the head and skull.

brain tumour
Description: a growth of abnormal cells in the brain, which may be malignant or nonmalignant and may be fatal. Because of its location, a nonmalignant brain tumour can cause very serious symptoms.
Persons most commonly affected: all age groups and both sexes but more common in adults.
Organ or part of body involved: brain.
Symptoms and indications: symptoms are variable, depending on the precise location of the tumour in the brain, and may be slow in onset. They include headache, vomiting, nausea, dizziness, poor coordination, disturbance of vision, weakness affecting one side of the body, mental changes and fits. Sometimes a tumour in a particular site may cause a more definite set of symptoms, leading to its

breast abscess

presence being suspected. A person with any symptoms of brain disorder should seek medical advice.

Treatment: depends upon the nature and precise site of the tumour. There are a range of treatments, including surgery, radiotherapy and the use of radioisotopes and chemotherapy. Continuing advances in medicine and surgery mean that more brain tumours can now be treated than was possible in the past.

Causes and risk factors: a brain tumour may arise as a secondary growth, resulting from a malignancy elsewhere in the body, or be a primary tumour. A brain tumour can be a result of TUBERCULOSIS or SYPHILIS and these diseases must obviously be treated if present. Preventative measures are primarily avoidance of the known risk factors associated with cancer. The most significant of these is avoidance of smoking.

breast abscess

Description: acute inflammation and infection with a collection of pus within the breast tissue.

Persons most commonly affected: women in the child bearing age group who have recently given birth.

Organ or part of body involved: breast.

Symptoms and indications: redness, heat, inflammation, hardness, tenderness and pain in infected part. Also, enlargement of lymph glands in the armpit and sharp pain when the infant sucks. If left untreated, the skin darkens and the abscess eventually bursts. The person may be feverish and feel unwell. A woman with symptoms of a breast abscess should seek medical treatment.

Treatment: involves supporting and bandaging the affected breast, expressing the milk and not feeding the baby on that side. Also, an antibiotic such as penicillin may be prescribed to fight the infection. Surgery to open and drain the abscess may be necessary and if the infection is very severe, breast-feeding may have to be abandoned.

Causes and risk factors: the cause of a breast abscess is a bacterial infection; usually a staphylococcus or streptococcus is the causal organism. The organisms enter through cracks in the nipple, particularly at the beginning of breast-feeding before the skin has 'toughened up'. Preventative measures to try to avoid cracking of the nipples include careful cleansing, use of cream or ointment, and not allowing the baby to suck for too long, or to 'comfort suck', especially during the early days of breast-feeding.

breast cancer

Description: a carcinoma (a cancer of the epithelium, the tissue that lines the body's internal organs and skin) or sarcoma (a cancer of the connective tissue), which is the commonest form of cancer in women. The incidence is lowest in countries such as Japan, where breast-feeding is prolonged, as babies are not weaned early, and where the intake of animal fats in the diet is low.

Persons most commonly affected: women, especially after the age of 30 years and more common in postmenopausal women.

Organ or part of body involved: breast and lymph nodes in armpit.

Symptoms and indications: the first sign of breast cancer that is usually noticed is a lump in the breast and/or node in the armpit. In addition, there may be a change in the usual appearance of the breast or a puckering of the skin in the region of the nipple. The breast may feel uncomfortable, and rarely there may be a discharge from the nipple. Most breast lumps are not serious, but a woman who detects a lump should always seek immediate medical attention.

Treatment: involves surgery, radiotherapy and chemotherapy, and usually a combination of these. Sometimes it is possible to remove the lump alone (popularly called 'lumpectomy'), but in other cases, surgery is more radical and the whole breast has to be removed, and lymph nodes under the arm. The degree of surgery depends on the size of the cancer and the extent to which it has spread. In addition to anticancer drugs, other drugs and hormone treatment may be necessary.

Causes and risk factors: as with most cancers, the exact cause is unknown, but some women are more at risk of developing the disease than others. There is a greater risk if a family member (especially mother, aunt or sister) has had breast cancer or if the woman has previously had benign breast tumours. Women who have not had children, and those aged 30 or over at the birth of a first baby, are at greater risk. Women who do not breast-feed are more likely to develop breast cancer. Smokers run a greater risk of developing all forms of cancer than people who do not smoke. Preventative measures include self-examination of the breasts to check for lumps, which should preferably be carried out just before the monthly period. In this way a woman becomes acquainted with the normal feel and appearance of her breasts and is more likely to detect a change. Also, women over 50 should regularly attend breast-screening clinics. Breast cancer can be completely cured if detected early enough but, as with many cancers, it can spread and set up secondary growths elsewhere. The survival time and treatment for those suffering from breast cancer has improved, and this cancer is a focus for intensive research.

brittle bone disease *see* OSTEOGENESIS IMPERFECTA

bronchiectasis

Description: a disease of the bronchi (tubes) of the lungs in which, as a result of infection, the passages become blocked with thick secretions causing the walls to dilate and become weakened.

Persons most commonly affected: all age groups and both sexes but more common in adults, although it may originate in childhood.

Organ or part of body involved: lungs and bronchi.

Symptoms and indications: the common, defining symptom is the frequent coughing up of foul, smelly secretions that are thick and green or yellow in colour and may be blood-flecked. The person suffers from frequent respiratory infections and is often breathless and unwell. In addition, the person may be abnormally tired and anaemic. A person with symptoms of bronchiectasis should seek medical treatment.

Treatment: the main treatment is the practice of postural drainage to eliminate the accumulated secretions. The person lies over the edge of the bed with the head hanging down so that the secretions pass into the trachea (windpipe) and can be coughed up. Also, surgery to remove a part of the lung (lobectomy) may be needed, and antibiotics to fight infections. Inhalations of aromatic substances, such as creosote, may be used to eliminate the smell. The person needs yearly immunisation against influenza.

Causes and risk factors: the initial damage to the bronchi may result from a number of different causes, including infections of the lungs e.g. pneumonia and chronic bronchitis, allergy (hay fever), inhalation of a foreign body e.g. a tooth, and tuberculosis. The secretions that accumulate lead to blockage and weakening of the bronchial walls, and accumulation of more material and secondary infections, which is bronchiectasis. Preventative measures for a person with bronchiectasis include a good diet, drinking plenty of fluids, avoidance of airborne pollutants (ideally living in an environment where there is clean, fresh air) and trying to avoid respiratory infections.

bronchiolitis or capillary bronchitis

Description: bronchitis (inflammation) affecting the bronchioles, the fine air passages that connect with the minute air sacs of the lungs where oxygen is given up to the blood circulation. This is a serious and potentially fatal condition, especially in young children and elderly persons.

Persons most commonly affected: all age groups and both sexes, especially infants and young children in whom it sometimes occurs in epidemics.

Organ or part of body involved: bronchioles.

Symptoms and indications: bronchiolitis usually develops as a result of a cold or upper respiratory tract infection. The symptoms are respiratory distress characterised by laboured, rapid, shallow breathing, constant hacking cough, flaring of the nostrils, wheezing and seesaw movements (called retractions) of the chest and abdomen. On listening to the chest, there are wheezing, crackling and bubbling sounds. The person may be feverish and restless or a child may be lethargic. Eventually the bronchioles and air sacs become blocked with secretions interfering with the passage of oxygen into the blood. The person shows signs of cyanosis with a bluish tinge to the skin, and death may follow from ASPHYXIA. In the young and old this can occur within 48 hours. A person with symptoms of bronchiolitis requires medical attention. Most patients can be treated at home under the doctor's supervision, but those showing signs of fatigue because of laboured breathing, cyanosis or dehydration need to be admitted to hospital for intensive nursing.

Treatment: at home, involves resting in bed, increasing the humidity in the air by means of steam or a humidifier to ease breathing, and drinking plenty of clear liquids. In hospital, oxygen is likely to be given by means of a tent or a face mask and fluids by intravenous drip. There may be a need for endotracheal intubation (a tube through the mouth or nose directly into the trachea) to deliver oxygen if the person is very ill. The secretions may have to be removed by postural drainage or suction through the trachea. The doctor may prescribe antibiotics if a secondary infection is present.

Causes and risk factors: the cause of the initial infection leading to bronchiolitis is normally a virus, especially respiratory syncytial virus or parainfluenza type 3 virus. Small children who have more than one attack of bronchiolitis may be more likely to develop ASTHMA and allergies.

bronchitis (acute)

Description: inflammation of the bronchi, the tubes that carry air to the lungs.

Persons most commonly affected: all age groups and both sexes.

Organ or part of body involved: bronchi and lungs.

Symptoms and indications: typically, the symptoms begin with those of the common cold but develop with painful coughing, wheezing, throat and chest pains and the production of purulent (pus-containing) mucus. The person is likely to be feverish and feels

bronchitis (chronic)

generally unwell, and crackling, bubbling and wheezing sounds can be heard when listening to the chest. A person with symptoms of bronchitis should seek medical advice.

Treatment: consists of rest and the taking of analgesics or a cough preparation that can be purchased over the counter. Also, inhalation of steam and a heating pad or hot-water bottle on the chest are very effective. Antibiotics may be needed to combat infection.

Causes and risk factors: the cause of bronchitis is a viral and/or bacterial infection, and there is a tendency for the condition to recur. There is a risk of the development of chronic BRONCHITIS or pneumonia. Preventative measures include not smoking, avoiding as far as possible cold, damp conditions and polluted air, drinking plenty of fluids and eating a good diet. Bronchitis is more likely to develop in a person who is 'run-down', with a lower resistance to infections.

bronchitis (chronic)

Description: a chronic inflammation and degeneration of the bronchi in the form of thickening and ulceration, and sometimes dilation of the tubes. It is the commonest cause of death in the UK.

Persons most commonly affected: all age groups and both sexes but more common in elderly persons.

Organ or part of body involved: bronchi and lungs.

Symptoms and indications: a persistent cough that, in the early stages of the disease, tends to occur in the winter months and disappear during the summer. However, as the bronchitis develops, the cough is present most of the time and is at its worst in the morning. There is an excessive, copious production of mucus, and the person is breathless. The sounds produced on listening to the chest are the same as those in BRONCHITIS (ACUTE). Usually there is less chest pain and feverishness than in the acute form. However, there may be periodic attacks of the acute form of bronchitis, which poses the greatest risk, especially to elderly people.

Treatment: preventative measures and attention to a susceptible person's general state of health are the most important factors. A susceptible person, especially if elderly, will need to be particularly careful with regard to keeping warm, eating a good diet and generally avoiding the risk factors that might worsen the condition.

Causes and risk factors: chronic bronchitis may arise as a result of repeated attacks of the acute form or through some other cause, often as a complication of heart disease. Several parameters are of direct consequence to its cause, including smoking, exposure to air pollutants, cold, wet climate, poor and damp housing, frequent respiratory infections and obesity. Hence, preventative measures involve trying to improve the consequences of these, where possible, particularly in the avoidance of cigarette smoking.

brucellosis or undulant fever or Malta fever or Mediterranean fever

Description: a disease of farm animals (pigs, cattle, goats) that can be passed on to human beings but is rare in Britain.
Persons most commonly affected: all age groups and both sexes.
Organ or part of body involved: liver, spleen, lymph glands, bone marrow.
Symptoms and indications: in humans it is characterised by fever, copious sweats, joint backache and headache, although the symptoms are not always clear cut. There may be enlargement of the spleen and liver. A person with symptoms of brucellosis should seek medical attention.
Treatment: the treatment consists of relief of the symptoms by means of analgesics and taking antibiotics, particularly tetracyclines, co-trimoxazole or gentamicin, to kill the infection. Sometimes a tetracycline and streptomycin are prescribed if the disease is present in chronic form.
Causes and risk factors: the cause is a species of bacteria belonging to the genus *Brucella*, and humans are usually infected by drinking nonpasteurised milk from cattle or goats with the disease. Hence, preventative measures are of prime importance, particularly the pasteurising of all milk for human consumption and keeping farm animals free from the disease. Brucellosis itself is rarely fatal, but there may be serious complications in the form of MENINGITIS or PNEUMONIA.

Buerger's disease or thromboangitis obliterans

Description: inflammation of the smaller and medium-sized blood vessels of the legs, especially of the lower limbs. This leads to clot formation and blockage, especially of the smaller arteries.
Persons most commonly affected: younger, adult men aged between about 20 and 45; rare in women.
Organ or part of body involved: arteries (and veins), particularly in lower limbs.
Symptoms and indications: pains in the legs, which come and go because of interruption of the blood circulation, are the main early symptoms. There may be a sensation of numbness, tingling or burning in the legs. GANGRENE may develop, and sometimes ulcers occur on the fingers and toes. A person with symptoms of Buerger's disease should consult a doctor.

bunions

Treatment: this is aimed at prevention as there is at present no cure for this condition. The measures recommended are similar to those for ATHEROSCLEROSIS (atheroma) and include not smoking, eating a diet low in cholesterol and salt, taking regular exercise and losing weight if obese. As this is a disease of smokers and is extremely rare in nonsmokers, the most important measure is to give up smoking. The symptoms of the disease can be alleviated in the early stages, and painkillers and drugs to dilate the blood vessels may be prescribed. An affected person should protect himself or herself against cold weather, being especially careful to keep hands and feet warm. Eventually, there may be a need for amputation if gangrene develops.

Causes and risk factors: the cause is unknown, but there is a definite association with smoking. The formation of blood clots in the veins (venous thrombosis) commonly occurs, and there is a risk of CORONARY THROMBOSIS.

bunions *see* CORNS

burns and scalds

Description: burns are damage to the skin and underlying tissues caused by dry heat, and scalds are similar injuries caused by wet heat. Formerly, burns were categorised by degrees (first, second and third) but are now usually described either as superficial, where sufficient tissue remains to ensure that the skin regrows, or deep, where grafting will be necessary.

Persons most commonly affected: all age groups and both sexes.

Organ or part of body involved: skin and underlying tissues.

Symptoms and indications: symptoms depend on the severity of the burn or scald. If it is relatively minor, there is pain and reddening of the skin, which may later blister or become white and peel off. In more severe burns there are raw wounds from which the skin peels off with a loss of fluid from the injury. Severe wounds of this nature can lead to shock and death, due to fluid loss at the burn site, and infection. All but the most minor burns should be seen by a doctor. In the case of extensive or severe burns and scalds, emergency medical help should be called.

Treatment: depends on the nature and severity of the burn or scald. Minor injuries can be effectively treated by running the affected part under cold water and then covering it with a dressing if needed. Slightly more severe burns should be treated by a doctor and require careful dressing and the use of antiseptics and antibiotics to combat likely infection. Serious and extensive burns are life-threatening and require emergency treatment, the most important part of which is transfusions to counter the fluid loss and maintain the circulation. The person is usually given strong pain relief, such as morphine, and antiseptics and antibiotics are needed to combat infection. Recovery is usually slow, and once the critical period is past, the person is likely to require skin grafting. The greater the extent of the burns and their depth, the poorer the chances of survival, and children and elderly persons are especially vulnerable. Chemical burns require special treatment to counteract the effects of the chemical involved.

Causes and risk factors: burns are caused by dry heat such as fire, sunburn, hot oil or fat in cooking, and also electrical currents and chemicals. Scalds are caused by very hot or boiling water and steam. Small children and the elderly are especially vulnerable to the risk of accidental burns in the home. Hence, the aim should be one of prevention and vigilance to eliminate areas of risk e.g. use of fireguards, cooker guards, safety kettles kept out of reach, fire-retardant clothing (especially pyjamas and nightdresses), installing smoke alarms and general awareness of fire danger.

bursitis

Description: inflammation of a bursa (a fluid-filled hollow surrounding and protecting a joint) e.g. housemaid's knee.

Persons most commonly affected: adults of all age groups and both sexes.

Organ or part of body involved: bursae of joints, especially the knees, elbows, shoulders, wrists, ankles.

Symptoms and indications: pain, especially on moving the affected part, resulting in restriction of normal activity. Also, there may be some swelling and heat. A person with symptoms of bursitis should seek medical advice.

Treatment: the most important aspect of treatment is to rest the affected part and avoid the activity that caused the condition, if this is known. Also, an injection of a corticosteroid preparation into the bursa may be needed to reduce inflammation.

Causes and risk factors: the cause may be obvious, as in the case of housemaid's knee, which is caused by excessive kneeling. Or there may be other repetitive activities that have put the joint under too much strain. However, sometimes the cause of the condition is less easy to discern. Occasionally, there may be infection in the bursa, which is then treated in the same way as an ABSCESS.

C

Caisson disease or **compressed air illness** or **'the bends'**
Description: a condition suffered by persons operating in high pressure in diving bells or divers at depth underwater if they surface too rapidly. Also, those who fly fast, high-performance aircraft.
Persons most commonly affected: adults who are divers or who work in the conditions outlined above e.g. in the oil industry, military aircraft.
Organ or part of body involved: blood and tissues throughout the body.
Symptoms and indications: pains in the joints (the bends), headache and dizziness (decompression sickness), chest pain, breathing difficulties, unconsciousness. Paralysis and death may occur if the person does not receive emergency medical attention.
Treatment: involves admittance to hospital, or a facility with a decompression chamber, until the person has recovered and been slowly readjusted to normal surface pressures.
Causes and risk factors: the cause of this condition is the formation of nitrogen bubbles in the blood, which then accumulate in different parts of the body. The nitrogen bubbles hinder the normal circulation of the blood in supplying the tissues with nutrients and oxygen. Treatment in a decompression chamber forces the nitrogen bubbles to redissolve into the blood. There is a risk of damage to the bones, lungs, brain and heart because of the interruption of the blood circulation, particularly if the person is severely or repeatedly affected. Those working in the occupations listed above, or who take up scuba diving, should receive adequate training and have access to proper medical facilities. The condition can be avoided by returning slowly from high to lower pressure, spending adequate time at each level.

calculi *see* KIDNEY STONES

cancer *see* BLADDER TUMOUR, BRAIN TUMOUR, BREAST CANCER, CERVICAL CANCER, EWING'S SARCOMA (bone), HEPATOMA (primary liver cancer), KAPOSI'S SARCOMA (AIDS-related skin cancer), LARYNGEAL CANCER, LIVER CANCER, LUNG CANCER, MESOTHELIOMA (cancer of the chest cavity [pleura]), OESOPHAGEAL CANCER, OSTEOSARCOMA (bone cancer), OVARIAN TUMOUR, PANCREATIC CANCER, PROSTATE GLAND CANCER, RECTAL TUMOUR, SKIN CANCER, STOMACH CANCER, TESTICULAR CANCER, UTERINE CANCER, VAGINAL CANCER.

candidiasis or thrush or moniliasis
Description: an infection of moist areas of the skin, i.e. skin folds or mucous membranes, caused by a fungus. When it occurs in the mouth or vagina it is called thrush.
Persons most commonly affected: young persons and adults of all age groups and both sexes.
Organ or part of body involved: mucous membranes of mouth and vagina; skin folds such as under the arms, breasts, genital area, etc.
Symptoms and indications: itchy, inflamed areas of skin with small pus-filled blisters that may 'weep' and crust over. In the mouth it forms white patches inside the cheeks and on the tongue and throat. Candidiasis is the most commonly occurring fungal infection and affected persons should consult a doctor.
Treatment: is by means of antibiotics, usually nystatin, which, depending upon the site of the infection may be in the form of oral preparations, cream or ointment, pessaries or inhalations.
Causes and risk factors: the causal organism is the fungus *candida albicans* and is generally easy to treat although it may recur. It may occur in people who are 'run-down' or who have recently had to take courses of antibiotics for other illnesses. It also tends to occur in persons with a depressed immune system, who have been taking immunosuppressive drugs, e.g. transplant patients. It may occur in patients suffering from AIDS.

capillary bronchitis *see* BRONCHIOLITIS

carbon monoxide poisoning
Description: carbon monoxide is an odourless and colourless gas that is highly dangerous when inhaled, leading to carbon monoxide poisoning.
Persons most commonly affected: all age groups and both sexes.
Organ or part of body involved: blood, all tissues and brain.
Symptoms and indications: the symptoms of poisoning include giddiness, flushing of the skin (due to carboxyhaemoglobin in the blood, which is bright red), nausea, headache, raised respiratory and pulse rate and eventual collapse, coma, respiratory failure and death. Carbon monoxide poisoning is an emergency and the person requires immediate medical help.
Treatment: the most important treatment is to immediately remove the person into fresh air and start artificial respiration if needed. Other emergency medical treatment may be needed in the form of giving of oxygen and assisted ventilation.
Causes and risk factors: in the blood, carbon monoxide has a much

greater affinity for oxygen (300 times higher) than haemoglobin and converts haemoglobin into carboxyhaemoglobin. (Haemoglobin is the red pigment present in the blood that picks up oxygen in the lungs and carries it in the circulation to all the tissues and organs of the body.) The tissues and organs of the body are quickly deprived of oxygen because there is no free haemoglobin left to pick it up in the lungs. Permanent damage is eventually caused to the ganglia at the base of the brain. Carbon monoxide is present in coal gas fumes and the emissions of vehicle exhausts. Domestic cases of accidental poisoning usually occur due to inadequate ventilation and ineffective maintenance of boilers and heating systems.

cardiac arrest

Description: the failure and stopping of the pumping action of the heart.
Persons most commonly affected: adults of all age groups and both sexes but particularly middle-aged and elderly persons. Less common in premenopausal women than in men but same incidence in women after menopause as in men.
Organ or part of body involved: heart.
Symptoms and indications: loss of consciousness, breathing and pulse stops, skin is pale and tinged with blue, pupils become dilated. Cardiac arrest or heart attack is a medical emergency and a person requires immediate aid.
Treatment: involves attempting to restart the heart by external cardiac massage (direct depressions of the breastbone) along with artificial respiration (mouth-to-mouth resuscitation). In hospital, defibrillation (electric shock) and direct cardiac massage (the chest wall is opened to allow massage of the heart) may be attempted as a last resort.
Causes and risk factors: causes include various forms of heart disease e.g. CORONARY THROMBOSIS, heartbeat irregularities, serious electrolyte (salts)/fluid imbalance and shock due to severe injury and haemorrhage. Also, electrocution, ANAPHYLACTIC SHOCK, lack of oxygen and respiratory arrest. Stress is believed to be a contributory factor, especially in people with existing heart disease or who are otherwise susceptible.

cardiomyopathy

Description: any disease or disorder of the heart muscle, which may arise from a number of different causes, leading to weak and ineffective pumping of the blood.
Persons most commonly affected: all age groups and both sexes but most common in older adults and in men.

Organ or part of body involved: heart muscle.
Symptoms and indications: the condition may lead to congestive heart failure, the symptoms of which include breathlessness, collection of fluid (oedema) in the legs, feet and ankles, palpitations and tiredness. Also there may be chest pain and a cough. A person with these symptoms should seek medical advice.
Treatment: depends upon whether the cause of the cardiomyopathy can be corrected. Symptoms can, however, be alleviated and drugs that may be prescribed include diuretics, digitalis, vitamin and mineral supplements, especially potassium. Some patients may require a heart transplant.
Causes and risk factors: causes include congenital abnormalities of the heart, dietary deficiencies (especially of potassium and thiamine [vitamin B_4]), viral infections and chronic alcoholism. However, the cause is not always known. Risks increase with severe obesity, smoking and alcoholism, which are reversible factors, and also with increasing age.

carpal tunnel syndrome

Description: a nerve disorder affecting the fingers, thumb and hand.
Persons most commonly affected: adults of both sexes but more common in women aged 30 to 60.
Organ or part of body involved: median nerve supplying hand.
Symptoms and indications: a tingling or burning sensation in the first three or four fingers of one or both hands, pains that may shoot up the arm, numbness and weakness in the hand. The symptoms are usually most severe at night. A person with these symptoms should seek medical advice.
Treatment: includes resting the hand and wrist, sometimes requiring a splint, which often resolves the condition. However, if it does not respond, surgery may be needed to divide the ligament in the wrist that is compressing the median nerve.
Causes and risk factors: the condition is caused by pressure on the median nerve by an overlying ligament in the wrist. This is brought about by trauma such as a lot of work with the hand and wrist, injury to the wrist or inflammatory conditions, especially arthritis. The condition can often be cured or improved.

catalepsy

Description: a mental disorder in which a person enters a trance-like state.
Persons most commonly affected: adults of both sexes and all age groups.

cataract

Organ or part of body involved: brain and central nervous system, whole body.
Symptoms and indications: the body becomes rigid like a statue and the limbs, if moved, stay in the position in which they are placed. There is no sense of recognition or sensation and a loss of voluntary control. The vital body functions are shut down to a minimum level necessary for life and, in fact, may be so low as to resemble death. The condition may last for minutes, hours or, rarely, several days. A person with catalepsy requires medical help.
Treatment: usually occurs in the context of the underlying disease or disorder with which the catalepsy is associated. (*See causes and risk factors.*)
Causes and risk factors: catalepsy may accompany severe mental illnesses such as schizophrenia. Also, it is brought on by severe mental trauma, either as a result of a sudden SHOCK or by a more prolonged depression. Occasionally it may accompany EPILEPSY.

cataract
Description: a condition in which the lens of the eye becomes hard and opaque, resulting in blurring of vision. (The lens is a flexible, clear structure enclosed in a thin capsule within the eye. It is responsible for focusing the incoming light rays onto the retina at the back of the eye where the image is formed.)
Persons most commonly affected: elderly persons of both sexes. Cataracts may affect younger people in certain circumstances and a congenital form can occur in newborn babies. (*See causes and risk factors.*)
Organ or part of body involved: lens of one or both eyes.
Symptoms and indications: the main symptom is blurring of vision, which may become progressively worse. A person with symptoms of cataract should consult a doctor.
Treatment: involves surgical removal of the whole or part of the affected lens.
Causes and risk factors: there are various causes of cataract. These include injury to the eye, metabolic disorders especially DIABETES, hypoparathyroidism and some others, congenital disorders, particularly Down's syndrome and GERMAN MEASLES (rubella), which if it affects a mother may cause cataracts in the baby. However, the commonest cause of cataracts is changes that occur in the eye as a result of advancing age. There are natural changes in the protein components of the lens leading to increased opacity and cataract formation. Preventative measures for other than age-related cataracts include seeking prompt attention for any infections or

condition involving the eyes, and having regular checkups and sight tests.

catatonia
Description: a state or syndrome in which a person becomes statue-like, remaining rigid, which is a feature of certain mental illnesses.
Persons most commonly affected: adults of all age groups and both sexes.
Organ or part of body involved: brain, nervous system, with whole body involvement.
Symptoms and indications: symptoms vary to a certain extent but include stereotyped behaviour (an action repeated over and over again in the same way), statue-like rigidity of the limbs, negativism (the person fails to cooperate and does the opposite of what is suggested) and CATALEPSY. A person showing signs of catatonia requires medical help.
Treatment: requires admittance to hospital for drug therapy and psychiatric help and counselling. The drugs that may be used include tranquillisers and, possibly, barbiturates given intravenously along with reassurance and counselling. Electroconvulsive therapy may sometimes be helpful. Patients normally require long-term support and help.
Causes and risk factors: the causes of profound mental disturbance are imperfectly understood. There are likely to be a number of causes at work including genetic factors, upbringing and family background, stressful events in life, physical illnesses and psychological trauma.

cat scratch fever
Description: a mild fever of viral origin resulting in swelling of the lymph glands.
Persons most commonly affected: all age groups and both sexes.
Organ or part of body involved: skin and lymph glands.
Symptoms and indications: swelling and slight infection at the site of a skin puncture. Slight swelling of lymph glands that usually subsides within a few days. Mild feverishness, discomfort and headache. It is advisable to consult a doctor if these symptoms are present.
Treatment: involves rest until the symptoms subside and the person feels better and drinking plenty of fluids. Medication is usually not necessary as the infection is caused by a virus. Occasionally, an ABSCESS may develop at the site of the wound, requiring further treatment. Complete recovery usually takes about one or two weeks.
Causes and risk factors: the cause of the infection is a virus that enters the body following a scratch from a cat, thorn or splinter or

cauliflower ear

other minor injury. In fact, a scratch from a cat is responsible for only about half the cases of cat scratch fever.

cauliflower ear
Description: a thickening of the external part of the ear that can lead to permanent deformity, caused by repeated injury suffered in sport.
Persons most commonly affected: men, especially those who are, or have been, boxers.
Organ or part of body involved: ear.
Symptoms and indications: a collection of blood (haematoma) following a blow or blows on the ear while playing sport. A person with the injury requires medical treatment as soon as possible to prevent permanent deformity.
Treatment: usually requires admittance to hospital where the blood is released to reduce the swelling. A firm bandage, which applies pressure to keep the swelling down, is then used. It is advisable to protect the ears and head during sports activities.
Causes and risk factors: thickening and deformity of the ears is a common injury among boxers.

cerebral palsy
Description: an abnormality of the brain that usually occurs before or during birth and results in severe physical, and often mental, disabilities.
Persons most commonly affected: detected after birth or in infancy and the person is affected for life. Both sexes are affected by congenital cerebral palsy, but it is more common in boys, and the incidence is in the order of 2 to $2\frac{1}{2}$ per thousand births. Less commonly, the illness may arise after birth due to a severe infection or trauma, and this type affects equal numbers of girls and boys.
Organ or part of body involved: brain, muscles.
Symptoms and indications: the severity of the symptoms varies greatly. The newborn baby may be floppy and have difficulty sucking but characteristically the child shows spastic paralysis of the limbs. Also, there may be involuntary writhing movements called athetosis, and balance and posture are also affected. There is often mental subnormality and speech impairment and sometimes EPILEPSY. Since a baby is closely monitored from birth, cerebral palsy is usually suspected or detected early on. A parent concerned in any way about the health of a baby should always call a doctor.
Treatment: the treatment required depends upon the severity of the symptoms and the degree to which the child is affected. The outlook is generally favourable and many children are able to enjoy a reason-

able or good quality of life. Treatment may involve some surgery but mainly physiotherapy, speech and occupational therapy and special education. It is now considered best to encourage the child to lead as normal and active a life as possible. Also, to expect and help the child to achieve as many aims and goals in life as possible, in spite of disability.

Causes and risk factors: it may arise as a developmental defect in the foetus due to genetic factors, or due to a viral infection during pregnancy. A lack of oxygen during a difficult labour or other trauma to the infant can result in cerebral palsy. After birth, the condition can result from HAEMOLYTIC DISEASE OF THE NEWBORN or infection of the brain e.g. MENINGITIS.

cervical cancer or cancer of the cervix

Description: cancer of the neck or cervix of the womb, which is one of the most common cancers affecting women.

Persons most commonly affected: women who are sexually active.

Organ or part of body involved: cervix – the neck of the womb.

Symptoms and indications: the precancerous and early stages of the disease may produce few or no symptoms. Later symptoms include abnormal vaginal discharge, which usually smells unpleasant and contains blood, and abnormal bleeding. If the cancer has spread to surrounding tissues and organs, further symptoms are likely to occur. Any abnormality in the cervix is normally detected by the cervical smear test offered to all women every three years in the UK. The woman is notified if any such signs occur and is given further investigation and treatment as required.

Treatment: is mainly aimed at prevention by means of the cervical smear test, which detects definite precancerous changes in the cells lining the surface of the cervix before cancer develops. At these early stages, the cancer is readily cured and treatment methods include cryosurgery, diathermy, laser treatment and electrocoagulation. One or a combination of more radical surgery, radiotherapy and chemotherapy are likely to be needed if the cancer has become established or has spread.

Causes and risk factors: the cause of this cancer is unknown but the sexual behaviour of a woman influences her risk of contracting the disease. The cancer does not occur in women who never have sexual intercourse. The earlier a woman or girl starts having sexual intercourse, and the greater the number of partners, are factors now recognised to increase her risk of contracting cervical cancer. However, the cure rate is high (about 95%) if detected and treated at an early stage.

Chagas' disease

Chagas' disease *see* SLEEPING SICKNESS

chicken pox (or varicella)
Description: a highly infectious viral disease that is normally mild and of fairly short duration.
Persons most commonly affected: children of both sexes; it can affect adults but this is uncommon.
Organ or part of body involved: the skin and the mucous membranes.
Symptoms and indications: there is an incubation period of two or three weeks and then usually the child becomes slightly feverish and unwell. Within 24 hours an itchy rash appears on the skin, which consists of fluid-filled blisters that vary in size. These may occur anywhere on the body including the scalp, inside the mouth and on the throat and in the genital area. Eventually these form scabs that fall off after about one week. The blisters are very itchy and tend to leave slight pock marks on the skin after healing, but these are not disfiguring. The symptoms are much more severe in adults accompanied by 'flu-like fever and aches and pains.
Treatment: involves keeping the child at home away from other children and relieving the itching by means of warm baths and soothing preparations. 'After-sun' preparations and calamine lotion are helpful in relieving itching. Children should be encouraged not to scratch, although this is difficult. Once scabs have formed and are drying and falling off, the child can start to resume normal activities but remains infectious until all the spots have gone.
Causes and risk factors: the cause of chicken pox is the varicella zoster virus and a childhood attack confers lifelong immunity as most children are exposed at some stage. Hence, the disease is uncommon in adults. Babies in the first few months of life usually have some immunity from the mother. After recovery from chicken pox the virus may remain within the system and become active later in adult life as SHINGLES.

chilblain or erythema pernio
Description: a round, itchy inflammation of the skin, usually occurring on the toes or fingers in cold weather.
Persons most commonly affected: all age groups and both sexes.
Organ or part of body involved: skin of the toes and fingers and sometimes the ears.
Symptoms and indications: round, red and itchy inflammation of the skin, which is especially troublesome when the feet or hands are warmed after having been chilled outside on a cold day.
Treatment: preventative treatment is best involving wearing good

warm gloves and footwear in winter weather. Keeping the feet and hands warm, eating a good diet and taking exercise to improve the circulation are helpful in the prevention of chilblains.

Causes and risk factors: chilblains tend to occur in people with defective circulation and may be an indication of poor health or inadequate nutrition. However, some people are more susceptible than others and in these persons, care and prevention are the best remedy.

cholecystitis or cholangitis

Description: inflammation and infection of the gall bladder and its ducts (bile ducts). Inflammation of the bile ducts is called cholangitis.

Persons most commonly affected: adults of both sexes and all age groups but less common in men. Rare in young people and children.

Organ or part of body involved: gall bladder and bile ducts.

Symptoms and indications: sharp, cramp-like pain in the upper part of the abdomen on the right-hand side. Pain may also be felt elsewhere. Abdominal discomfort, feverishness, nausea and vomiting, flatulence. Sometimes there may be jaundice and itching of the skin, and stools may be pale in colour. A person with symptoms of cholecystitis should seek medical advice.

Treatment: mild attacks may only require rest in bed and a course of antibiotics until the symptoms subside. However, often admittance to hospital and a surgical operation to remove the gall bladder (cholecystectomy) is necessary.

Causes and risk factors: the cause of cholecystitis is usually GALL-STONES causing blockage, inflammation and infection of the bile ducts. Hence, preventative measures to avoid the formation of gallstones are helpful e.g. eating a low-fat diet.

cholera

Description: a severe bacterial infection of the small intestine. Cholera remains a serious killer disease in many countries, especially in conditions of overcrowding and poor sanitation e.g. refugee camps. During epidemics, the death rate exceeds 50% with children and elderly persons being at particular risk. The disease is rare in the UK and such cases that occur are contracted abroad. Strict standards of hygiene, sanitation and nursing ensure that the infection does not spread, and prevent an epidemic. Early and prompt detection and treatment enable most patients to make a full recovery. This vigilance remains necessary because cholera caused thousands of

deaths in the last century during widespread epidemics in many countries.
Persons most commonly affected: all age groups and both sexes.
Organ or part of body involved: digestive system – whole body.
Symptoms and indications: there is considerable variation in the severity of symptoms and in the manner in which they present themselves. In mild cases, the patient may hardly feel ill, whereas in those severely affected during epidemics, death may occur very rapidly within a few hours. In most cases, three stages of cholera are recognised. During the first stage, there is copious diarrhoea and vomiting, with the production of characteristic 'rice water stools' containing flakes of fibrin (a protein substance formed in the blood during blood clotting). There are severe pains and cramps, extreme thirst and increasing signs of dehydration. In the second stage, death may occur due to dehydration and collapse. The person's skin is cold and wrinkled, the eyes are sunken, the pulse becomes imperceptible and the voice is a hoarse whisper ('vox cholerica'). During the third stage, the person may start to recover and gradually improve and the symptoms subside. Relapse is still possible at this stage, particularly in the form of a fever. A person who has travelled abroad and has any signs of illness should seek medical advice.
Treatment: requires isolation of the patient and scrupulous attention to hygiene during nursing. This includes treatment and very careful disposal of the body waste of the infected person, to prevent the spread of the disease. Treatment of the patient involves bed rest and the taking of tetracycline or other sulphonamide drugs to kill the cholera bacteria. The patient requires salt solutions to counteract the dehydration that occurs, and these are taken by mouth and/or given intravenously. Prevention of cholera is by means of vaccination but this is only effective for about six months.
Causes and risk factors: the disease is caused by the bacterium vibrio cholerae. It is spread by contamination of drinking water by faeces of those affected by the disease, and also by flies landing on infected material and then crawling on food. In countries where cholera is present, drinking water must be treated or boiled and strict standards of hygiene used in food preparation. Efforts should be made to eliminate flies from houses and to ensure that they do not come into contact with food. Risks remain wherever there are conditions of overcrowding, poverty and poor sanitation.

cirrhosis of the liver
Description: a disease of the liver in which fibrous matter resembling scar tissue is produced as a result of damage and death to the

cells. The liver becomes yellow-coloured and nodular in appearance, and there is a loss of its normal function that may eventually lead to complete failure.
Persons most commonly affected: adults of both sexes and all age groups but more common in men.
Organ or part of body involved: liver.
Symptoms and indications: there are various symptoms, which include loss of appetite and weight, digestive upset, weariness, enlargement of liver, ANAEMIA, dark urine, JAUNDICE, HAEMORRHAGE and blood in the stools. Also, bruising, fine, red spidery veins in skin, fluid retention, bloating (oedema) and red hands. Also, the spleen enlarges and there may be baldness and breast enlargement in men. Eventually, there may be collapse, coma and death from liver failure. A person with any symptoms of liver disease should seek medical advice.
Treatment: the progress of the disease can be halted if the cause is known, although nothing can be done to repair the damage to the liver that has already taken place. Excess consumption of alcohol is the most common cause of cirrhosis of the liver. Hence, if this is the cause, no more alcohol should be consumed. The affected person should eat a diet that is high in protein and carbohydrates but low in fat and salt. Iron, vitamins, (B and K) and mineral supplements may also be necessary. Provided that the liver damage is not too great, it should be possible for the person to lead a normal life as long as the progress of the disease is halted.
Causes and risk factors: as stated above, the most common cause of cirrhosis of the liver is excess consumption of alcohol over a long period of time. Other causes are viral HEPATITIS (post necrotic cirrhosis) and cirrhosis of unknown cause (cryptogenic cirrhosis). Exposure to toxic chemicals at the workplace is a further potential risk.

coeliac disease or gluten enteropathy
Description: a wasting disease occurring in childhood, an allergic condition in which the intestines are unable to absorb fat.
Persons most commonly affected: begins in infancy when the child is weaned, affecting infants and children of both sexes and remaining throughout life.
Organ or part of body involved: digestive system.
Symptoms and indications: loss of appetite, failure to thrive or weight loss, pains in abdomen, foul-smelling, pale stools, flatulence, dietary deficiencies and possibly anaemia. The symptoms appear after the child is introduced to foods containing gluten, which is found in

cold sores

wheat and rye flour. A baby or child who has symptoms of coeliac disease should be seen by a doctor.
Treatment: consists of eating a gluten-free diet throughout life. The child should start to thrive again once gluten is excluded, but may need vitamin, mineral and iron supplements to regain lost ground.
Causes and risk factors: the cause of coeliac disease is a congenital sensitivity or intolerance to gluten, causing damage to the lining of the intestines. The intestines are then unable to absorb fat, leading to excretion of an excess of fat and then other symptoms described above. There may be a family history of coeliac disease or a link with other allergic conditions. *See also* SPRUE.

cold sores
Description: an infectious inflammation of the skin and mucous membranes, characterised by the development of small blisters.
Persons most commonly affected: both sexes and all age groups, usually first appearing before the age of five. Once present, the virus persists for life.
Organ or part of body involved: skin, lips and mouth area. The lesions sometimes occur on the genitals and, rarely, occur on the cornea or conjunctiva of the eyes.
Symptoms and indications: there is a characteristic development of small, painful, fluid-filled blisters surrounded by a reddish area. In a few days, the eruptions dry up and heal completely, normally without scarring. If the eyes are affected, there may be some scarring and damage to the eye. A person with symptoms of an eye infection should always seek medical advice.
Treatment: various ointments and topical preparations are available without prescription for the treatment of cold sores. Occasionally, a secondary bacterial infection occurs, which requires treatment with an antibiotic preparation. If the eyes are involved, the person requires treatment by an eye specialist and may be prescribed an antiviral agent such as acyclovir.
Causes and risk factors: the cause of the infection is a HERPES SIMPLEX virus that is contracted from a person already having the virus. The virus is passed on through close physical contact e.g. kissing, and so may affect several members of a family. It often lies dormant for a long period of time before flaring up to produce cold sores. These then tend to occur from time to time throughout life. A person may be more susceptible to infection if 'run-down' or under stress in any way.

colic
Description: spasmodic, severe abdominal pain, which occurs in

waves with brief interludes in between. Infantile colic is common in young babies in the first few months of life.
Persons most commonly affected: adults and children of all ages and both sexes. Infantile colic affects babies between the ages of about two weeks and four months.
Organ or part of body involved: digestive tract.
Symptoms and indications: cramping, spasmodic waves of pain; usually the symptoms last for a fairly brief period. Infantile colic characteristically causes the baby to cry loudly for several hours, especially in the evening, and the legs may be drawn up in pain. Colic is painful but usually short-lived. A doctor should be consulted if the symptoms continue for a long time. Infantile colic can be alarming and parents often need reassurance that there is nothing seriously wrong with their baby. However, this condition does not require medical intervention.
Treatment: involves finding the most comfortable position to relieve the pain and resting until the symptoms subside. A hot-water bottle is also helpful. An attack of colic is generally not serious but can result in a twisting of the bowel that must receive immediate medical attention in hospital. Colic-type pain may also be caused by a tumour in the bowel, which again requires urgent medical treatment. Infantile colic is best coped with by general measures to try to comfort the baby. To try to prevent colic, the baby should be 'winded' during feeding and prevented from overfeeding or taking milk too quickly. Infantile colic generally stops after three or four months of age.
Causes and risk factors: the cause of colic is usually the presence of some indigestible food that causes the contraction of the intestinal muscles. Infantile colic is due to wind associated with feeding. In adults, provided that there is no more serious underlying cause, attacks are usually brief and infrequent.

colitis (ulcerative)
Description: inflammation of the colon, that may lead to ulceration and that is a severe chronic condition with a tendency to recur.
Persons most commonly affected: younger adults in the age range 16 to 45, especially women.
Organ or part of body involved: colon, bowel.
Symptoms and indications: abdominal discomfort and pain, watery diarrhoea containing blood, anaemia and fever. Also, there is a lack of appetite and loss of weight and sweating. A person with symptoms of colitis should consult a doctor. Occasionally, there may be serious complications as a result of this condition, which can prove fatal.

compressed air illness

Treatment: is by means of bed rest, drug treatment with corticosteroids and sulphasalazine, iron supplements to correct the anaemia and a bland, low-roughage diet. Another drug that may be prescribed is azathioprine and after recovery, it may be necessary to continue with sulphasalazine to prevent the recurrence of the condition. Rarely, surgery may be needed to remove part of the colon. Preventative treatment includes a low-roughage diet and avoidance of cold, damp weather conditions whenever possible.

Causes and risk factors: the cause of colitis is not known but there may be a genetic or family susceptibility, and the risk increases with an overconsumption of alcohol. There is a risk to the patient's life if the blood loss or wasting is excessive, or if infection such as PERITONITIS sets in as a result of serious ulceration. Also, there is a greater risk of contracting cancer of the colon.

compressed air illness *see* CAISSON DISEASE

concussion

Description: a loss of consciousness due to a blow to the head, causing bruising of the brain.

Persons most commonly affected: all age groups and both sexes.

Organ or part of body involved: brain.

Symptoms and indications: the symptoms vary in severity and reflect, to some extent, the force of the blow. There may be confusion, headache and dizziness in a case of mild concussion, or the person may fall into unconsciousness and remain in that state for seconds, hours or even weeks. It may be possible to rouse the person to some extent, but he or she is extremely irritable and does not answer questions correctly and soon becomes unconscious again. When the person comes round from the state of unconsciousness he or she usually suffers from a severe headache and irritability and these symptoms can last for some time. A person suffering from concussion usually needs to be admitted to hospital and a doctor should be called.

Treatment: depending upon the severity of the concussion, the patient requires admittance to hospital for rest and observation. There is a danger of bleeding caused by the blow on the head, which could result in serious, life-threatening damage to the brain. When the unconsciousness persists for some time the person requires careful monitoring, nursing and observation. Once the person has regained consciousness, even in mild cases of concussion, rest is needed until the headache subsides.

Causes and risk factors: the cause of concussion is a sudden knock to the head causing a compression wave that momentarily interrupts the blood supply to the brain. As indicated above, there is a risk of bleeding and further brain damage. The person normally makes a good and complete recovery but there may be memory loss, irritability and a tendency to headaches, lasting for several months. Also, there may be a risk or tendency in some people to EPILEPSY.

congenital nephroblastoma *see* WILM'S TUMOUR

conjunctivitis
Description: inflammation and infection of the mucous membrane (conjunctiva) that lines the inside of the eyelid and covers the front of the eye.
Persons most commonly affected: all age groups and both sexes.
Organ or part of body involved: conjunctiva of the eyes.
Symptoms and indications: reddening, watering and itching of one or both eyes. Discharge from the eye, which may be clear or yellowish, and forms crusts that glue the eyelids together after sleeping. There may be eye pain and discomfort. Symptoms vary according to the cause of the conjunctivitis and some forms are more serious than others. A person with symptoms of conjunctivitis should seek medical advice.
Treatment: depends upon the cause and nature of the condition but usually involves the application of eyedrops or ointment to relieve the symptoms and to kill infection. Drugs used include sodium cromoglycate, chloramphenicol and tetracycline antibiotics, penicillin and acycloguasine. Recovery from the milder forms of conjunctivitis is normally complete.
Causes and risk factors: there are various causes of conjunctivitis, including allergy, bacteria, viruses e.g. Herpes simplex and the microorganism, chlamydia. Chlamydia conjunctivitis (chlamydia trachomatis) is a common cause of blindness in some Third World countries. A baby may be infected by chlamydia or gonococcal infection (GONORRHOEA) as it passes through the birth canal, leading to the development of conjunctivitis in the first weeks of life.

constipation or costiveness
Description: the condition in which the bowels are opened too infrequently and the faeces become dry, hard and difficult and painful to pass.
Persons most commonly affected: all age groups and both sexes.
Organ or part of body involved: colon and rectum.
Symptoms and indications: infrequent opening of the bowels and the faeces passed are hard, dry, very dark and small. There may be

convulsions

bleeding, straining and pain, swelling of the abdomen due to retained faeces and a feeling of bloatedness. A person with persistent constipation should seek medical advice, as the condition itself may be a symptom of an underlying condition.

Treatment: involves making changes to lifestyle, including eating more roughage such as fruit, raw vegetables, wholemeal bread and bran, drinking at least eight glasses of water a day and taking more exercise. In addition, laxatives and enemas may be needed to relieve the condition. It is helpful to respond promptly to the urge to open the bowels and to encourage one daily bowel movement. These measures also help to prevent a recurrence of the condition.

Causes and risk factors: the cause is usually an inappropriate diet, inadequate fluid intake and inattention to the need to open the bowels. Sometimes the cause lies in the colon itself. Too much water may be absorbed quickly (a 'greedy colon'), leading to the production of dry, hard faeces. Or, in the case of a 'spastic colon', the muscles are in spasm (*see* IRRITABLE BOWEL SYNDROME). Sometimes the muscles of the colon do not work properly because of a lack of vitamin B in the food intake. Prolonged bouts of constipation may result in the development of piles or in a HERNIA or prolapse of the rectum or uterus.

convulsions or fits

Description: involuntary and rapidly alternating muscular contractions and relaxations throwing the body and limbs into contortions. Convulsions are themselves a symptom triggered by some underlying cause.

Persons most commonly affected: babies from about the age of six months and young children up to four years. Both sexes may be affected. Convulsions can also affect adults of both sexes.

Organ or part of body involved: brain and central nervous system; muscles.

Symptoms and indications: in young children, convulsions usually accompany a fever. Hence, the child is often already unwell and feverish. During the convulsion itself, there is uncontrolled twitching and jerking of the limbs, body, head and face, and unconsciousness. The person may lose control of bladder and bowel function and be irritable on regaining consciousness. Following the convulsion, the person usually sleeps for several hours. The convulsion normally only lasts for a few minutes. A person who has had a convulsion should be seen by a doctor.

Treatment: depends upon the underlying cause of the convulsion. If triggered by fever, as is often the case in young children, measures

to reduce the temperature and treat any infection are usually required. If the underlying cause is EPILEPSY, as is commonly the case in adults, then this requires appropriate treatment. If the convulsions continue, an injection of barbiturates or other sedative drug may be required.
Causes and risk factors: as indicated above, the commonest cause of convulsions in young children is fever. However, breath-holding, which is quite common in infants and very young children, is another cause. Also, breathing difficulties, which may occur, for example, during a bout of WHOOPING COUGH, may trigger a convulsion. More serious causes include inflammation and diseases of the brain such as MENINGITIS and ENCEPHALITIS, and head injury. In adults, the commonest cause is epilepsy. Convulsions are alarming to observe but unless caused by a serious disease or infection, in themselves they are rarely life-threatening.

Cooley's anaemia *see* THALASSAEMIA

corneal foreign bodies
Description: a foreign body lodging on the cornea or outer surface of the eye.
Persons most commonly affected: all ages and both sexes.
Organ or part of body involved: cornea.
Symptoms and indications: intense irritation and watering of the eye and photophobia (profound sensitivity to light).
Treatment: removal of foreign body and application of antibiotic drops or ointment. An eye patch may be worn until any damage has healed (usually about 24 hours).
Causes and risk factors: usually dust or material thrown up by mechanical tools. Can be avoided by wearing suitable eye protection when at risk e.g. when riding a motor cycle or when using power tools. If foreign bodies are not removed quickly from the eye, serious damage may be caused to the sight.

corns (and **bunions, hammer toe**)
Description: a corn is a small, localised portion of hardened, thickened skin occurring on or between the toes, which is cone-shaped. The point of the cone, known as the 'eye' points inwards and causes pain. A bunion occurs over the joint at the base of the largest toe. The joint between the toe and the first metatarsal bone becomes swollen and forms a lump beneath thickened skin (a callus). A hammer toe is similar but involves the second toe, which becomes bent at the joint to resemble a hammer.
Persons most commonly affected: adults of all groups and both sexes.
Organ or part of body involved: foot

Symptoms and indications: thickened skin and painful lumps or bumps on or between the toes.
Treatment: preventative measures are to ensure that shoes are always of a good fit with plenty of room for the toes. Corns and bunions can be treated at home by soaking in warm water to soften the area of thickened skin and, after drying, rubbing down with a pumice stone. Corn plasters can be used on the corn to reduce pain and pressure on the toe. It is often advisable to have corns and bunions treated professionally by a qualified chiropodist.
Causes and risk factors: the causes of corns and bunions are ill-fitting, tight footwear. There is an overgrowth of cells, due to pressure, leading to a thickening of the skin and the development of a lump.

coronary artery disease or coronary heart disease or ischaemic heart disease

Description: any abnormal condition that affects the coronary arteries that supply blood to the heart and arise from the aorta. The commonest disease is coronary ATHEROSCLEROSIS, resulting in narrowing or blockage that causes serious or fatal damage to the heart.
Persons most commonly affected: adults of both sexes but much less common in premenopausal women. There is equal incidence in adults during later years of life.
Organ or part of body involved: coronary arteries.
Symptoms and indications: often there are no or few symptoms until the arteries are severely narrowed. The disease advances until it causes ANGINA PECTORIS or CORONARY THROMBOSIS (which leads to heart attack). These conditions both require immediate medical attention.
Treatment: requires admittance to hospital and balloon angioplasty (a procedure for dilating the arteries), or coronary bypass surgery may be needed. Various drugs may be prescribed, including painkillers, beta-adrenergic blockers, VASODILATORS, anticoagulants, and nitroglycerin. The diet should be low in fat and salt and the person should undertake a programme of moderate exercise under doctor's advice. Preventative measures include no smoking, eating a low-fat, low-salt diet, taking regular exercise, and measures to avoid stress.
Causes and risk factors: the cause of the disease is not certain but the risk increases with the lifestyle factors mentioned above, i.e. smoking, poor diet, lack of exercise, stress and obesity. Also, persons with DIABETES, high blood pressure (HYPERTENSION) or previous heart

problems run a greater risk of developing the disease. The condition is a serious one, which may ultimately shorten life, although many people make a good recovery once the initial crisis has passed.

coronary thrombosis or **heart attack** or **myocardial infarction**
Description: a sudden blockage of one of the coronary arteries by a blood clot or thrombus that interrupts the blood supply to the heart. This causes death of myocardial (heart muscle or myocardium) cells due to interruption of the blood supply.
Persons most commonly affected: men, especially aged over 40, but also occurs in women.
Organ or part of body involved: arteries and heart.
Symptoms and indications: severe and agonising chest pain that may spread to involve the left arm, upper back, neck and jaw. Breathlessness and a crushing feeling on the chest, vomiting and nausea. A rise in temperature and pale and clammy skin, rapid pulse and collapse. A person suffering a coronary thrombosis requires urgent medical help and the emergency services should be called. If the person stops breathing and the heart stops, mouth-to-mouth resuscitation and external cardiac massage must be given until help arrives. Provided that a person receives prompt medical help, and survives the critical hours following a first heart attack, a good recovery is possible and normal activities can be gradually resumed. However, a severe heart attack may be fatal and the outlook is less favourable if the onset of treatment is delayed.
Treatment: following admittance to hospital, consists of giving strong pain relief, such as injections of morphine, oxygen and thrombolytic drugs to break up blood clots. The person requires intensive nursing in a coronary care unit. Various other drugs designed to restore the function of the heart are likely to be required, including anti-arrhythmics, beta-adrenergic or calcium channel blockers, digitalis, nitroglycerin and other antianginal preparations.
Causes and risk factors: the cause is a final sudden blockage or occlusion of one of the coronary arteries that has previously become narrowed (*see* CORONARY ARTERY DISEASE). This causes an interruption of the blood supply to part of the heart muscle, which dies, and this is known as myocardial infarction. The heart ceases to pump blood effectively, with the symptoms described above. The risk of heart attack increases with smoking, a poor diet high in fat and salt, obesity, high blood pressure (HYPERTENSION), stress, lack of exercise and raised levels of cholesterol in the blood.

costiveness *see* CONSTIPATION

Crohn's disease

Crohn's disease
Description: inflammation of a part of the ileum, which is the lower part of the small intestine, leading to ulceration and thickening.
Persons most commonly affected: young adults of both sexes between the ages of 20 and 40.
Organ or part of body involved: ileum, lymph tissue and glands.
Symptoms and indications: spasmodic abdominal pains of a colicky type that may be mistaken for APPENDICITIS. Slight fever, nausea, loss of weight and appetite. There may be diarrhoea and distension of the abdomen with tenderness and pain. There is a thickening of the ileum, which can sometimes be felt externally. A person with symptoms of Crohn's disease should seek medical advice. Attacks of symptoms tend to recur at intervals over a long period of time, although the disease may disappear.
Treatment: consists of rest and eating a low-fibre diet that is high in vitamins. Pain-relieving drugs and vitamin supplements may be prescribed, and also antibiotics and corticosteroid drugs. Occasionally, if there is a complete blockage or a failure to respond to medical treatment, admittance to hospital for surgical removal of the affected part may be necessary.
Causes and risk factors: the cause is unknown, although there may be a tendency for Crohn's disease to occur in families and hence a genetic link. People with food allergies are more likely to develop the disease. There is a possibility of infection or ABSCESS, perforation of the severely inflamed part, FISTULA and increased risk of the development of cancer of the ileum. *See also* ILEITIS.

croup
Description: a group of diseases characterised by infection, swelling and partial obstruction and inflammation of the entrance to the larynx, occurring in young children.
Persons most commonly affected: young children of both sexes up to the age of about six years.
Organ or part of body involved: larynx, windpipe (trachea) and bronchial tubes (leading to the lungs).
Symptoms and indications: harsh, strained breathing producing a characteristic crowing sound, accompanying a cough and fever. There may be pains in the chest or throat and the child is generally restless and unwell. Attacks usually occur at night. If the child is experiencing severe difficulties in breathing, emergency medical attention is required. Milder cases can be treated at home but a doctor should be consulted.
Treatment: mild cases can be relieved by taking the child into the

bathroom and turning on the hot water taps to produce a steamy atmosphere. The condition can be relieved by inhalation of steam from a bowl or basin of hot water to which a soothing preparation, such as tincture of benzoin, can be added. Mild sedatives and/or painkillers may be prescribed by a doctor. The child should be encouraged to drink plenty of fluids. Rarely, the obstruction becomes dangerous and completely blocks the larynx. The outcome is rapidly fatal, unless the child has been admitted to hospital, where nasotracheal intubation or emergency tracheostomy to restore the airway can be carried out.

Causes and risk factors: DIPHTHERIA used to be the most common cause of croup but it now usually results from a viral infection of the respiratory tract (laryngotracheobronchitis), or less commonly, a bacterial infection. A child normally makes a good recovery from croup but attacks are likely to recur. The child should be discouraged from playing outside in cold, damp weather, as this may cause an attack in some cases.

Cushing's syndrome

Description: a metabolic disorder that results from the presence in the body of excessive amounts of corticosteroids, which are hormones produced by the cortex of the adrenal glands. The production and regulation of these hormones is controlled by the pituitary gland at the base of the brain. There may be an inability to regulate adrenocorticotrophic hormone or cortisol, produced by the pituitary gland, which itself controls the production of corticosteroids by the adrenal glands. Or, the problem may lie in the adrenal glands themselves.

Persons most commonly affected: all age groups and both sexes but more common in adults and in women.

Organ or part of body involved: pituitary gland and adrenal glands.

Symptoms and indications: reddening of face and neck with puffiness, growth of body and facial hair, obesity, OSTEOPOROSIS and, possibly, mental disturbances. Also, there may be menstrual irregularities in women, high blood pressure, DIABETES MELLITUS and the development of peptic ulcers. There may be an increased susceptibility to infections and stretch marks on the abdomen. A person with Cushing's syndrome requires careful monitoring and often needs long-term medical treatment.

Treatment: depends upon the source of the problem but may involve surgery to remove a tumour and hormone replacement therapy if glands have to be taken out. Also, drugs to correct high blood pressure (HYPERTENSION) and calcium supplements to counteract osteoporosis may be required. Occasionally, treatment may include irradiation of the pituitary gland. Depending upon the cause, Cushing's syndrome can be cured but the person usually needs continuing medication throughout life.

Causes and risk factors: the commonest cause of Cushing's syndrome is a tumour of the pituitary gland or adrenal gland. Also, a malignancy elsewhere e.g. in the lung, which has required extensive and prolonged treatment with corticosteroid drugs can produce Cushing's syndrome. If these are gradually and carefully withdrawn, the symptoms may improve. There is a risk of fractures due to the osteoporosis that accompanies Cushing's syndrome and affected persons should take care to avoid accidental injury.

cystic fibrosis (CF)

Description: an inherited (genetic) disease, the defective gene responsible for it being located on human chromosome no. 7.

Persons most commonly affected: children of both sexes.

Organ or part of body involved: the disease affects all the mucus-secreting glands of the lungs, pancreas, mouth and gastrointestinal tract and also the sweat glands of the skin.

Symptoms and indications: a thick mucus is produced that affects the production of pancreatic enzymes and causes the bronchi to widen (bronchiectasis) and become clogged. The child has a constant, severe cough but the mucus is thick and difficult to cough up. Respiratory infections are common. The stools contain a lot of mucus and are slimy, with a foul smell. The child loses weight and the sweat contains abnormally high levels of sodium and chloride. The liver and spleen become enlarged. The diagnosis of cystic fibrosis is usually made early in the child's life by analysis of the stools, but there is no antenatal test that can detect the condition.

Treatment: the disease is incurable but the outlook for affected children has greatly improved with increasing numbers of patients surviving into adult life. Treatment involves physiotherapy to relieve the bronchial congestion, particularly daily postural drainage that can be carried out at home. Humidifiers may be needed in the home to keep the air moist, which helps to thin the mucus. Any respiratory infection should be treated promptly by a doctor and may require antibiotics. The child may need a special diet that is high in protein and low in fat. Vitamin supplements and pancreatic enzyme tablets are normally required. The child may need frequent admittance to hospital for intensive nursing during infections. The child should be encouraged to lead as normal a life as possible.

Causes and risk factors: the cause is a genetic abnormality that affects about one child in every 2000. Many people carry the gene for cystic fibrosis and if there is a family history of the disease, a couple may need to seek advice before having children.

cystitis

Description: inflammation and infection of the bladder, normally caused by a bacterium.
Persons most commonly affected: females of all age groups. The condition is much less common in males.
Organ or part of body involved: bladder.
Symptoms and indications: characteristically, there is a need to pass urine frequently accompanied by a burning, painful sensation. There may be cramp-like pains in the lower abdomen with dark, strong urine that contains blood. A person with symptoms of cystitis should seek medical advice.
Treatment: involves taking a course of antibiotics and also drinking a lot of fluids, possibly with the addition of bicarbonate of soda which counteracts the acidity of the urine, thereby easing the pain. The increase in fluid makes the urine more dilute, thus helping to flush out the bacteria, making it less likely that they will grow again and cause a further attack. Recovery is usually rapid although cystitis may recur from time to time.
Causes and risk factors: the cause of the infection is usually the common bacterium that normally inhabits the bowel, *E. coli*. The prevalence of cystitis in females is due to the fact that the urethra is much shorter in women than in men, and the bacteria (which are harmless in the bowel) are more likely to gain access both to the urinary tract and vagina. In the bladder, the bacteria cause inflammation and infection with the symptoms of cystitis, as described above. There is a slight risk of the infection spreading up to the kidneys, which is a more serious condition, hence cystitis should always be treated promptly.

D

deafness

Description: partial or total loss of hearing in one or both ears. Deafness may be congenital (present from birth), conductive (an abnormality of the outer or middle ear, preventing the passage of

delirium

sound waves to the inner ear) or nerve deafness (an abnormality of the inner ear, the auditory nerve or the brain).
Persons most commonly affected: congenital deafness: from birth and both sexes. Conductive deafness: any age and both sexes. Nerve deafness: any age, but increasingly common in people over 50. Both sexes.
Organ or part of body involved: ears.
Symptoms and indications: gradual or sudden loss of hearing. In congenital deafness, this may be noticed as a lack of response to sounds, or when the child is older, poor or absent speech.
Treatment: for congenital deafness, early testing of the hearing is important. A hearing aid may be fitted, and special training for parent and child for hearing and speech may be used. Conductive deafness may be treated by an operation, or fitting a hearing aid. Nerve deafness may be helped by use of a hearing aid.
Causes and risk factors: Congenital deafness: in most cases, the cause is unknown, but may be inherited, caused by the mother catching rubella (GERMAN MEASLES) in the first 16 weeks of pregnancy, some drugs during pregnancy, brain damage at birth or SYPHILIS in the mother. Vaccination against rubella for girls between the ages of 11 and 14 should give immunity for life, and is an important means of prevention. Conductive deafness: is most commonly caused by OTITIS MEDIA. Nerve deafness: in most cases there is no definite cause, but some are due to exposure to excessive noise, for example, gunfire explosions or working in a very noisy place.

delirium
Description: an acute mental disorder, in which there is disorientation, confusion and hallucination, with several causes.
Persons most commonly affected: all age groups and both sexes.
Organ or part of body involved: brain.
Symptoms and indications: incoherence, confusion, restlessness, fear, anxiety, often hallucinations or illusions and sometimes delusions. If the delirium is caused by ALCOHOLISM, it is called *delirium tremens*.
Treatment: usually by treating the cause. If this is fever, then sponging the patient with tepid water to reduce the temperature will help. Fluid intake and nutrition must be maintained, and if the cause is withdrawal from alcohol dependence, sedation may be required.
Causes and risk factors: a wide range of metabolic disorders, postpartum (after childbirth) or postoperative stress, ingestion of toxic substances (including alcohol), physical or mental stress or exhaustion may all cause delirium.

dementia
Description: mental impairment, caused by a variety of diseases, leading to a permanent deterioration of the brain.
Persons most commonly affected: adults over 60 of both sexes.
Organ or part of body involved: brain.
Symptoms and indications: increasing forgetfulness, especially of recent events, confusion, unpredictable behaviour, loss of interest in events and personal appearance and poor judgement.
Treatment: neurological examination to determine the cause of the dementia. The only help that can be given is in providing care and attention for the sufferer.
Causes and risk factors: the cause is unknown. If the person affected is young or middle-aged, the cause may be ALZHEIMER'S DISEASE.

dengue
Description: also known as break-bone fever or dandy-fever, this is a tropical fever.
Persons most commonly affected: all ages and both sexes.
Organ or part of body involved: skin and joints.
Symptoms and indications: these occur in two stages. In the first, there are normally joint pains, fever, extreme weakness and headache. This is then followed by a day or two of remission and then the fever returns, usually accompanied by a rash.
Treatment: the joint pains can usually be relieved with aspirin, sometimes used together with codeine, although in severe cases, pethidine may be used. Calamine lotion eases the rash. Bed rest is needed and fluid intake should be kept up. In some cases, the fever may return more than once, and the weakness and joint pains may take months to disappear.
Causes and risk factors: the virus causing the fever is transmitted to man by the mosquito *Anopheles*. In areas where there is a risk of being bitten by these mosquitoes, use of an insect repellent and mosquito nets should help to reduce the risk.

dermatitis
Description: an inflammation of the skin that can have many different causes. If the cause is an allergic reaction to something, this form of dermatitis is usually called ECZEMA.
Persons most commonly affected: all ages and both sexes.
Organ or part of body involved: skin.
Symptoms and indications: the skin turns red and in some cases may be itchy. The skin may develop small blisters.
Treatment: the first line of treatment must be to remove the cause of the dermatitis. This may be contact with a substance that irritates

dermatomyositis

the skin (contact dermatitis) or sunlight (light dermatitis). In mild cases, an application of calamine lotion may be sufficient to bring relief, but in more severe cases a topical (applied to the area being treated) corticosteroid may be used. This is an artificial hormone preparation that reduces the body's production of antibodies, which lessens inflammation.

Causes and risk factors: contact dermatitis: is caused by contact between the skin and an irritant substance. There are many substances that may irritate the skin, including soaps and detergents; industrial chemicals; some metals, cosmetics and plants, and for babies, urine, causing nappy rash. People who know that their skin is sensitive to a particular substance must try to avoid further contact with it. Light dermatitis: particularly in children, this may have no specific cause, other than a particular sensitivity to sunlight. However, in many sufferers, the condition is caused either by use of some drugs, or sometimes, a particular chemical in lipstick or a perfume in cosmetics.

dermatomyositis *see* POLYMYOSITIS

diabetes insipidus

Description: a rare disorder of the pituitary gland (a hormone-producing gland in the brain).
Persons most commonly affected: all ages and both sexes.
Organ or part of body involved: pituitary gland and endocrine (hormone) system.
Symptoms and indications: great thirst and passing of large quantities of pale urine. Dry hands and constipation.
Treatment: if caused by tumour, then surgery is needed, otherwise treatment with antidiuretic hormone, or ADH, (a drug that constricts blood vessels and reduces the passing of urine).
Causes and risk factors: lack of ADH, caused by injury, tumour, intracranial (within the head) bleeding, ANEURYSM or KIDNEY DISEASE.

diabetes mellitus

Description: a condition in which the body cannot use sugar and carbohydrates (starches) from foods, because the pancreas (an organ in the abdomen, producing digestive juices) does not produce enough of the hormone insulin. This means that sugar accumulates in the blood and body tissues, causing defects in various parts of the body.
Persons most commonly affected: usually people under 30, but it may begin at any age. It can also frequently affect the middle-aged and elderly, particularly if they are obese. Both sexes.
Organ or part of body involved: pancreas.

Symptoms and indications: thirst, fatigue, weight loss, and increased appetite and thirst. Frequent urination, itching genitals, boils, and, if advanced, deterioration of vision.

Treatment: aims to restore the blood sugar level to as near normal as possible. In younger people, the condition is usually more severe and the only treatment is with insulin injections to lower blood sugar levels and by control of the diet to regulate the carbohydrate/insulin balance. In older people diet alone may be sufficient.

Causes and risk factors: the causes are mostly unknown, although there seems to be an inherited tendency to developing diabetes. However, it may be triggered by stress or viral infection. Some women develop diabetes during pregnancy, but it normally disappears after the baby's birth. Missing meals may lead to hypoglycaemia (too low a level of glucose in the blood). The sufferer will be hungry and may sweat and become confused. An immediate intake of glucose will usually return them to normal. Too low a level of insulin may lead to coma and death if not corrected. Sufferers of diabetes are at risk of eye and kidney problems, and they have to be very careful to look after their feet, as any foot infection, if not dealt with immediately, may lead to GANGRENE.

diarrhoea *see* FOOD POISONING, GASTRITIS, GASTROENTERITIS

diphtheria

Description: a very contagious, but in western countries, very rare, throat infection.

Persons most commonly affected: people over five. Both sexes.

Organ or part of body involved: throat, skin, heart, central nervous system.

Symptoms and indications: early symptoms are a sore throat, fever and swollen neck glands. If untreated, this may lead to airway obstruction, caused by a film forming in the throat, and shock.

Treatment: the first immediate treatment is an injection of antitoxin, and a course of antibiotics. The patient should be quarantined, and bed rest is required. If the disease is in an advanced stage, a tracheotomy (an incision in the trachea or airway) may be required to help breathing.

Causes and risk factors: a bacterial germ causes the disease, but immunisation offers protection against infection.

discoid lupus erythematosus *see* LUPUS ERYTHEMATOSUS

dislocation

Description: a bone wrenched out of place at a joint is said to be dislocated. If the dislocation is minor, it may be called subluxation.

Persons most commonly affected: all ages, both sexes.
Organ or part of body involved: any joint, but most commonly the jaw, shoulder, knee and spine. Some children are born with hip dislocation.
Symptoms and indications: the joint is very painful and swollen and may show bruising. There is usually difficulty in moving the joint.
Treatment: relocation of the joint by a doctor and then immobilisation of the joint for a few weeks. Occasionally, surgery may be required, but this is normally only if dislocations happen repeatedly.
Causes and risk factors: dislocation is usually accidental. It may sometimes be caused by a shallow or poorly formed joint surface (usually congenital) or arthritis.

diverticular disease
Description: diverticulosis is a condition where there are diverticulae (small pouch-like swellings through weak points in the wall of the colon). Diverticulitis is the inflammation or infection of diverticulae.
Persons most commonly affected: adults of both sexes, becoming more common with increasing age.
Organ or part of body involved: colon.
Symptoms and indications: there are usually no symptoms of diverticulosis. However, there may be pain in the left side of the lower abdomen and disturbed bowel habit, caused by muscle spasms in the colon. The symptoms of diverticulitis are intermittent cramping in the abdomen, often becoming severe pain. There is often fever and nausea and there may be tenderness of the affected area.
Treatment: a high-fibre diet. X-rays of the colon are usually taken to ensure that the symptoms are not caused by cancer of the colon. If the diverticulae are infected, treatment with an antibiotic is required. If a diverticula has ruptured, surgery to mend the colon is required.
Causes and risk factors: this disease cannot be prevented, but the risk of getting it can be reduced by making sure that the diet is well balanced, with low salt and fat intake and a high fibre intake.

drowning
Description: the immediate aftereffects of prolonged submersion in water.
Persons most commonly affected: all ages and both sexes.
Organ or part of body involved: lungs, blood and heart.
Symptoms and indications: there is a lack of spontaneous breathing. The patient has a blue colour and has no pulse.

Treatment: the patient must be removed from the water. If there are any foreign bodies in the mouth, such as weed, mud or false teeth, they must be removed. A check must be made to determine whether the patient is breathing, and whether he or she has a pulse or not. Artificial respiration and external cardiac massage (cardiopulmonary resuscitation or CPR) must be started at once if required, and help sent for. The CPR should be kept up until either the patient recovers enough to breathe unaided, in which case they should be put in the recovery position, or until the emergency services arrive to take over.

Causes and risk factors: water entering the lungs. In 15% of cases, submersion in water causes a spasm of the larynx. To avoid drowning accidents, learn to swim. Do not swim after drinking alcohol, or too soon after eating. Do not swim in deep water to cool down on a hot summer day, as the water may be very cold, resulting in a sudden and disabling cramp. Do not dive or jump into unknown water; there may be underwater obstructions like weed or rocks, or in a swimming pool, underwater hazards. Do not leave small children alone in the bath, or in gardens with ornamental pools, as a child can drown in just a few inches of water. When taking part in water sports, like boating or water-skiing, wear a life jacket.

drug abuse

Description: the misuse of a mood-changing substance for pleasure, often leading to addiction. Some of the most common substances used are nicotine, alcohol (*see* ALCOHOLISM), amphetamines, barbiturates, cocaine, opium alkaloids, glues and solvents, cannabis and psychedelic drugs. Drugs may also be abused by athletes keen to improve their performance. In this case, it is usually stimulants or anabolic steroids.

Persons most commonly affected: all ages (except early childhood) and both sexes.

Organ or part of body involved: central nervous system, blood, liver and kidneys.

Symptoms and indications: these depend on the substance being abused, but most of them give altered behaviour. There may be increased sensitivity to sights and sounds and unpleasant symptoms when the substance is withdrawn. The use of heroin and cocaine makes the pupils of the eyes contract to pinpoints.

Treatment: the first step in treatment has to be the desire of the abuser to stop. Professional help will probably be needed and counselling. In the case of narcotic abuse, a doctor may prescribe

methadone, a less potent drug, to decrease the severity of withdrawal symptoms.
Causes and risk factors: drug abusers risk accidental injury while under the influence of the substance. They risk serious infections if using non-sterile needles for injected drugs, such as HEPATITIS, BLOOD POISONING and HIV. There is a high risk of death caused by overdose, and body organs may suffer irreversible damage. There is also a high risk of losing their job, friends, home and family.

duodenal ulcer
Description: an ulcer (a breach of the membrane, which does not heal easily) in the duodenum (the tube between the outlet of the stomach and the small intestine).
Persons most commonly affected: adults and both sexes, but especially those of blood group O, or those with a family history of duodenal ulcers.
Organ or part of body involved: duodenum.
Symptoms and indications: a burning, gnawing pain below the ribs. It may wake the sufferer in the early hours. There is usually pain one to two hours after meals, which continues until the next meal and is only relieved by milk, antacids (medicines that reduce the acidity of the stomach) and food.
Treatment: stopping smoking, antacids, barium meal, possibly surgery.
Causes and risk factors: stress, excess acid and smoking.

dysentery (amoebic and bacillary)
Description: an inflammation of the intestine, especially the colon, caused by bacteria (bacillary dysentery) or protozoa (amoebic dysentery).
Persons most commonly affected: all ages and both sexes.
Organ or part of body involved: digestive tract, but especially the colon.
Symptoms and indications: bacillary dysentery: severe diarrhoea, with the passage of blood and mucus. There may be nausea, cramp and fever, and the symptoms may last for about a week. Amoebic dysentery: symptoms may appear within a week of infection, or may take years to appear. The onset is very gradual, with weight loss, ANAEMIA and indigestion, and eventually, passing of bloody stools.
Treatment: bacillary dysentery; bed rest, rehydration with plenty of water, and great care to ensure that any soiled clothing or bedding is either destroyed or thoroughly cleaned and disinfected. Amoebic

dysentery; treatment with nitroimidazole drugs, followed by diloxamide furoate.
Causes and risk factors: bacterial dysentery is caused by infection from bacteria, amoebic by infection by protozoa. Both can be avoided by protecting food from flies, avoiding contaminated water and taking care to see that sanitation is good. Known carriers of either disease should not be allowed to handle food. Complications in bacillary dysentery only occur in severe cases, when the intestine may perforate and bleed. This may also happen with amoebic dysentery, where there is also a risk of abscesses forming in the liver, brain, bone or testes.

E

ear infection *see* OTITIS MEDIA (MIDDLE EAR), OTITIS EXTERNA (OUTER EAR)

eclampsia of pregnancy
Description: CONVULSIONS (fits) arising in pregnancy.
Persons affected: females during pregnancy.
Organ or part of body affected: cardiovascular system (blood system).
Symptoms and indications: an early sign is raised blood pressure, with headaches and marked swelling of the ankles. (Slight swelling of the ankles is quite common in the advanced stages of pregnancy.) There may be an unexplained weight gain. The condition can be confirmed by the presence of protein in the urine. If untreated, convulsions will follow. The condition is usually discovered when the mother is in the early stages of the disease, when it is called PRE-ECLAMPSIA.
Treatment: bed rest is necessary, with careful monitoring of the foetus. If the condition is severe, an emergency Caesarian section may be required.
Causes and risk factors: these are unknown. It is more likely to happen in a first pregnancy, or where the mother is older. The mother may also be obese, have had previous HYPERTENSION or have DIABETES MELLITUS. She may also be carrying twins, or a Rhesus-incompatible baby. No hereditary link has been established but it is recommended that a pregnant woman inform her midwife or doctor of any history of the condition in her family.

ectopic pregnancy

Description: a pregnancy where the fertilised egg grows outside the uterus, usually in one of the Fallopian tubes joining the ovary to the uterus. As the egg grows, it stretches the tube and eventually ruptures it.
Persons affected: females during pregnancy.
Organ or part of body involved: usually Fallopian tubes.
Symptoms and indications: if a period is two to three weeks overdue, sudden severe pain in the abdomen. Sometimes, there is less severe pain and bleeding from the vagina. If no action is taken at this stage, there may finally be collapse from bleeding into the abdomen.
Treatment: immediate admission to hospital for surgery to remove the affected tube. If the blood loss has been large, a blood transfusion will be necessary.
Causes and risk factors: an ectopic pregnancy is more likely to happen if the Fallopian tube has suffered previous damage from infection. It is also more likely if there is a contraceptive coil in the uterus. As only one tube is affected by an ectopic pregnancy, it is still possible to conceive again.

eczema

Description: an inflammation of the skin, usually caused by allergy. Eczema is a form of DERMATITIS. The most common forms of eczema are atopic or infantile eczema and discoid eczema.
Persons most commonly affected: all ages and both sexes.
Organ or part of body involved: skin.
Symptoms and indications: atopic eczema: this usually starts at the age of three to four months. Reddening of the skin starts on the scalp, spreading to the face and in some cases to other parts of the body. The skin erupts with small spots, which weep and are very itchy. Approximately 70% of children affected by this form of eczema have a family history of ASTHMA, HAY FEVER or eczema. Discoid eczema: in this form of eczema, small coin-shaped patches of skin become itchy and blistered. This is more common in young adults or middle life.
Treatment: atopic eczema: the application of 1% hydrocortisone ointment may be prescribed, and if the itching is very severe, a sedative to prevent the sufferer scratching. Discoid eczema: a prescription for coal tar ointment may help the itching.
Causes and risk factors: atopic eczema is usually inherited and the cause of discoid eczema is unknown.

embolism
Description: blocking of a small blood vessel, usually by a THROMBO-EMBOLISM, but occasionally by fat after a bone fracture, or by air after an injection or a diving accident. It is usually in the lung (a PULMONARY EMBOLISM), but may be elsewhere.
Persons most commonly affected: all age groups and both sexes.
Organ or part of the body involved: circulatory system.
Symptoms and indications: for a pulmonary embolism, these are shortness of breath, a sudden cough and chest pain that may be slight to very severe. Sometimes the lips turn blue (cyanosis), or there may be blood in the sputum. In severe cases, there may be symptoms of SHOCK or unconsciousness.
Treatment: X-rays are taken to check the position of the embolism, and anticoagulants are given to prevent further clots. In severe cases, a patient may be admitted to hospital for oxygen and anticoagulant therapy, and sometimes surgery may be needed to remove the clot.
Causes and risk factors: it occurs most often after surgery and other treatment involving long stays in bed. It can be partially prevented by moving about as soon as possible after surgery, childbirth or injury. For some operations that carry a higher risk, anticoagulants may be prescribed before treatment. People who have had previous emboli may take regular anticoagulants. Large embolisms can cause sudden death, medium embolisms usually heal, leaving no permanent disability and small embolisms are usually harmless and often heal without their presence being recognised.

emphysema
Description: overinflation of the tiny air sacs in the lungs, which can rupture to form larger sacs. Over time the total surface area available for gaseous exchange is diminished and so less oxygen is available for the body.
Persons most commonly affected: older people of both sexes.
Organ or part of body involved: lungs.
Symptoms and indications: wheezy breathing and shortness of breath, which is even worse after exercise. In severe cases, the patient may become blue, bloated and 'barrel-chested'.
Treatment: oxygen may help and antispasmodics may be of use during attacks of breathlessness.
Causes and risk factors: almost all cases of emphysema are caused by smoking, giving rise to BRONCHITIS. Nothing can be done to reduce existing damage to the lungs. Since a reduced level of oxygen reaches the blood from the damaged lungs, strain may be put on the heart.

encephalitis

Description: inflammation of the brain.
Persons most commonly affected: all age groups and both sexes.
Symptoms and indications: initial symptoms include fever, headache and neck stiffness, generalised aches and pains, fatigue, weakness and irritability. As the condition worsens, the affected person may become confused and disorientated and there may be convulsions, paralysis and eventually coma. Anyone with the symptoms of encephalitis requires emergency medical attention as it is a serious, life-threatening condition.
Treatment: Although there is no specific treatment for encephalitis the condition can be improved by relieving the pressure around the brain (it is increased pressure caused by the inflammation that causes the symptoms). Admittance to hospital is necessary for intensive medical and nursing care.
Causes and risk factors: encephalitis is most commonly caused by a viral infection of the brain which can also lead to the inflammation of the meninges and the development of MENINGITIS. It can also be a complication of a number of infectious diseases such as MEASLES and CHICKEN POX. Japanese encephalitis is caused by the bite of an infectious mosquito. There is a risk of permanent brain damage resulting from the condition.

endocarditis

Description: inflammation of the endocardium (the inner lining of the heart).
Persons most commonly affected: all age groups and both sexes, but bacterial endocarditis is very rare before the age of five.
Organ or part of body involved: heart.
Symptoms and indications: sometimes shows as an unexplained fever, and there are symptoms of HEART BLOCK and/or EMBOLISM.
Treatment: antibiotic therapy.
Causes and risk factors: caused by bacterial or viral infection, usually in a previously damaged heart. This damage may be congenital ('hole in the heart') or caused by RHEUMATIC FEVER. The infection enters the bloodstream and is carried to the damaged heart. This can occur most easily during dental treatment involving extractions or scaling. The condition can be prevented if the dentist is informed and a course of antibiotics taken before treatment. Recovery from endocarditis is not certain.

endometriosis

Description: a condition where cells from the endometrium (the

lining of the uterus) are found elsewhere in the body, usually in the Fallopian tubes, ovaries or uterine muscle.
Persons affected: menstruating females between puberty and menopause.
Organ or part of body involved: reproductive organs, and sometimes bowel.
Symptoms and indications: pelvic pain, often of long duration, usually worse during menstruation. Lower back pain, heavy periods and pain during sexual intercourse.
Treatment: surgery or hormone treatment.
Causes and risk factors: causes are unknown, but the condition may lead to infertility or pelvic cysts.

enterobiasis *see* THREADWORMS

entropion
Description: inward turning of the eyelid, causing the eyelashes to rub and irritate the cornea.
Persons most commonly affected: both sexes, usually older people.
Organ or part of body involved: eyelid.
Symptoms and indications: sore, watering, red eyes.
Treatment: involves admittance to hospital for surgery to correct the condition.
Causes and risk factors: may be caused by inflammation or scarring following injury, but is usually caused by spasms or slackening of the eyelid muscle, which can occur as the muscles age.

epidural abscess *see* BRAIN ABSCESS

epiglottitis
Description: a relatively rare inflammation and swelling of the epiglottis (the cartilage separating the back of the tongue and the entrance to the airway, which closes off the airway when swallowing).
Persons most commonly affected: both sexes, usually children aged one to six, but may occur in other age groups.
Organ or part of body involved: epiglottis.
Symptoms and indications: fever, noisy difficult breathing, cough, excessive saliva and rapid pulse developing quickly over a few hours.
Treatment: admission to hospital and antibiotic therapy. If obstruction to breathing is severe, the patient may be need to be intubated (have a tube inserted into the airway) or in very severe cases a tracheotomy (an incision into the trachea) may be necessary. Oxygen is usually given.
Causes and risk factors: it is caused by a bacterial infection, but it is rarely transferred between children.

epilepsy (or falling sickness)

Description: a neurological disorder characterised by the occurrence of CONVULSIONS or seizures and a loss of consciousness or momentary loss of awareness.

Persons most commonly affected: all age groups and both sexes. Usually, it starts in children between the ages of 2 and 14 and quite frequently below the age of 5.

Organ or part of body involved: brain.

Symptoms and indications: there are several forms of epilepsy and usually the symptoms arise suddenly. Occasionally, the person has a warning that an attack is about to occur. This is called *aura epileptica* and takes the form of odd or unpleasant sensations of sound, sight or smell, a change of mood, or pain or trembling in the muscles.

Grand mal seizure: this affects all age groups and involves a sudden loss of consciousness. The person falls to the ground, the muscles are stiff and he or she has a rapid pulse, poor pallor and dilated pupils. The body is then thrown into spasm by violent jerking of the muscles. The person may gnash the teeth, bite the tongue and froth at the mouth, and the eyes roll in the head. Breathing is noisy and the person may lose control of the bladder and bowel function. The attack usually lasts up to a few minutes and the body then relaxes. The person may regain consciousness to a certain extent but is usually very confused and soon falls into a deep sleep that may last for a few hours. On waking, the person may be restored to normal or feel tired, subdued and depressed.

Petit mal seizure: this often occurs in children and is characterised by a loss of awareness. The person suddenly stops the activity in which he or she is engaged and looks blank and is not aware of his or her surroundings. There may be some odd muscular movements or changes of expression. The attack lasts for a very short time and the person usually comes round and resumes previous activity, often being unaware of the episode.

Temporal lobe epilepsy: the affected person suddenly changes and behaves in an abnormal and inappropriate way, becoming angry or aggressive or agitated. Such behaviour is unusual and abnormal for that person.

Focal epilepsy: one part of the body is thrown into muscular spasm, although this may spread to involve the whole body, but there is no loss of consciousness.

A person who has an epileptic seizure requires immediate medical attention.

Treatment: is tailored to each individual's requirements and the person will require monitoring and periodic checkups. Various anticonvulsive drugs are used to control epilepsy, including phenytoin, primidone, methoin, clonazepam, sodium valproate and carbamazepine. The type and dose that is most effective varies between individuals. A person who suffers from epilepsy should not drink alcohol and may not be allowed to drive until two years have passed without an attack. Usually, seizures can be prevented and controlled and a person suffering from epilepsy can expect to lead a normal life. However, the condition generally cannot be cured except in those cases where surgery or other treatment can correct a brain disorder.

Causes and risk factors: there are a number of different causes, including brain injury, tumour or inflammation, and infection, disorders of metabolism such as hypoglycaemia, brain haemorrhage and birth trauma. Many people suffer a fit or convulsions at some stage in life, but most do not develop epilepsy.

Epstein Barr virus *see* GLANDULAR FEVER

erythema

Description: any one of a number of skin conditions, characterised by the engorgement of superficial blood vessels and the appearance of red inflamed patches. Types include *erythema ab igne*, *erythema pernio* (*see* CHILBLAIN), *erythema nodosum*, *erythema multiformae* and *erythema infectiosum* ('slapped-cheek' disease).

Persons most commonly affected: all age groups and both sexes depending upon type.

Organ or part of body involved: skin, especially legs, arms, hands, face.

Symptoms and indications: erythema ab igne – red inflammation of the legs in a network pattern caused by sitting too close to a fire. Erythema nodosum – more common in females, and characterised by the appearance of painful, red nodules and swellings, which are quite large and usually occur on the lower legs. There may be fever, malaise and swollen, painful ankles and knees. Erythema multiformae – more common in children and young people, especially girls. Red blotches, lumps and blisters appear on the hands, arms and body but the characteristics vary. Erythema infectiosum – affects children, especially during the months of spring. A bright red rash appears on the cheeks and spreads to other parts of the body. It usually subsides after about three weeks. A person with symptoms of erythema should seek medical advice.

Treatment: depends to a certain extent on the cause and type of

erythema pernio

erythema and the severity of symptoms. Corticosteroid or nonsteroidal anti-inflammatory drugs may be prescribed, along with analgesics. Preparations for bathing affected skin may be recommended along with rest and avoiding extremes of heat and cold.
Causes and risk factors: erythema nodosum – allergic reaction to certain drugs (sulphonamides) and bacterial infections e.g. streptococcus, mycobacterium tuberculosis and sarcoidosis. Erythema multiformae – allergic reaction to the use of some drugs e.g. barbiturates and sulphonamides or caused by a virus. Erythema infectiosum – highly contagious and thought to be caused by a virus.

erythema pernio *see* CHILBLAIN

erythroderma
Description: also known as exfoliative DERMATITIS. It is an abnormal thickening and flaking of the skin.
Persons most commonly affected: both sexes, but three times more common in men than women. It is rare before the age of 50.
Organ or part of body involved: skin.
Symptoms and indications: red patches of skin, which gradually thicken and then peel.
Treatment: corticosteroids.
Causes and risk factors: it occurs half the time in people with existing skin conditions, usually chronic ECZEMA or PSORIASIS. In a third of cases, there is no cause. For the rest, the condition may be as a result of HODGKIN'S DISEASE or LEUKAEMIA.

erythromelalgia
Description: also called red NEURALGIA. It is a condition of red or purple blotches on fingers or toes, which are warm and painful.
Persons most commonly affected: both sexes, mainly middle-aged.
Organ or part of body involved: skin.
Symptoms and indications: a burning sensation and red blotches on hands and feet, occasionally spreading to limbs. It can last for a few minutes to several hours.
Treatment: reduction in temperature by the use of fans and removal of clothes or bedclothes that have triggered the attack. Aspirin usually gives relief.
Causes and risk factors: it may be without cause, but is often associated with HYPERTENSION (high blood pressure). Prevention includes keeping hands and feet cool in summer and by staying out of the sun, and not wearing thick socks or gloves in winter.

Ewing's sarcoma
Description: a rare, very malignant cancer of bone.
Persons most commonly affected: both sexes, children and young adults.
Organ or part of body involved: bone, usually starting in limbs or pelvis.
Symptoms and indications: pain, swelling and tenderness. There may be a high temperature, and the white blood cell count may be raised.
Treatment: irradiation and chemotherapy. Surgical amputation of a limb may be necessary in some cases.
Causes and risk factors: males are more often affected than females and it occurs at a younger age than any other bone tumour, peaking between the ages of 10 and 20 years. Combined therapy results in the cure of over 60% of cases, with localised Ewing's sarcoma.

exanthem subitum *see* ROSEOLA INFANTUM

exophthalmos
Description: forward displacement of one or both eyeballs. Also called 'pop eyes'.
Persons most commonly affected: both sexes, but ten times more common in women than in men. All ages, but most common in the third decade.
Organ or part of body involved: eyeball.
Symptoms and indications: protruding eyes.
Treatment: surgery may be necessary to remove a blood clot, tumour or ANEURYSM. Drugs may be prescribed if the cause is an infection or HYPERTHYROIDISM.
Causes and risk factors: causes include thyrotoxicosis (GRAVES' DISEASE) or a tumour pushing onto the eyeball (in this case, it is only ever one eye).

F

fascioliasis
Description: a disease caused by the liver fluke, *Fasciola hepatica*, which affects the liver and bile ducts.
Persons most commonly affected: all ages and both sexes.
Organ or part of body involved: liver and bile ducts.
Symptoms and indications: the disease is diagnosed by finding eggs

of *Fasciola* in the stools. The symptoms include fever, loss of appetite, indigestion and abdominal pain, nausea and vomiting, diarrhoea and coughing. It is possible that the liver may be damaged in more serious or prolonged cases, and there may also be jaundice.
Treatment: most cases are mild and treatment with the drugs chloroquine and bithionol leads to recovery. Emetine may also be used although this can itself irritate the stomach. The most important treatment is preventative, e.g. wild watercress should never be eaten.
Causes and risk factors: the liver fluke is found in cattle and other herbivores and the disease is passed to man via snails. Eggs from the parasite pass out in the faeces of the animal. The eggs are taken up by snails and a larval stage is deposited on vegetation, especially wild watercress, which if eaten causes infection and a renewal of the parasite's life cycle.

favism
Description: a type of haemolytic ANAEMIA, i.e. anaemia caused by the breakdown of red blood cells by the body's own system, but sooner than would normally occur (which is usually at the end of the 'life span' of a red blood cell).
Persons most commonly affected: there is a particular geographic pattern to the disease, those affected most being in Iran, parts of the Mediterranean, a high proportion of Yemenite Jews in Israel and some African Americans.
Organ or part of body involved: blood.
Symptoms and indications: anaemia with the symptoms fever, headache, dizziness, vomiting, JAUNDICE, diarrhoea.
Treatment: blood transfusion in the case of severe anaemia.
Causes and risk factors: favism is brought on by eating a particular broad bean (*Vicia fava*) because a chemical in the bean causes the haemolysis (breakdown of the red blood cells). However, it only occurs when the affected person has an inherited genetic defect resulting in the absence of an enzyme, glucose-6-phosphate dehydrogenase, which would otherwise protect the red blood cells. The defect is sex-linked and, because it also carries increased resistance against MALARIA, it tends to be perpetuated.

A similar reaction can also occur with the antimalarial drugs primaquine and pamaquine, and other compounds such as sulphonamides and some vitamin K analogues.

fever
Description: a rise in body temperature above normal (37.4°C orally, 37.6°C rectally). Also called pyrexia.

Persons most commonly affected: may affect all ages and both sexes.
Organ or part of the body involved: any part of body may be involved.
Symptoms and indications: at the outset a fever is frequently marked by shivering that can become quite violent. In addition, in the early stages there is accompanying headache, sickness, thirst, diarrhoea or constipation, and possibly back pains. This is usually followed by an increase in pulse and breathing, hot dry skin, a marked thirst and loss of appetite and reduced urination. In severe cases where the body temperature continues to rise, there will be DELIRIUM. Loss of strength and some wasting of muscles may occur in prolonged cases.
Treatment: because a fever is a symptom of another condition or illness, it is vital that the underlying condition is treated. At the same time, some steps may be taken in an attempt to reduce the body temperature directly. The affected person may be sponged with tepid water or placed in a bath in which the water temperature is gradually lowered.

Certain antipyretic drugs, such as paracetamol and quinine, act on the controlling centres of the brain causing greater heat loss through the skin.
Causes and risk factors: fevers are caused primarily by viral or bacterial infections and may occur with any infection, however minor. Fever is the primary outcome of many diseases caused by a toxin in the system e.g. scarlet fever or typhoid, and the toxins are produced by bacteria in the body. Fever may also be associated with tumours, autoimmune diseases or SHOCK.

The risk increases in cases of poor nutrition, in areas with poor sanitation, or where there is polluted water. Delirium occurs above a body temperature of 40.5°C. Excessive fever or hyperpyrexia occurs at 41.1°C and is regarded as dangerous while death usually results if the temperature remains above 41.7–42.2°C.

fibroid

Description: a benign (noncancerous) growth of cells in the wall of the uterus.
Persons affected: menstruating women over 30. Fibroids do not form after the menopause.
Organ or part of body involved: uterus.
Symptoms and indications: quite often there are no symptoms. However, there may be pain and excessive menstrual bleeding; also more frequent menstruation, bleeding between periods and an increase in vaginal discharge. There may be anaemia.

Treatment: small fibroids may be enlarged by contraceptive pills that have a high oestrogen content, so it may be necessary to change this contraceptive method. If fibroids are troublesome, causing bleeding, discomfort, etc, then they are usually removed surgically. This can be done without removing all of the uterus, but sometimes this is necessary. In addition, if blood loss associated with the fibroids is high, an iron supplement may be necessary.

Causes and risk factors: the cause of fibroids is unknown, but they may be hereditary, and their growth may be enhanced by contraceptive pills containing oestrogen.

In a very small number of cases there may be a malignant change that is indicated by rapid growth. However, this is very rare, occurring in under 0.5% of cases.

fibrositis

Description: also called muscular rheumatism. An inflammation of muscles, particularly in the back, that may also affect the chest, shoulders, arms, hips or thighs. The term fibrositis is to some extent being superseded by fibromyalgia.

Persons most commonly affected: adults, usually over 30 years. It tends to be more common in females.

Organ or part of body involved: muscles.

Symptoms and indications: a gradual onset of stiffness and pain with sudden muscle spasms that can be quite painful. There are tender points, or nodules, which are sensitive to touch. Associated symptoms include fatigue, loss of sleep, IRRITABLE BOWEL SYNDROME symptoms and anxiety.

Treatment: the application of heat to specific areas can help relieve pain whether by means of hot baths, showers, heat lamps or other methods. In addition, gentle massage, exercises and more sleep (encouraged by medication) will all help. In some cases, aspirin may ease discomfort and injection of a local anaesthetic (such as lignocaine) with hydrocortisone can be applied to tender points.

Causes and risk factors: the cause is unknown but there are certain conditions or circumstances that may stimulate the condition. These include stress or trauma, exposure to cold or dampness, muscle injury or a viral infection. Also it may be associated with another disease that causes joint inflammation, such as RHEUMATOID ARTHRITIS. Cases of localised fibrositis develop in men who suffer a strain due to their occupation or participation in sport.

fistula

Description: a channel or connection between an organ or similar

natural cavity and the surface, or between two organs or cavities, where no such connection should exist.
Persons most commonly affected: no one group is more susceptible than another.
Organ or part of body involved: depends on the site, commonly the anus.
Symptoms and indications: there are several types of fistula but the commonest is the anorectal, where the connection is from the anal canal to the skin. It may follow a history of abscesses with some discharge. A urinary fistula causes urinary infections and may connect with the skin or elsewhere e.g. uterus, vagina, small intestine or abdominal wall. A salivary fistula causes saliva to run out onto the cheek instead of into the mouth, and an arteriovenous fistula (i.e. a connection between an artery and a vein) will cause arterial or venous insufficiency and a warm mass can be felt if near the surface.
Treatment: in all cases, surgery is the first choice for treatment. In some cases, such as the anorectal fistula, this can be quite difficult if the condition has been present for some time. The operation restores the natural connection and when this is achieved, the fistula heals quite quickly. However, in the case of an anorectal fistula, healing is slowed and complicated by the entrance of material into it from the bowel.
Causes and risk factors: there are numerous causes. It may be congenital but usually is due to injury or illness. An anorectal fistula generally forms due to an abscess and a urinary fistula may occur in women following an injury during a prolonged delivery. Blockage of the salivary duct may lead to a salivary fistula.

fits *see* CONVULSIONS, ECLAMPSIA OF PREGNANCY, EPILEPSY

food poisoning
Description: poisoning resulting from eating contaminated foods or ingesting poisonous chemicals, fungi or berries. *See also* BOTULISM.
Persons most commonly affected: both sexes and all ages.
Organ or part of body involved: primarily the digestive system.
Symptoms and indications: in general, food poisoning results in nausea and vomiting, diarrhoea, abdominal pain and possibly headache and fever. The symptoms and the time of onset vary with the type of food poisoning, but will usually commence between one and twenty-four hours of intake.

Staphylococcal food poisoning from meat, milk or egg products generates symptoms abruptly within two to eight hours and the attack is usually short-lived (three to six hours) with complete recovery. Only susceptible individuals (young, chronically ill or the elderly) are likely to be at risk. *Clostridium perfringens* is associated with food poisoning from meat and meals that are reheated, and symptoms are produced within eight to twenty-four hours.

Numerous species of *Salmonella* cause food poisoning with symptoms following eight hours to three days after ingestion. Such infections are found in the meat and/or milk of domesticated cows, pigs and poultry and also in uncooked or lightly cooked hen's eggs.
Treatment: in the main, treatment is more preventative than curative, i.e. affected foods should be avoided and preparation and storage of foods should comply with good practice and appropriate regulations. Depending upon the severity of the attack, treatment may just involve bed rest, or, if there is severe vomiting, intravenous infusions of electrolytes may be required. Thereafter, the diet should be bland until recovery is assured.
Causes and risk factors: *Salmonella* (and also *Listeria*) are bacteria causing the symptoms. Although the animals mentioned above may be infected, they do not necessarily display symptoms, but products made from them create the poisoning. *Salmonella* bacteria are generally killed by heating to 60°C for about 15 minutes. Staphylococcal and clostridial food poisoning are caused by toxins released by the bacteria and in these cases, heating does not destroy either the toxin (staphylococcal) or the bacteria (clostridial). It is therefore essential that hygienic conditions prevail at all stages of food production.

Although the number of outbreaks of food poisoning has increased over recent years, it is not usually a fatal condition, but certain groups of people will be at greater risk, i.e. babies and the very young, pregnant women, the elderly and the chronically ill.

fracture *see* BONE FRACTURE

framboesia *see* YAWS

Friedreich's ataxia
Description: a hereditary disease producing gradual degeneration of the nerve cells of the spinal cord and brain.
Persons most commonly affected: usually children, between the ages of five and fifteen.
Organ or part of body involved: spinal cord and brain.
Symptoms and indications: intitial symptoms include an unsteady walk and loss of the knee-jerk reflex, followed by slurring and other speech difficulties. Progressively, the disease causes some tremor, severe arching of the feet and spinal deformity (curved spine). There

may also be progressive heart disease. The sufferer may live for 20 to 30 years, the symptoms becoming gradually worse, leaving the individual quite helpless.
Treatment: there is no treatment.
Causes and risk factors: the disease is caused by a recessive gene on chromosome nine.

frostbite
Description: damage to tissue caused by exposure to freezing conditions.
Persons most commonly affected: no one particular group.
Organ or part of body involved: the extremities: toes, fingers, etc.
Symptoms and indications: the first symptoms of frostbite are when the affected area, be it toes, fingers or face, goes white and numb and all feelings of cold or pain disappear. As the severity of the condition worsens, there can be blisters on the frozen area, with a hardening and blackening of the skin. Swelling of the tissue produces tingling and sometimes severe pain. In very serious cases, the affected part becomes swollen and discoloured (blue/grey) and infection may set in.

Associated symptoms include shivering, slurred speech and possible loss of memory.
Treatment: shelter should be found immediately. The affected area should *not* be massaged, but warmed by putting in warm water, clothing or similar, but not by placing near an open fire or by applying direct heat. A general warming of the body may be required, by means of hot drinks and insulation e.g. a sleeping bag. Any blisters should not be opened and the affected area should be cleaned carefully. It may be appropriate to give antibiotics to combat infection and analgesics to relieve pain. Anyone with a badly affected foot should not walk.
Causes and risk factors: frostbite results from the formation of ice crystals in the tissues causing tissue injury or tissue death in an extreme case. It is therefore essential that anyone who may be at risk is well clothed and equipped for the conditions and if frostbite does occur, can seek shelter and assistance quickly. A possible risk is that dead or infected tissue, be it finger, toe, nose or ear, may have to be amputated, but in mild cases (usually called frosting) full recovery is possible.

frozen shoulder
Description: a painful condition in which the shoulder joint becomes stiff.

furuncle

Persons most commonly affected: usually between the ages of 50 and 70 in both sexes.
Organ or part of body involved: shoulder.
Symptoms and indications: pain and stiffness that limit considerably the normal movement of the joint.
Treatment: there is no particular treatment but gentle exercise may help. An injection of corticosteroid into the joint may also help in some cases.
Causes and risk factors: the cause is not known and the condition usually occurs gradually for no reason. However, it may also develop after a stroke or myocardial infarction (heart attack).

furuncle *see* BOIL

G

gallstones
Description: stones of varying composition that form in the gall bladder. There are three types of stone: cholesterol, pigment and mixed, the latter being the most common. Calcium salts are usually found in varying proportions.
Persons most commonly affected: adults of both sexes but twice as common in women as in men. They are more common with increasing age, hence more prevalent in middle-aged and older people.
Organ or part of body involved: gall bladder and bile ducts.
Symptoms and indications: in many cases, gallstones may be present for years without causing any symptoms. However, when symptoms do occur they include severe pain of a colic type, particularly on the upper right-hand side of the abdomen. The pain may also be felt in the upper part of the back. There may be nausea, vomiting and indigestion. If the stones pass into the common bile duct, the resulting obstruction can cause JAUNDICE. A person having symptoms of gallstones should seek medical advice.
Treatment: gallstones, particularly small ones, may be treated with ultrasound waves to break them up, or drugs may be prescribed (which are derived from bile salts) to dissolve them. The drugs may need to be taken for about two years before the stones disappear and they can produce some side effects. Surgical treatment to remove the gall bladder may be required and this is carried out either by conventional methods or by making small incisions and using fibreoptic

instruments (fibreoptic endoscopy). Prior to surgery, during an attack of pain from gallstones, treatment consists of bed rest and taking painkillers until the symptoms subside. Most patients make a good recovery following cholecystectomy (removal of the gall bladder).
Causes and risk factors: the exact cause is unknown but their formation seems to be due to a change in bile composition, rendering cholesterol less soluble. Stones may also form around a foreign body and calcium salts are usually found in varying proportions. Stones are more likely to form if the gall bladder fails to empty effectively or if any infection of the bile ducts has occurred. *See also* CHOLECYSTITIS.

gangrene or mortification

Description: death of tissue due to loss of blood supply or bacterial infection. There are two types of gangrene, dry and moist, and gas gangrene, which is caused by a particular type of bacterial infection.
Persons most commonly affected: all age groups and both sexes.
Organ or part of body involved: gangrene can affect any part of the body and is very serious if it involves the main organs within the abdomen. Often, the fingers, hands, arms, toes, feet and legs are the sites most likely to be affected.
Symptoms and indications: dry gangrene – the affected part becomes cold and turns dark red then brown and black, and there is an obvious line between living and dead tissue. This line of demarcation shows as an area of reddening and slight inflammation. There may be a slight smell but no pain or fever, and eventually, the gangrenous part drops off.

Moist gangrene – there is putrefaction (bacterial decomposition of tissue) and an issuing of fluids from the affected tissues, accompanied by an obnoxious smell but not much pain. The affected area becomes swollen and eventually blackened in places. Its extent is not always clear and is likely to spread. The patient is likely to suffer from a serious fever and there is a risk of death from blood poisoning.

Gas gangrene – this occurs when a wound is present that is infected by a particular form of bacterium that produces gas. The bacteria produce toxins that cause decay and putrefaction with the generation of gas. The gas spreads into muscles and connective tissue, causing swelling, pain, fever and, possibly, toxic DELIRIUM. If untreated, the condition quickly leads to death.

A patient with gangrene requires prompt medical treatment, usually in hospital.
Treatment: usually involves amputation and also the taking of antibiotics if infection is involved. The bacteria causing gas gangrene

are anaerobic (exist without air or oxygen). Hence, surgical incisions that allow the penetration of air, along with oxidising agents, antitoxin and penicillin are all used in treatment to prevent the spread of the gangrene. A person can usually be cured if gangrene is treated early, but is left with disfigurement due to amputation.

Causes and risk factors: dry gangrene is caused purely by loss of blood supply and is a late-stage complication of DIABETES MELLITUS, in which ATHEROSCLEROSIS is present. Moist gangrene is caused by bacterial infection, and gas gangrene by infection with soil bacteria of the genus *Clostridium*. Gangrene may occur following injury, particularly crushing of a limb cutting off the circulation. Also, as a result of atherosclerosis and FROSTBITE.

gastric erosion
Description: degeneration and minor ulceration of the lining of the stomach.
Persons most commonly affected: adults of both sexes and all age groups but more common in men.
Organ or part of body involved: stomach.
Symptoms and indications: black stools owing to the presence of blood. Vomiting blood, which may appear red or as black grains (coffee grounds), anaemia. A person with these symptoms should seek prompt medical advice.
Treatment: involves identifying the cause of the problem, often a drug being taken for some other condition, which may then need to be withdrawn and the prescription changed. Iron supplements and preparations to inhibit the production of acid in the stomach may be required. Foods that may irritate the stomach, and alcohol, should be avoided until the lining heals. Recovery is usually good, and healing may take one or two weeks. However, it may return.
Causes and risk factors: the most common cause is a type of drug that is being taken for some other condition, which may erode the stomach lining in susceptible people. Drugs likely to cause this include those prescribed for arthritic conditions or ASTHMA, aspirin, alcohol and non-steroidal anti-inflammatory drugs. Rarely, serious bleeding or even perforation of the wall of the stomach can occur, which require corrective surgery, and are potentially life-threatening, especially in elderly patients.

gastric ulcer *see* STOMACH ULCER

gastritis
Description: inflammation and/or infection of the stomach lining (mucosa).

Persons most commonly affected: all age groups and both sexes.
Organ or part of body involved: stomach.
Symptoms and indications: symptoms include vomiting, nausea, diarrhoea, abdominal pains, discomfort and tenderness, wind and loss of appetite. There may be feverishness and the person may feel unwell and generally lethargic. Rarely, there may be vomiting of blood or blood in the stools, which are then black in colour. There may be dehydration due to diarrhoea, which can be serious, especially in children. A person with symptoms of gastritis should seek medical advice.
Treatment: depends upon the cause and if it is drugs, alcohol or other irritant substance, then these need to be withdrawn and avoided. Plenty of fluids should be drunk and food avoided on the first day that gastritis begins. The person should carefully and gradually resume a normal diet, avoiding foods that may irritate, and alcohol. Recovery is normally complete within about one week.
Causes and risk factors: causes include excess consumption of alcohol or indigestible foods, drugs that are being taken for some other condition, and viral infection. There is a slight risk of serious bleeding or perforation of the stomach wall, requiring corrective surgery, which are potentially life-threatening, especially in elderly patients.

gastroenteritis
Description: inflammation and infection of the stomach and intestines.
Persons most commonly affected: all age groups and both sexes.
Organ or part of body involved: stomach and intestines.
Symptoms and indications: diarrhoea and sometimes vomiting, nausea, abdominal pains and tenderness, loss of appetite and fever. There may be dehydration if diarrhoea is severe and prolonged. Young children and elderly persons with gastroenteritis should be seen by a doctor, as should any person showing signs of dehydration.
Treatment: an attack of gastroenteritis is normally short-lived, symptoms subsiding after two to five days. The person should rest in bed and avoid all food but take frequent small quantities of water, gradually increasing the amount as diarrhoea and vomiting subside. Children may need sachets of salts, as prescribed by a doctor, added to drinking water. As symptoms subside, very small quantities of easily digestible solid food can be tried and if this is tolerated, a normal diet can be gradually resumed as the appetite returns. If a person, especially a young child or elderly patient,

genital herpes

becomes dehydrated, admittance to hospital may be needed so that fluids can be given by intravenous drip. Scrupulous attention should be paid to hygiene (especially washing hands frequently), as the condition is often very contagious. Recovery is usually good, occurring within a short space of time, although it may be two or three weeks before the person regains a normal appetite.

Causes and risk factors: the most common cause is a bacterial or viral infection but also parasites and food poisoning may be responsible. It is common in persons experiencing a total change of environment, as occurs when visiting a different country. Very young children and babies and the elderly are at greatest risk and this condition is a common cause of death where people are crowded together in poor, inadequate housing with inadequate sanitation.

genital herpes *see* HERPES SIMPLEX INFECTION

German measles (rubella)

Description: a highly infectious viral disease, occurring mainly in childhood, which is mild in effect.

Persons most commonly affected: children, but can occur in adults.

Organ or part of body involved: skin, respiratory system, glands in neck.

Symptoms and indications: there is an incubation period of two or three weeks before symptoms appear. These include headache, shivering and a sore throat, with a slight fever. There is some swelling of the glands in the neck and soon after a rash of tiny pink spots appears, initially on the face and/or neck and subsequently spreading over the body. The rash disappears in roughly one week but the condition remains infectious for three or four more days. The symptoms are normally mild and it may be difficult to identify the disease in the early stages. Its most marked feature, although short-lived, is the swelling of the neck. A pregnant woman should consult a doctor if concerned about German measles.

Treatment: no specific treatment is necessary other than keeping the child at home until three or four days after the spots have disappeared and the disease is not infectious. The child can be given mild painkillers, if needed, and bed rest if feeling unwell. Plenty of fluids should be drunk and a normal diet offered. Recovery is usually complete after a week or ten days.

Causes and risk factors: the cause of the disease is a virus and an attack normally confers lifelong immunity. However, German measles poses a risk of foetal abnormalities in the early stages of pregnancy, if the mother catches the infection. The risk is considered to be greatest during the first 16 weeks of pregnancy. Any woman who has not had the disease in childhood and who is considering pregnancy, should be vaccinated, after a lack of immunity has been established by a simple blood test. Young girls are now routinely immunised around the age of 12 or 13. It is a wise precaution for any pregnant woman to avoid contact with anyone who is suffering from German measles or who may have been exposed to the disease.

giardiasis
Description: inflammation of the duodenum (the first portion of the small intestine) and the upper part of the small intestine.
Persons most commonly affected: all age groups and both sexes, most of which occur in people who have recently travelled in Russia or the Middle East.
Organ or part of body involved: small intestine.
Symptoms and indications: sudden copious diarrhoea, nausea and pain in the abdomen, pale, foul-smelling stools that are fatty, and fever. In some cases there may be little diarrhoea and mild abdominal discomfort. A person with these symptoms should seek medical advice.
Treatment: consists of rest and a course of the drug metronidazole or mepacrine, which kills the causal parasite. Alcohol should be avoided and plenty of fluids should be drunk. Strict attention should be paid to hygiene, especially washing the hands. Recovery is normally good and occurs naturally within about one month, but is much quicker with drug treatment.
Causes and risk factors: the cause is the parasite *Giardia lamblia*, which inhabits the small intestine, often without causing harm. It is contracted from drinking untreated water or water that has not been treated to a high standard, or from streams. To prevent infection, any suspect water should be boiled or treated with purifying tablets. Foods such as fruit or salad vegetables should be washed in treated water. Particular care should be taken when travelling abroad, especially if camping.

glandular fever or infectious mononucleosis
Description: an infectious viral disease, the symptoms and effects of which can be quite long-lasting.
Persons most commonly affected: adolescents of both sexes in mid-teenage years and young adults under 40 years.
Organ or part of body involved: lymph nodes, liver, spleen, throat.

glaucoma

Symptoms and indications: include a sore throat, swelling of lymph nodes in the neck and also in the armpits and groin, and fever. Also, headache, loss of appetite, and fatigue. The liver and spleen may become enlarged, and occasionally jaundice develops. The person feels generally unwell and tired. A person with symptoms of glandular fever should be seen by a doctor. The disease is diagnosed by the large numbers of monocytes (white blood cells) in the blood.

Treatment: consists of rest in bed and the taking of painkillers to relieve symptoms, as advised by the doctor. Plenty of fluids should be drunk and the patient should try to eat a good balanced diet. Complications are normally rare but total recovery may take many weeks, the person often continuing to feel unusually tired.

Causes and risk factors: the disease is caused by the Epstein Barr virus, which is contracted from close physical contact (such as kissing) with an infected person. It is thought to be prevalent in adolescents because their immune system is not fully mature and also due to the nature of transmission. It is more likely to arise when young people are crowded together and sharing living conditions, as in colleges, student flats, military establishments, etc. A rare complication is a ruptured spleen, requiring surgery and recovery in hospital.

glaucoma (open-angle and narrow-angle)

Description: a serious group of conditions affecting the eyes. They are all characterised by high pressure within the eye (intra-ocular pressure) and may result in blindness.

Persons most commonly affected: adults of both sexes aged over 40 years, with those aged more than 60 being at particular risk.

Organ or part of body involved: eye.

Symptoms and indications: open-angle glaucoma or chronic glaucoma – there are no or few symptoms until the condition is well advanced and then the person normally experiences some form of vision disturbance. This may take the form of partial loss, particularly of peripheral vision or blurring of vision, which tends to get worse. The person may perceive halos around lights and have poor vision in the dark. The intra-ocular pressure within the eye is raised but the angle between the iris and cornea stays open. A person with these symptoms should consult a doctor and will need continuing treatment.

Narrow-angle glaucoma or acute glaucoma – symptoms include seeing a halo of coloured light around lamps, blurring of vision, severe pain around eye and throbbing headache. There is increasing interference with vision, the eyeball is hard and tender and the angle between the iris and cornea is closed. The eye may be red and swollen. The symptoms are caused by increasing pressure in the eye because fluid cannot drain away. This condition requires emergency medical treatment in hospital.

Treatment: open-angle glaucoma or chronic glaucoma – treatment consists of the application of eye drops several times a day, and taking tablets, which cause the intra-ocular pressure to fall. Some patients may require a surgical operation, called trabulectomy, which helps fluid to drain from the eye more easily.

Narrow-angle glaucoma or acute glaucoma – treatment consists of admittance to hospital and intensive use of drops and tablets to lower the intra-ocular pressure. Surgery is then required to prevent the condition occurring again.

Glaucoma can be successfully treated and the symptoms controlled if caught early but failure to do this can result in total blindness.

Causes and risk factors: the cause of all types of glaucoma is a restriction in the outflow of fluid (aqueous humour) within the eye, leading to a buildup of pressure, which causes damage to the retina and optic nerve, resulting in visual loss or blindness. The reason why this occurs is not known but genetic (hereditary) factors, stress, smoking and increasing age are likely to increase the risk of a person developing glaucoma. An eye test carried out at regular intervals can detect glaucoma.

glomerulonephritis (acute, postinfectious and chronic)
Description: inflammation of the glomeruli of the kidneys. A glomerulus is a small round knot of blood capillaries that brings water, salts, urea and other waste products to the kidney tubules, so that the material can be filtered and excreted. Each kidney contains about 1,000,000 glomeruli.

Persons most commonly affected: all age groups and both sexes, but most common in children from one to eleven years.

Organ or part of body involved: kidneys.

Symptoms and indications: acute – symptoms include oedema (fluid retention), with swelling and puffiness of the eyelids, face and ankles, raised blood pressure, reduction in the amount of urine passed that contains protein, blood and albumin. The child is likely to feel generally restless and unwell, may be feverish and have pains and headaches, and suffer from vomiting and nausea, with a lack of appetite. Recovery is normally complete but may take several weeks.

Chronic – this is a very serious condition and the symptoms are those of renal failure. There is nausea and vomiting, pains in muscles and bones, fatigue and the production of large amounts of urine.

gluten enteropathy

The person requires kidney dialysis and, eventually, a kidney transplant. A person with symptoms of glomerulonephritis requires medical treatment and may need admittance to hospital, depending upon the nature and severity of the illness.

Treatment: for the acute condition, treatment is aimed at maintenance of the salt/water balance of the body. While the kidneys are producing small amounts of urine, fluid and salt intake need to be restricted. The amount of fluids drunk can be gradually increased as the kidneys recover and the output of urine becomes greater. It is necessary for the person to rest in bed while symptoms persist, as this maintains a good blood supply to the kidneys. Often penicillin or other antibiotic is needed to kill off the initial throat infection. (*See causes and risk factors.*)

The chronic disease usually results from different causes and treatment is by means of dialysis and kidney transplant, necessary because of failure of the kidneys.

Causes and risk factors: the cause of acute glomerulonephritis is the deposition of soluble immune complexes in the walls of the fine capillary blood vessels of the glomeruli. These are formed as a result of the activation of the body's immune system by antigens (substances foreign to the body). The antigens responsible are usually streptococcal bacteria, which have already caused a sore throat. The child usually develops glomerulonephritis two or three weeks after an initial streptococcal throat infection. Hence, there is a potential risk of this condition in respiratory infections known to involve streptococcus bacteria.

gluten enteropathy *see* COELIAC DISEASE

goitre

Description: a swelling of the neck due to thyroid gland enlargement. There are four main types: simple or endemic, nodular, lymphadenoid and toxic.

Persons most commonly affected: all age groups and both sexes.

Organ or part of body involved: thyroid gland.

Symptoms and indications: a swelling in the front of the neck that may be soft or firmer, depending upon the type of goitre. A person with symptoms of goitre should seek medical advice.

Treatment: depends upon the type and cause of the goitre. It may be due to a deficiency of iodine in the diet and this is remedied by increasing the intake of iodine. Iodine is necessary for the production of thyroid hormones, which are manufactured by the thyroid gland. Thyroid production is itself regulated by the pituitary gland at the base of the brain. This manufactures and releases thyrotrophin stimulating hormone, which stimulates the thyroid gland to produce its hormones. Simple goitres are treated by thyroid hormone replacement therapy with thyroxine, one of the hormones produced by the thyroid. Treatment for nodular goitre consists of surgery to remove the thyroid gland (thyroid-ectomy) and that for toxic goitre, as in GRAVES' DISEASE. The treatment for lymphadenoid goitre is with thyroid hormone replacement therapy, with thyroxine.

Causes and risk factors: the cause of simple goitres is overproduction of thyrotrophin stimulating hormone by the pituitary gland, which has the effect of producing thyroid gland enlargement. Lymphadenoid and toxic goitres are examples of autoimmune conditions. For reasons that are not understood, the immune system loses its ability to distinguish between 'self' and 'non-self' and produces antibodies against its own tissues. Lymphadenoid goitres are more likely to occur for the first time in people in their 30s and 40s. Simple goitres often arise at times when there is a greater demand by the body for thyroid hormones, such as at puberty and during pregnancy.

gonorrhoea

Description: the most common venereal disease, which is primarily spread by sexual intercourse, i.e. a sexually transmitted infection.

Persons most commonly affected: young adults of both sexes but can affect any age group.

Organ or part of body involved: men – urethra and possibly spreading to affect bladder, prostate gland and testicles. Women – urethra and reproductive organs. The joints, especially wrists and elbows, ankles and knees, are commonly affected. Occasionally, the blood circulation (BLOOD POISONING), heart valves (ENDOCARDITIS) and eyes (CONJUNCTIVITIS) may be affected. The eyes are affected if infected discharge is accidentally passed to them via the hands or a contaminated towel. (*See causes and risk factors.*)

Symptoms and indications: men – burning pain on passing urine, which is cloudy and may contain pus, thick yellowish-green discharge from the penis (gleet), enlargement of glands in the groin. If untreated, fibrous tissue may form causing narrowing of the urethra and difficulty in passing urine. There may be pains in the joints and other organs, the bladder, testicles and prostate gland may become inflamed and tender. Women – may have fewer symptoms than men and these include yellowish-green vaginal discharge (gleet), burning pain on passing urine, which may contain pus. Also the Bartholin's

gout

glands (which are sited near the opening of the vagina) often become ulcerated and inflamed. If untreated, the infection and inflammation spreads to the main reproductive organs, the womb, Fallopian tubes and ovaries. The damage is likely to cause infertility and other long-term problems, and occasionally, life-threatening peritonitis from an infected Fallopian tube. A person showing any symptoms of gonorrhoea or who has cause for concern should consult a doctor immediately.

Treatment: the patient is usually referred to a hospital clinic specialising in venereal diseases, and diagnosis is confirmed by examination of a sample of the discharge. Treatment is usually very effective through the taking of penicillin, sulphonamides or tetracycline, and can be cured within one or two weeks. The person may need checks for a few more weeks to make sure that the infection has totally cleared. During the course of treatment, the person should refrain from sexual activity, be scrupulous in personal hygiene and not share towels, etc. The person should wash the hands frequently and especially avoid rubbing or touching the eyes. Sexual partners should be informed.

Causes and risk factors: the cause of the infection is the bacterium *Neiseria gonorrhoea*, which is spread mainly by sexual intercourse but occasionally through contact with infected discharge or underwear, towels, etc. The risk of contracting the infection increases if a person has sexual intercourse with many partners, without the use of condoms, but this is a common disease that can affect anyone. There is a danger of sterility and other complications through spread of the infection within the body, especially if it is not caught and treated in the early stages. A newborn baby may acquire a serious form of conjunctivitis during its passage through the birth canal if the mother has gonorrhoea. This is called ophthalmia neonatorum and was, until recently, a major cause of blindness.

Preventative measures are obviously important, including the use of condoms and non-promiscuity.

gout

Description: a disorder caused by an imbalance of uric acid (an organic acid containing nitrogen, which is the end product of the metabolism of protein) in the body. It leads to deposition of this substance as salts (urates) of the acid, in the joints, causing inflammation.

Persons most commonly affected: adults of both sexes and all age groups, but particularly men aged over 60. Uncommon below 40 years of age unless there is high incidence within a family.

Organ or part of body involved: joints.
Symptoms and indications: inflammation, swelling, reddening, tenderness and severe pain of infected joints (gouty arthritis). The kidneys may also be damaged, with formation of stones. Deposits of the salts (called 'tophi') may reach the stage where they prohibit further use of the joints, causing hands and feet to be 'set' in a particular position. A person with symptoms of gout should seek medical advice.
Treatment: during an attack treatment is usually by taking colchicine, which relieves the inflammation and pain and has been in use (as colchium) for 3000 years. Prevention of future attacks is by means of drugs that increase the excretion of the waste salts or slow their formation, such as probenecid and allopurinol respectively. Also, analgesic and non-steroidal anti-inflammatory drugs may be prescribed for this condition. The person should rest, keeping weight off the affected joint, until the symptoms of the attack subside. Gout cannot be prevented but symptoms and future attacks can be controlled with medication and treatment.
Causes and risk factors: as stated above, the cause is high-circulating blood levels of uric acid leading to the formation and deposition of urates in the joints. There is often a genetic, family predisposition towards the development of the condition, and this is usually the case in a young person with gout. Some blood diseases such as leukaemia and the use of certain drugs and antibiotics may increase the likelihood of a person developing gout.

granuloma annulare

Description: a chronic skin disease characterised by the appearance of ring-shaped lesions on the lower limbs, hands and feet.
Persons most commonly affected: children of both sexes aged less than 12 years.
Organ or part of body involved: skin on back of hands, arms, elbows, soles of feet, back of lower legs and knees.
Symptoms and indications: formation of raised papules (bumps) that are reddish in colour, do not itch and are arranged in a ring formation. The shape of the rings may change and alter in size as the condition progresses. A person with symptoms of this condition should seek medical advice.
Treatment: the doctor may prescribe topical steroids in order to hasten the healing of the skin. This condition is self-limiting and heals spontaneously in less than two years but treatment speeds up recovery.
Causes and risk factors: the cause is not known but the risk increases with trauma and injury to the skin such as sunburn.

Graves' disease

Description: a disorder characterised by thyroid gland overactivity (HYPERTHYROIDISM), enlargement of the gland (*see* GOITRE) and protruding eyes.

Persons most commonly affected: all age groups and both sexes but particularly people aged over 30 and more common in women than in men.

Organ or part of body involved: thyroid gland.

Symptoms and indications: the symptoms are goitre, protruding eyes and signs of excess metabolism due to hyperthyroidism (because thyroid hormones control the body's metabolism). These symptoms include nervousness, tremor, hyperactivity, rapid heart rate and palpitations, muscular weakness, breathlessness, intolerance of heat and sweating, irritability and blurring of vision. A person with symptoms of Graves' disease requires medical treatment.

Treatment: this may follow one of three courses. Usually, antithyroid drugs are tried first, which inhibit the production of excess thyroid hormones. These include methimazole, carbimazole and propylthiouricil. These can be effective for about two years but often there is a relapse of the condition. Hence, surgery to remove part or three quarters of the thyroid gland (partial thyroidectomy) may be required and this is usually undertaken if the person has a large goitre. The third type of treatment is by means of radioactive iodine therapy, which is taken as a tasteless clear drink. This tends eventually to make the thyroid gland underactive (hypothyroidism), but this can be easily remedied by taking thyroxine tablets (thyroxine is a hormone produced by the thyroid gland). Hence, after treatment with radioactive iodine, the person will need periodic checkups for the development of hypothyroidism. In general, treatment of Graves' disease is very successful.

Causes and risk factors: Graves' disease is thought to be an example of an autoimmune disorder. For reasons that are not understood, the immune system loses the ability to distinguish between 'self' and 'non-self' and produces antibodies that attack its own tissues. These mechanisms are responsible for the hyperthyroidism and bulging eyes of Graves' disease. There is a family connection and prevalence of autoimmune thyroid disorders among relatives of people with Graves' disease. If the disease is not properly treated or controlled, life-threatening complications can result, due to the effects on the body's metabolism.

Grawitz tumour *see* HYPERNEPHROMA

Guillain-Barré syndrome or GBS or infectious or acute idiopathic polyneuropathy or polyneuritis

Description: a severe and often rapidly progressive form of polyneuritis (or polyneuropathy) characterised by the development of a symmetric pattern of muscle weakness and paralysis.

Persons most commonly affected: all age groups and both sexes, especially adults between the ages of 30 and 50.

Organ or part of body involved: nerves and muscles.

Symptoms and indications: muscle weakness, which begins in the lower limbs and moves to the arms and other parts of the body within 72 hours. There may be life-threatening involvement of respiratory muscles leading to paralysis and respiratory failure. There may be blood-pressure changes, heartbeat irregularities and complete paralysis. A person with symptoms of Guillain-Barré syndrome requires immediate emergency medical attention.

Treatment: involves admittance to hospital for intensive nursing and, possibly, artificial respiration. Fluid and salt levels require careful monitoring and adjustment. Patients who are seriously ill are given plasmapheresis (blood is drawn off, plasma is removed and blood cells are then returned to the circulation). Heat is used for the relief of pain and, as soon as possible, massage, physiotherapy and exercise of muscles and joints are started. Various mechanical devices are likely to be needed while paralysis persists.

Causes and risk factors: the cause is unknown but it is thought to be an autoimmune disorder. (A condition in which the immune system loses the ability to distinguish between 'self' and 'non-self' and produces antibodies that attack its own tissues). Guillain-Barré syndrome often develops shortly after a mild infection, routine immunisation or surgery. Recovery is prolonged, with many patients still having some weakness even after two or three years.

H

haemolytic disease of the newborn

Description: a serious disease affecting foetuses and newborn babies, which is characterised by haemolysis (destruction of red blood cells).

Persons most commonly affected: newborn babies of both sexes.

Organ or part of body involved: blood.

Symptoms and indications: ANAEMIA, JAUNDICE and oedema (fluid retention), which is called hydrops foetalis. The amount of a pigment

called bilirubin, derived from haemoglobin in red blood cells, builds up in the baby's blood and can cause brain damage if left untreated.
Treatment: high levels of bilirubin in the blood are treated with ultraviolet light (phototherapy). In severe cases of the disease, it may be necessary to give the baby an exchange blood transfusion. The whole of the baby's blood is replaced with Rhesus negative blood of the right blood group.
Causes and risk factors: the usual cause is incompatibility between the blood of the mother and that of the baby. Generally, the baby has Rh- positive red blood cells (i.e. they contain the Rhesus factor) while that of the mother is Rh- negative. The mother produces antibodies to the Rh factor present in the foetal blood and these are passed to the foetus in the blood circulation via the placenta. This then causes the destruction or haemolysis of the baby's red blood cells.

The incidence of the disease has been greatly reduced by giving a Rh-negative mother an injection of anti-D immunoglobulin following the birth of a Rh-positive baby. This prevents the formation of the antibodies that would harm a subsequent baby and is also given to Rh-negative women following miscarriages or abortions.

haemophilia
Description: a hereditary disorder of blood coagulation in which the blood clots very slowly. There are two types of haemophilia, due to a deficiency of either one of two coagulation factors in the blood. Haemophilia A is caused by deficiency of factor VIII and haemophilia B by deficiency of factor IX, called Christmas factor. The severity of the disease depends upon how much less of the coagulation factor than normal is present in the blood.
Persons most commonly affected: males; the disease is a sex-linked recessive disorder carried on the X chromosome.
Organ or part of body involved: blood.
Symptoms and indications: the severity of the symptoms depends upon the extent of the deficiency of the coagulation factor. Symptoms are prolonged, severe bleeding following wounds or injury and bleeding into joints, muscles and other tissues. In severe cases, there may be spontaneous internal bleeding and serious bleeding after only a minor wound.

Those less severely affected only bleed seriously after a greater wound or injury. Haemophilia is likely to be diagnosed at an early stage and the child will require ongoing treatment throughout life.
Treatment: is by means of injections of transfusions of plasma containing the missing coagulation factor. Freeze-dried preparations

can be kept at home in a refrigerator for reconstitution and injection intravenously, when required. Special pre-operative treatment is required for haemophiliacs needing planned surgery to raise the levels of coagulation factor in the blood. In the past, haemophiliacs suffered great pain due to internal bleeding, which caused deformity of joints and muscles. Many did not survive into adult life. Now, the outlook is good, although the person obviously has to be aware of, and take greater precautions against, the dangers of accidental injury. However, with care, a sufferer can hope to lead a much more normal life.

Causes and risk factors: as stated above, haemophilia is a sex-linked recessive condition carried on the X chromosome; hence, it affects males, with females being the carriers. Half the daughters of a mother carrying the haemophilia gene will also be carriers and half of her sons will be haemophiliacs. The sons of a haemophiliac father and non-carrier mother will not have haemophilia but half of the daughters will be carriers.

haemorrhage

Description: haemorrhage means bleeding – a flow of blood from a ruptured blood vessel, which may occur externally or internally. A haemorrhage is classified according to the type of vessels involved: arterial H – bright red blood spurts in pulses from an artery. Venous H – a darker coloured steady flow from a vein. Capillary H – blood oozes from torn capillaries at the surface of a wound. In addition, a haemorrhage may be primary, i.e. it occurs at the moment of injury. Or, it is classed as reactionary when it occurs within 24 hours of an injury and results from a rise in blood pressure. Thirdly, a secondary haemorrhage occurs after a week or ten days as a result of infection (sepsis). Haemorrhage at specific sites within the body are designated by special names, e.g. haematuria (from the kidney or urinary tract), haemoptysis (from the lungs) and haematemesis (from the stomach).

Persons most commonly affected: all age groups and both sexes.

Organ or part of body involved: any blood vessel.

Symptoms and indications: the symptoms are, obviously, bleeding from the blood vessels involved but this may only be apparent if the haemorrhage is external. Internal haemorrhage may produce a range of symptoms depending upon the part of the body involved and the person is likely to be seriously ill. Haemorrhage from a major artery is the most serious kind, as large quantities of blood are quickly lost and death can occur within minutes from organ failure and SHOCK. A person with a haemorrhage needs emergency medical treatment and admittance to hospital.

Treatment: is aimed at arresting the bleeding. For an external haemorrhage there are four approaches to stopping the bleeding.
1. Direct pressure on the point of the bleeding.
2. Direct pressure on the artery or blood vessel.
3. Raising the wounded part (if a limb).
4. Application of substances (called styptics) to help the blood to clot or to constrict the blood vessels.

Hot water at a temperature between 46° and 49°C and, also, water that is ice cold, can be helpful in this respect.

For internal haemorrhage, it is important to keep the person lying down, as the heart then pumps the blood with less force and the blood pressure is lowered. Also, the patient should be kept calm and warm until emergency medical help arrives. Morphine is often given by injection.

A person with haemorrhage will require further treatment in hospital, which may include surgery and blood transfusions, depending upon the nature of the injury or other cause of the condition.

Causes and risk factors: the most obvious cause of haemorrhage is a wound or other injury. However, there are many others, including ulcers or drugs that may cause inflammation or bleeding in the digestive tract, haemorrhage after childbirth and certain diseases or conditions, such as haemophilia.

hammer toe *see* CORNS

haemorrhoids or piles

Description: varicose and inflamed veins around the lower end of the bowel, situated in the wall of the anus. They are classified as internal, external and mixed, depending upon whether they appear beyond the anus.

Persons most commonly affected: adults in middle and older age of both sexes.

Organ or part of body involved: veins at the lower end of the bowel (called the haemorrhoidal veins) in the wall of the anus.

Symptoms and indications: symptoms include bleeding, pain and itching, and the distended vein, may be felt as a lump. Bleeding is generally slight but can occasionally be more persistent and cause anaemia. A person with haemorrhoids should seek medical advice.

Treatment: is by means of creams, injections and suppositories. Attention should be paid to lifestyle, especially the diet and taking regular exercise. It is important to eat a healthy diet containing plenty of fibre and to drink water to avoid constipation. Also, taking regular exercise to improve the blood circulation, and avoiding sitting down for long periods are helpful in preventing and improving piles. In severe cases that do not respond to these measures, admittance to hospital for surgical removal of haemorrhoids may be needed. Symptoms of piles can normally be successfully relieved, although there is a tendency for the condition to recur.

Causes and risk factors: piles are commonly caused by constipation and straining when passing stools, especially in middle-aged and elderly persons. Hence it is important to avoid constipation and a sedentary life style. They are also common in pregnancy, disappearing again after the baby is born. However, piles may be a symptom of other disorders affecting the bowel or blood circulation. They often occur in persons with liver disease, such as CIRRHOSIS, heart and congestive disorders.

hand, foot and mouth disease

Description: a highly contagious viral infection affecting the mucous membranes within the mouth, the feet and hands.

Persons most commonly affected: infants and young children of both sexes.

Organ or part of body involved: mucous membranes of the mouth, throat, feet, especially the toes, and palms of the hands.

Symptoms and indications: painful blisters and ulcers that appear in the areas described. The child often has a sore throat and fever and loss of appetite. A child with hand, foot and mouth disease should be seen by a doctor.

Treatment: consists of bed rest, encouraging the child to drink plenty of fluids and use of pain-relieving drugs such as paracetamol. Sucking ice cubes and eating ice cream or sipping iced drinks will help to relieve the pain from mouth and throat ulcers and help fluid intake. Complete recovery usually takes about four or five days. Special care should be taken with hygiene and washing of utensils used by the child.

Causes and risk factors: the cause of the infection is a virus, the Coxsackie A16 virus, which is highly infectious. Hence, there is usually an outbreak among a number of children and the incubation period, before symptoms appear, is three to five days.

hay fever

Description: an allergic reaction to pollen e.g. that of grasses, trees and many other plants, which affects numerous individuals.

Persons most commonly affected: all age groups and both sexes.

headache

Organ or part of body involved: nose, throat, eyes, respiratory system.
Symptoms and indications: symptoms include a blocked and runny nose, sneezing, watering eyes that are itchy and red and may swell. The person may sometimes wheeze and have slight breathing difficulties. A person with severe symptoms of hay fever should seek medical advice.
Treatment: is by means of antihistamine drugs and if the allergen (the substance causing the symptoms) can be identified, desensitisation may be successful. This involves injecting or exposing the individual to controlled and gradually increasing doses of the allergen until antibodies are built up.
Causes and risk factors: the cause of the symptoms is the release of a naturally occurring chemical substance in the body, called histamine. This is widely found throughout all the body tissues and is responsible for the dilation of blood vessels (small arterioles and capillaries) and the contraction of smooth muscle, including that of the bronchi of the lungs.

headache
Description: a pain felt within the head. Most people experience headaches at one time or another and the causes and significance of these vary tremendously. *See* MIGRAINE.
Persons most commonly affected: all age groups and both sexes.
Organ or part of body involved: head.
Symptoms and indications: pain or ache in the head, the site of which varies according to the cause of the headache. A headache is often a symptom of illness or disorder. In this case, it may well be accompanied by other symptoms, such as nausea and vomiting. A person with a severe headache should seek medical advice if the pain persists or if worried in any way.
Treatment: depends upon the underlying cause. If the headache is a symptom of an underlying disease or disorder, then this must be identified and treated. Other forms of headache can be relieved using painkillers such as paracetamol.
Causes and risk factors: there are many causes of headache and some are more serious than others. Common causes are stress, tiredness, feverishness accompanying an infection such as a cold, an excess of close work involving the eyes, dyspepsia (indigestion and digestive disorders), overexposure to hot sun (sunstroke or heatstroke) and hunger. Other more serious causes include uraemia and kidney failure, high blood pressure, rheumatic diseases, GLAUCOMA, brain disorders and infections such as MENINGITIS, encephalitis, small

inflammation of the brain, TUMOUR and ANEURYSM. Also, a headache is a common symptom following brain injury or CONCUSSION. The arteries that supply it with blood, meninges (membranes) that cover it and the fibrous partitions within the brain are capable of transmitting the sensation of pain. It is thought that stretching and dilation, or other pressure on the arteries (called the intracranial arteries) may be the cause of headaches due to the disorders or diseases listed above.

head injury
Description: any injury to the head that may or may not be accompanied by a wound or fracture of the skull.
Persons most commonly affected: all age groups and both sexes.
Organ or part of body involved: head.
Symptoms and indications: the danger of a head injury lies with possible damage to the brain itself. Hence, there may be bleeding and swelling if there is a wound, but also other symptoms that indicate that the brain has suffered trauma. These include drowsiness, nausea and vomiting, confusion and memory loss, blurring of vision, lapses into unconsciousness, headaches, effects on the pupils of the eyes and irritability (*see also* CONCUSSION). A person who has suffered a head injury should always be seen by a doctor and may require emergency treatment and admittance to hospital.
Treatment: the person requires admittance to hospital for observation, and may need further treatment, including surgery, depending upon the nature of the injury and development of symptoms.
Causes and risk factors: normally caused by an accident of some sort. It is important to wear proper protective headgear and helmets when taking part in various sporting activities, such as cycling, horse riding, etc.

heart attack *see* CORONARY THROMBOSIS.

heart block
Description: a condition in which there is a failure in the conduction of electrical impulses from the natural pacemaker (the sinoatrial node) through the heart, which can lead to a slowing of the pumping action. There are three types: in first-degree (partial or incomplete) heart block, there is a delay in conduction between the atria (the two thin-walled, upper chambers of the heart) but this does not cause slowing. In second-degree heart block, there is intermittent slowing because not all the electrical impulses are conducted between the atria and ventricles (the lower thick-walled, muscular main pumping chambers of the heart). In third-degree (or complete) heart block,

heartburn

there is no electrical conduction, the heartbeats are slow and the ventricles beat at their own inbuilt low rhythm.

Persons most commonly affected: men in middle and older age and postmenopausal women. However, can occur in people in younger age groups.

Organ or part of body involved: the electrical conduction system of the heart, which regulates the contraction of heart muscle.

Symptoms and indications: slow, irregular heartbeats, blackouts (Stokes Adams syndrome) and possible heart failure. A person with symptoms of heart block requires medical treatment.

Treatment: for second- and third-degree heart block, treatment involves admittance to hospital and the fitting of an artificial pacemaker that overrides and replaces the natural pacemaker of the heart. Although there can occasionally be a problem with electrical interference to the artificial pacemakers, the treatment is, on the whole, highly successful and abolishes all symptoms.

Causes and risk factors: heart block is more common in elderly people where degenerative changes have occurred (*see* ATHEROSCLEROSIS). However, it is sometimes an inborn (congenital) disorder or may accompany other forms of heart disease, such as myocarditis (inflammation of the heart muscle), CORONARY THROMBOSIS, CARDIOMYOPATHY and heart valve disease. As with many forms of heart disease, risks increase with smoking, a poor diet which is high in salt and cholesterol, stress and lack of fitness and exercise. Also, persons with high blood pressure (HYPERTENSION), DIABETES MELLITUS, an imbalance of salts (electrolytes) within the body and previous heart disease are at a greater risk of developing heart block. The use of certain drugs such as quinidine, digitalis and beta-adrenergic blockers increase the risk of heart block.

heartburn

Description: a burning pain or discomfort felt in the region of the heart and often rising upwards to the throat.

Persons most commonly affected: adults of all ages and both sexes. Pregnant women.

Organ or part of body involved: stomach and oesophagus (gullet).

Symptoms and indications: unpleasant burning sensation in stomach, gullet and throat.

Treatment: the treatment is relieved by taking antacid tablets or alkaline substances such as sodium bicarbonate.

Causes and risk factors: the cause is usually regurgitation of the stomach contents, the burning being due to the acid in the gastric juice. Also, it may be caused by inflammation of the oesophagus (oesophagitis) or ulcers in the oesophagus. In order to prevent heartburn, it is advisable to avoid overeating or food and drink that might lead to an increased production of stomach acid. These foods include spicy curries, acid fruits, alcohol and coffee. The risk of developing heartburn increases with age, obesity, excess consumption of alcohol, poor diet and some drugs, such as aspirin and preparations taken for ARTHRITIS.

heart disease *see* AORTIC VALVE DISEASE, ANGINA PECTORIS, ATHEROSCLEROSIS, CARDIOMYOPATHY, CORONARY ARTERY DISEASE, ENDOCARDITITS, MITRAL INCOMPETENCE.

heat exhaustion
Description: exhaustion and collapse due to overheating of the body and loss of fluid following unaccustomed or prolonged exposure to excessive heat.
Persons most commonly affected: all age groups and both sexes but more common in elderly persons.
Organ or part of body involved: all body systems.
Symptoms and indications: in the mildest form, which is heat collapse, blood pressure and pulse rate fall and this is accompanied by fatigue, light-headedness and, possibly, muscular cramps. The person urinates less frequently and is usually pale, but the skin may be moist and the temperature near to normal. A person showing these symptoms should receive treatment immediately and be seen by a doctor.
Treatment: involves rest in the shade away from the sun and taking extra fluids. Drinks of salt solution may be required, or this may need to be given intravenously. Recovery is normally good, occurring in about one or two days.
Causes and risk factors: the cause of heat exhaustion is unaccustomed or prolonged exposure to excessive heat. It is more common in hot climates and results from excessive sweating, leading to loss of fluids and salts and disturbance of the electrolyte balance in body fluids. It can be prevented by gradual acclimatisation to the heat, especially if hard physical work is to be carried out, and drinking lots of fluids. The risk increases with gastrointestinal disorders where there has been vomiting and diarrhoea, and if conditions are humid as well as hot. Any illness such as diabetes may make this condition more likely to occur and elderly people should be especially careful (*see also* HEATSTROKE).

heatstroke or heat hyperpyrexia
Description: a severe condition that follows overexposure of the body to excessive heat.

Persons most commonly affected: all age groups and both sexes with elderly persons most at risk.
Organ or part of body involved: all body systems.
Symptoms and indications: failure of sweating and all temperature regulation, headache, muscular cramps, hot, dry skin and high body temperature. The heartbeat rate is rapid, and there is a loss of consciousness, followed by coma and death, which can occur quite quickly. The person requires immediate emergency attention to save his or her life and admittance to hospital.
Treatment: the body is overheated and must be cooled immediately by sponging or immersion in cool water, and fanning. The body may be wrapped in wet sheets. Once the temperature has returned to just above normal (38.9°C), the person should be dried and wrapped in a dry blanket. When consciousness returns, drinks and salt solutions are needed or may have to be given intravenously. Convalescence may take some time and it may not be possible for the person to continue former activities in the prevailing climate.
Causes and risk factors: the cause of the symptoms is loss of fluid and salt through excessive sweating, leading to disruption of the salt/water balance, lowered blood volume, metabolic disturbance and shock. Preventative measures include taking enough time for acclimatisation to the heat and increasing the amount of fluids drunk. People who are required to carry out hard, physical work need to drink salt solutions to compensate for the loss that occurs in profuse sweating.

hepatitis

Description: inflammation of the liver due to the presence of toxic substances or infection caused by viruses. Hepatitis may be 'acute', causing a flare-up of symptoms, or chronic, with similar symptoms that persist for years. Other forms of hepatitis are designated A, B, C, D and E, according to the type of virus that causes them. Fulminant hepatitis is a rare and very severe form that is often fatal.
Persons most commonly affected: all age groups and both sexes.
Organ or part of body involved: liver.
Symptoms and indications: acute and chronic hepatitis – symptoms include abdominal pain, JAUNDICE, nausea, itching, malaise and fever. The chronic condition may persist for years and eventually lead to CIRRHOSIS. Hepatitis A (infectious hepatitis) and Hepatitis E – these produce symptoms of fever, sickness, malaise and jaundice. Serum hepatitis (viruses B, C and D) – the symptoms include chills, fatigue, headaches and jaundice.

All these viruses may persist in the blood for a long time and if

B is involved, the condition is known as chronic type B hepatitis.

Fulminant hepatitis – the symptoms are very severe with great destruction of liver cells, retention of fluid, unconsciousness, serious jaundice and liver and kidney failure. Coma and death may follow unless a liver transplant can be carried out. A person with any symptoms of hepatitis should always seek immediate medical advice.

Treatment: treatment for many forms of hepatitis includes bed rest and drinking plenty of fluids. Various drugs are used to combat viral hepatitis, including interferon. Surgery in the form of a liver transplant operation may be the only option in severe forms of the disease. Recovery from many types of hepatitis is good and complete although may take some time. Infection with and recovery from viral hepatitis normally confers immunity from a future attack.

Causes and risk factors: causes are various and include those viruses listed above. Also, other viral infections, such as glandular fever and HIV can produce symptoms of hepatitis. Some drugs cause liver inflammation and hepatitis, especially alcohol and paracetamol in excess. Alcohol abuse is the most common cause of hepatitis in the UK. Infectious hepatitis is transmitted by eating food contaminated by a person who has the virus and is common in conditions of poor hygiene and sanitation. With serum hepatitis, the route of infection is blood or blood products and is most common where infected needles have been shared among drug addicts. The infection may also be passed on by tattooing needles and also through sexual intercourse with an infected individual.

hepatoma or heptocellular carcinoma

Description: a malignant tumour of the liver that is rare in western countries except among persons with CIRRHOSIS. It is prevalent in parts of the Far East and Africa.

Persons most commonly affected: adults of both sexes but more prevalent in men.

Organ or part of body involved: liver.

Symptoms and indications: malaise, loss of appetite and weight, abdominal discomfort, jaundice, retention of fluid in the abdomen, feverishness. There may be an enlargement of the spleen and it may be possible to detect a hard mass in the abdomen. There may be unexplained bleeding from the gastrointestinal tract. A person with symptoms of hepatoma should seek medical treatment as soon as possible.

Treatment: may involve admittance to hospital and surgery to remove the tumour, if possible. Also, various drugs including painkillers may be prescribed to relieve the symptoms. The disease is incur-

heptocellular carcinoma

able but ongoing research is being carried out to further understanding and to improve treatment methods.

Causes and risk factors: the risk of this form of cancer increases with excessive consumption of alcohol and cirrhosis of the liver. Also, there is a greater risk with previous HEPATITIS, particularly infection with the hepatitis B virus. Hepatoma is common in parts of the Far East and Africa and a suspected cause is the aflatoxin (produced in the spores of the fungus *Aspergillus flavus*) which contaminates stored peanuts and cereals.

Hepatoma often produces alpha fetoprotein (a type of protein normally produced in the liver and gut of a foetus), which is detectable in the blood and can be tested for as an indicator of the presence of the malignancy. Preventative measures include not drinking alcohol, especially for those who have had previous liver diseases.

heptocellular carcinoma *see* HEPATOMA

hernia

Description: the protrusion of a part or whole of an organ from out of its normal position within the body cavity. Most commonly, a hernia involves part of the bowel. There are various types of hernia described according to their nature and origin.

- Congenital hernia – present at birth, a common one being an 'umbilical hernia', in which abdominal organs protrude into the umbilical cord.
- Acquired hernia – occurs after birth, a common example being an 'inguinal hernia' in which part of the bowel bulges through a weak part of the abdominal wall (known as the inguinal canal).
- HIATUS HERNIA – the stomach passes through the hiatus (a hole allowing passage of the oesophagus) from the abdomen into the chest cavity.
- Reducible hernia – one that is freely movable and can be returned by manipulation into its proper place.
- Irreducible hernia – one that cannot be returned by manipulation into its proper place.
- Incarcerated hernia – one that has become swollen and fixed in its position.
- Obstructed hernia – one involving the bowel. The contents of the hernia are unable to pass further down and are held up and obstructed.
- Strangulated hernia – the most dangerous type, in which the blood supply has been cut off due to the protrusion itself.

Persons most commonly affected: all age groups and both sexes.

Organ or part of body involved: any organ may be involved except the liver and pancreas. Usually, however, a hernia involves the bowel and digestive tract.

Symptoms and indications: a protruding lump that often can be returned to its normal position by manipulation. (However, not all hernias produce a lump that can be felt on the body's surface.) There may be slight discomfort or pain and a feeling of weakness. A strangulated hernia is a life-threatening condition causing severe pain, feverishness and vomiting, and eventually turning gangrenous. This requires immediate emergency surgery as there is a risk of PERITONITIS and death. A person with symptoms of a hernia should always seek medical advice.

Treatment: a reducible hernia may be treated by pushing back into place and support. Curative treatment is by means of surgery to return and retain the protrusion in its proper place (hernioplasty). It may be necessary for a person to go on a diet or have other treatment to reduce the size of a large hernia before surgery is performed. Treatment and recovery from all but a strangulated hernia is usually good and complete.

Causes and risk factors: the cause of a hernia is a weakness or injury in retaining muscles or connective tissue. There may be a congenital weakness, or stretching and tearing may occur along a line of weakness, such as a previous operation scar (incisional hernia). The risk of development of a hernia increases with age, pregnancy and obesity, and also inappropriate lifting and straining. In the latter case, the hernia may appear suddenly but usually its development is gradual.

herpes simplex infection or genital herpes

Description: an infection of the genital region caused by a herpes virus.

Persons most commonly affected: sexually active adults of both sexes and all age groups.

Organ or part of body involved: genitals.

Symptoms and indications: itching of genital area, followed by the development of small, painful blisters or ulcers. The person feels generally unwell, the lymph glands are enlarged and there may be slight fever. Urination is painful due to the presence of the ulcers. A person with genital herpes should consult a doctor.

Treatment: involves rest until symptoms subside and possibly the antiviral drug acyclovir. Scrupulous attention should be paid to personal hygiene and warm baths may help to relieve symptoms. The

herpes zoster

virus remains in the body throughout life and tends to flare up from time to time, although some people are more susceptible to recurrent attacks than others. These are more likely to occur when the person is suffering from, or recovering from, some other debilitating condition when the body has been under stress. During an attack, the person should refrain from sexual intercourse until one month after all symptoms have disappeared. Also, it is advisable to use condoms.
Causes and risk factors: the cause of the infection is herpes simplex viruses types I and II. Herpes type I virus causes COLD SORES. The virus is transmitted by sexual relations with a person who has an active herpes infection (either cold sores or genital herpes). The infection is especially damaging in those taking anticancer drugs or other drugs that suppress the immune system. A newborn baby who acquires the virus from an infected mother during birth may become seriously ill with a general infection. Hence, a pregnant woman who has previously had an active infection should inform the doctor.

herpes zoster *see* SHINGLES

hiatus hernia
Description: a hernia in which part of the stomach passes through the hiatus (a hole allowing the passage of the oesophagus through the diaphragm) from the abdomen into the chest cavity.
Persons most commonly affected: adults of both sexes over the age of 50 but can affect younger people.
Organ or part of body involved: oesophagus, diaphragm, stomach.
Symptoms and indications: the symptoms are usually felt after eating a meal and include heartburn, wind and discomfort. A person with symptoms of hiatus hernia should seek medical advice.
Treatment: includes the taking of antacid preparations to alleviate the symptoms of heartburn, eating small meals, avoidance of hot, spicy foods and, as with all hernias, avoidance of straining. Corrective surgery may be required to repair the hernia.
Causes and risk factors: there may be a congenital or inborn weakness in the diaphragm or this may be due to pressure or injury. The symptoms of heartburn are caused by backflow of gastric juice from the stomach into the oesophagus. The risk of the development of a hiatus hernia increases with age, obesity and inappropriate lifting or straining of the abdominal muscles.

high blood pressure *see* HYPERTENSION

hip fracture
Description: the hip joint is a 'ball-and-socket' joint made up of the

head of the femur (thigh bone), which rests inside a deep, cup-shaped cavity (the acetabulum) in the hip bone. The hip bone (or innominate bone) is itself made up of three fused bones, the pubis, ischium and ilium, which form part of the pelvis. A hip fracture involves a break of some sort in the femur.
Persons most commonly affected: all age groups and both sexes but especially older persons, particularly women with OSTEOPOROSIS.
Organ or part of body involved: femur and other elements of the hip joint.
Symptoms and indications: severe pain, swelling and inability to walk following a fall or injury. A person suffering this injury requires immediate emergency medical treatment in hospital.
Treatment: is by means of surgery to repair the joint, securing the damaged portions by means of steel pins. Elderly patients may need a hip-replacement operation. Convalescence and recovery may take some time especially in older people.
Causes and risk factors: the cause is an accidental injury or, in the elderly, a fall. Care should be taken to avoid the possibility of falls and the diet should include adequate amounts of calcium. Women should consider hormone replacement therapy after the menopause to minimise the risk of osteoporosis. As with all injuries of this nature, there is a risk of poor healing, infection, and damage to nerves and blood vessels, especially if the fracture is severe or complicated. These are particularly dangerous in elderly people.

Hodgkin's disease
Description: a malignant disease affecting the lymphatic system in which there is a gradual and increasing enlargement of lymph glands and nodes throughout the body.
Persons most commonly affected: both sexes and all age groups but more common in men and rare in young children under ten years.
Organ or part of body involved: lymphatic system including nodes, glands and spleen.
Symptoms and indications: loss of weight, sweating, anaemia and a characteristic type of fever (known as Pel-Ebstein fever). This is an intermittent type of fever, coming on for a short period then subsiding for a few days before returning again. The person becomes gradually weaker and the glands enlarge and may attain a very great size. A person with symptoms of Hodgkin's disease requires immediate medical treatment.
Treatment: is by means of surgery, radiotherapy and chemotherapy (a combination of drugs being used). The outlook is generally good,

hookworm disease

especially if the disease is detected early. Some treatment methods may cause side effects, usually relatively short-lived.

Causes and risk factors: the cause of the disease is unknown but there is a possibility that a virus may be involved in some cases. There are no particular preventative measures but it is wise not to smoke.

hookworm disease or ancylostomiasis

Description: a disease caused by infestation with a parasitic nematode worm of which there are two kinds. *Ancyclostoma duodenale*, also called the tunnel worm, occurs mainly in the Mediterranean and the Middle and Far East, while *Necator americanus* is found in the Far East, many parts of Africa and South and Central America. However, because of increasing international travel, cases of hookworm infestation may occur elsewhere.

Persons most commonly affected: all age groups and both sexes.

Organ or part of body involved: intestine via bloodstream and lungs.

Symptoms and indications: gastrointestinal upset, pain in abdomen, diarrhoea, intestinal bleeding causing anaemia, fatigue and general malaise. A person with symptoms of hookworm infestation should seek medical advice.

Treatment: various drugs are effective against hookworm, including mebendazole, kephenium hydroxynaphthoate, and pyrantel embonate. The accompanying anaemia also requires appropriate treatment, and the person may need to rest until fully recovered.

Causes and risk factors: hookworm larvae inhabit the soil and infect people by burrowing through the skin of the feet. Alternatively, they may gain direct access to the gastrointestinal system through the drinking of contaminated water. They enter the bloodstream and travel to the lungs and thence to the intestine via the windpipe and oesophagus. Once in the intestine, the worms mature and burrow into the wall, causing damage and bleeding with the symptoms outlined above. They are a cause of death among poor people suffering from malnutrition, who live in overcrowded and insanitary conditions. Care should be exercised in a country where hookworm is prevalent, with regard to eating, drinking and personal hygiene.

Huntington's chorea

Description: an inherited condition characterised by DEMENTIA and involuntary jerking movements.

Persons most commonly affected: the usual age for symptoms to develop is between 35 and 45 and it affects people of both sexes.

A few people develop symptoms at a much younger age.
Organ or part of body involved: nervous system, brain, muscles.
Symptoms and indications: early symptoms include behavioural changes such as apathy, increased irritability and, in some cases, more profound psychiatric disturbances. Early physical signs include flicking movements of fingers and toes, unsteadiness in walking, contortion of facial muscles and muscle spasms. The disease progresses inexorably over a number of years, leaving the person completely mentally and physically disabled. A person with symptoms of Huntington's chorea should seek medical advice.
Treatment: there is no treatment to cure or halt the progress of the disease but drugs can be used to diminish the muscle spasms (chorea).
Causes and risk factors: the cause is unknown and the disorder cannot be prevented. Each child of an affected parent has a 50% chance of developing the disease and should receive genetic counselling before having children.

hydrocephalus
Description: an abnormal collection of cerebrospinal fluid within the skull.
Persons most commonly affected: children of both sexes but can occur in adults.
Organ or part of body involved: brain.
Symptoms and indications: in children, the chief indication is a gradual abnormal increase in the size of the head, the growth being disproportionate to that of the rest of the body. Other symptoms are drowsiness, irritability and eventual mental subnormality. In severe cases there may be loss of vision and hearing, paralysis and death. The condition is often congenital and is usually detected during medical and developmental checks on the child.
Treatment: involves surgery to redirect the fluid but this is not always successful. About 50% of children survive if the progress of the condition is halted and one third of these go on to enjoy a normal life with little or no physical or mental impairment.
Causes and risk factors: hydrocephalus results either from an excessive production of fluid or from a defect in the mechanism for its reabsorption, or from a blockage in its circulation. The cause is frequently congenital and it often accompanies spina bifida in babies, or infection (MENINGITIS), or the presence of a tumour. The collection of fluid in hydrocephalus causes pressure on the brain, with the resultant damage and loss of mental and physical abilities.

hyperemesis gravidarum

Description: a rare condition of pregnancy characterised by severe vomiting, which is greatly in excess of that of 'morning sickness'.
Persons affected: pregnant women.
Organ or part of body involved: gastrointestinal tract.
Symptoms and indications: severe vomiting leading to dehydration, disturbance of the electrolyte/fluid balance in the body and damage to the liver. If untreated, it can result in coma and death. The person suffers severe vomiting, may have a headache and pale dry skin, show signs of confusion and have a rapid heartbeat rate. A pregnant woman with any of these symptoms requires immediate medical treatment.
Treatment: involves replacement of fluids and electrolytes. This may need to be carried out in hospital by means of an intravenous drip. Recovery is normally good if the person is treated early.
Causes and risk factors: the cause is not known but is more likely with a multiple pregnancy and may be linked to the production of high levels of the hormone human chorionic gonadotrophin. There is a possibility that it may recur in any subsequent pregnancy.

hypernephroma or renal cell carcinoma or Grawitz tumour

Description: a malignant growth affecting kidney cells, which resembles tissue of the adrenal glands (suprarenal glands) and was thought at one time to originate from them.
Persons most commonly affected: adults of both sexes, especially men in middle and older age groups.
Organ or part of body involved: kidney.
Symptoms and indications: the malignancy may be present for some time without causing symptoms. Eventually symptoms are produced, including feverishness, lower abdominal pain, blood in the urine, possibly vomiting and enlargement of the abdomen. The tumour may go on to cause KIDNEY FAILURE if not detected and treated early, and is liable to spread and produce secondary growths elsewhere. A person with any symptoms of kidney disease should seek medical advice.
Treatment: involves surgery to remove the tumour and, possibly, radiotherapy, chemotherapy and use of hormones (testosterone and progestogens) to inhibit growth. The outcome is generally favourable if the tumour is dealt with early and has not spread.
Causes and risk factors: the cause is not known. There is a likelihood of spread of the tumour via the blood system and small growths can occur along the renal vein. Other organs affected include the liver, lungs (where a characteristic growth is produced), bones and

brain. These secondary growths may already be present before the hypernephroma is diagnosed.

hypertension or high blood pressure

Description: an increase above normal in the pressure exerted by blood circulating through the arteries. It may be a condition in itself or a symptom of underlying disease. There are two types: essential hypertension and malignant hypertension (which may be an end stage of essential hypertension).

Persons most commonly affected: essential hypertension – adults aged over 40 years, especially males, most commonly occurring or between 50 and 60 years. Malignant hypertension – younger adults of both sexes. Hypertension affects people in western countries far more commonly than those in the east.

Organ or part of body involved: heart, blood vessels (arteries), kidneys.

Symptoms and indications: both forms of hypertension may present no symptoms in the early stages. Symptoms arise because complications have developed (see below).

Essential hypertension – later stages or when symptoms are present, headache, especially on waking but wearing off through the day and returning in the evening. The headache is often felt at the back of the head. There may be noise or ringing in the ears (tinnitus) and dizziness. If not treated, death may follow, due to kidney failure, heart attack, stroke or cerebral haemorrhage.

Malignant hypertension – as well as the above symptoms, characteristically there is a high diastolic blood pressure. (Diastole is the point at which the heart relaxes between contractions, when the ventricles fill with blood. It usually lasts about half a second, at the end of which the ventricles are about three quarters full. Diastolic blood pressure is that exerted during this period and it should normally be at the lowest point). Also, there is swelling of the first part of the optic nerve in the eye (called the optic disc, or papilla) because of high intracranial pressure within the head. This is called papilloedema. Malignant hypertension is fatal in a short period of time if it is not treated, often due to kidney failure. A person with symptoms of hypertension should seek immediate medical advice.

Treatment: involves lifestyle changes particularly as regards diet (a low-salt, low-saturated-fat diet is usually recommended), exercise and avoidance of stress. Smoking should be avoided and those who are obese usually need to lose weight. Many antihypertensive drugs are available including beta adrenoreceptor blockers, thiazide diuretics, angiotensin inhibitors such as captopril, guanethedine,

methyldopa and others. Some drugs produce side effects. With early detection and treatment of hypertension the outcome is usually good and the development of fatal complications can be averted.
Causes and risk factors: the cause is generally unknown but the risk of the development of hypertension increases with stress, smoking, obesity, a high salt, high saturated fat diet, and the lack of exercise and fitness. Also, there are hereditary factors in many cases. Preventative measures include avoidance of the risk factors outlined above.

hyperthyroidism

Description: excessive activity of the thyroid gland – an overactive thyroid. *See also* GRAVES' DISEASE.
Persons most commonly affected: adults of both sexes in younger age groups below 50. More common in women than in men.
Organ or part of body involved: thyroid gland – an important endocrine (hormone-producing) gland essential for the regulation of metabolism and affecting many body functions.
Symptoms and indications: symptoms include flushing, sweating and feeling warm, itchy skin, anxiety and overactivity, insomnia, rapid heartbeat, breathlessness, weight loss or gain, gastrointestinal upset, protrusion of eyes, goitre and weariness. A person with symptoms of thyroid gland disorder should seek medical advice.
Treatment: includes the taking of antithyroid drugs to depress thyroid gland activity. Also, radioactive iodine therapy and surgery to remove part of the thyroid gland may be necessary.
Causes and risk factors: causes include a tumour of the thyroid gland, pituitary gland disease or other disorder, and there may be a family history of hyperthyroidism.

hyperventilation

Description: breathing at an abnormally rapid rate when at rest, resulting in a fall in the concentration of carbon dioxide in the blood.
Persons most commonly affected: all age groups and both sexes.
Organ or part of body involved: respiratory system, central nervous system and whole body.
Symptoms and indications: hyperventilation is characterised by rapid, shallow breathing and the person may be agitated and then feel faint with tingling or numbing sensation in the hands, feet and face. If not checked, the person falls into unconsciousness. A person suffering from these symptoms should seek medical advice.
Treatment: hyperventilation often accompanies extreme anxiety. The affected person must be reassured and helped to calm down and

breathe normally. Breathing into and out of a paper bag is helpful (the expired air contains more carbon dioxide). Hyperventilation may also occur if the carbon dioxide level in the blood is abnormally high due to impaired gas exchange in the lungs, as in PULMONARY OEDEMA and PNEUMONIA, and subsides when these conditions are treated and controlled.

Causes and risk factors: hyperventilation may occur as a result of extreme stress or anxiety or a sudden shock, as a symptom of a panic attack. The person may need counselling to deal with stress if the condition is a recurring problem.

hypothermia

Description: hypothermia describes the bodily state when the core temperature falls below 35°C due to prolonged exposure to cold.
Persons most commonly affected: all age groups and both sexes but especially likely in elderly persons.
Organ or part of body involved: whole body – all metabolism.
Symptoms and indications: early signs of hypothermia include shivering and the heart works harder to increase the flow of blood around the body. The person feels cold, the body temperature drops and there is mental confusion and tiredness. Eventually, shivering ceases and, with increasing chilling, the function of the body organs becomes disturbed and cardiac output falls. The tissues require less oxygen as their functions start to fail, but eventually the heart is unable to supply even this reduced demand. The symptoms are a further drop in body temperature and unconsciousness, leading to death. A person suffering from even mild hypothermia requires emergency medical treatment.
Treatment: consists of warming the person to restore body temperature to normal. If the core temperature has fallen very low (below 28°C) great care has to be exercised in moving the patient, who is susceptible to ventricular FIBRILLATION. Warming is done by means of insulating blankets, warm water baths, heating pads, etc. The person may be given warm moist air or oxygen to breathe. However, peritoneal, gastric or bladder dialysis with warm saline solutions may be needed to save the life of an unconscious patient who is very severely chilled. The salt and water balance of the body is disrupted and requires careful monitoring and appropriate treatment along with ECG monitoring of the output of the heart. The person requires intensive care treatment and nursing until consciousness returns and the body temperature approaches a normal level.
Causes and risk factors: the cause of hypothermia is prolonged

hypothyroidism

exposure to severe cold. This is an obvious problem outdoors in winter especially if there is a cold wind. However, people may suffer from hypothermia when wet, even if the weather is not severely cold, or in accidents involving falling into the sea or other very cold water. Elderly persons can suffer hypothermia in their own homes when heating is inadequate. Preventative measures include the obvious ones of preparing for outdoor winter activities by wearing adequate protective clothing. Elderly people must keep their homes warm or live and sleep in one room that can be kept adequately heated. In some surgical operations (heart and brain surgery) a state of deliberate hypothermia may be induced while a particular procedure is carried out.

hypothyroidism *see* MYXOEDEMA

I

ichthyosis
Description: a generally hereditary skin condition, in which the skin is very dry and looks cracked, producing a resemblance to fish scales.
Persons most commonly affected: both sexes, present for life.
Organ or part of body involved: skin.
Symptoms and indications: there are various types of ichthyosis and the appearance of the skin varies according to the severity of the condition and the parts affected. The skin lacks oil and looks rough and dry, and dirt collects easily in the cracks. The scales may be quite thin, or thicker, depending upon the type and severity of the icthyosis. The skin may improve in summer and be especially hard in winter. A person with this condition often requires prolonged treatment to improve the condition and appearance of the skin.
Treatment: the most important treatment is the ongoing use of emollient preparations, particularly petroleum-based or mineral oils, to replace the natural oils the skin lacks. Special bath preparations and creams and ointments containing vitamin A acid and retinoic acid may be prescribed. Synthetic tretinoin preparations (vitamin A) taken by mouth, such as etretinate and isotretinoin may be prescribed under specialist supervision.
Causes and risk factors: the cause of ichthyosis is generally genetic, although it may occur in some other disease, such as leprosy, LYMPHOMA, AIDS and MYXOEDEMA. Inherited forms are due to a

defect in keratinisation (a natural process in which the nails, hair and outer layers of the skin become filled with keratin, a fibrous protein).

idiopathic polyneuropathy *see* GUILAIN-BARRÉ SYNDROME

ileitis
Description: inflammation of the ileum (the lower part of the small intestine).
Persons most commonly affected: younger adults of both sexes but can occur in other age groups.
Organ or part of body involved: ileum and gastrointestinal tract.
Symptoms and indications: generally similar to those of CROHN'S DISEASE, including abdominal pains and tenderness, bowel irregularity and loss of weight. The intestine may become thickened and this can sometimes be felt externally. If the thickening is to a great extent, a blockage may occur, necessitating an immediate emergency operation. A person with symptoms of ileitis should seek medical advice.
Treatment: involves bed rest, eating a low-fibre diet that is high in vitamins, and taking various medications, which may include corticosteroids, antibiotics, analgesics and vitamin supplements. An operation to remove the thickened part of the ileum (ileostomy) may be needed. Treatment is relatively successful in relieving symptoms but the condition may recur.
Causes and risk factors: the specific cause is not known but ileitis may occur in association with TUBERCULOSIS, bacterial infection (by *Yersinia enterocolitica*), Crohn's disease, ulcerative colitis and TYPHOID FEVER. Complications arising from this condition are similar to those of Crohn's disease, including blockage of the ileum, abscess formation, bleeding and ANAEMIA. *See also* CROHN'S DISEASE.

impetigo
Description: a common, infectious bacterial skin disease.
Persons most commonly affected: babies and children of both sexes but can occur in older persons e.g. scrum-pox in players of rugby football. A severe form in infants is called pemphigus neonatorum.
Organ or part of body involved: skin on face and limbs.
Symptoms and indications: the infection starts as a red patch that forms pustules that join to create crusted yellowish sores. The contents of the sores are highly infectious and easily spread by direct contact or via towels, etc. The scabs usually dry up, fall off and do not cause scarring. However, in pemphigus neonatorum serious blistering of the skin occurs, and treatment should begin as soon as

infectious mononucleosis

possible. A person or child with this condition requires prompt medical treatment.

Treatment: is by means of scrupulous attention to hygiene and taking a course of antibiotics such as penicillin. Treatment should begin as soon as possible as the infection may spread and continue for months if not treated. Special solutions and lotions may be prescribed for treating the affected areas of skin. The condition usually responds well to antibiotic treatment. Affected children should be kept away from others until the infection has completely cleared.

Causes and risk factors: the cause is usually a staphylococcus bacterium, although, occasionally, a streptococcus may be involved.

infectious mononucleosis *see* GLANDULAR FEVER

influenza

Description: a highly infectious disease caused by a virus that affects the respiratory tract.

Persons most commonly affected: all age groups and both sexes.

Organ or part of body involved: respiratory tract.

Symptoms and indications: symptoms include headache, weakness, fever, sneezing and coughing, sore throat, aches and pains in limbs and joints, and loss of appetite. It may be necessary to seek medical advice if the symptoms are very severe or if the patient is elderly.

Treatment: the symptoms subside more quickly with complete rest. Painkillers such as paracetamol can be taken to relieve the symptoms and plenty of fluids should be drunk. The person should endeavour to eat some light meals until the appetite returns. In the absence of complications, symptoms usually subside in one or two weeks.

Causes and risk factors: the cause of the infection is usually one of three main strains of influenza virus, designated A, B and C, which are each sometimes responsible for epidemics of the disease occurring in cycles. Characteristically, infection with one strain does not confer immunity against another. Also, the virus quickly produces new variants or characteristics so that an attack of one is unlikely to provide protection against a later bout of the disease. Sometimes, complications can arise as a result of influenza in the form of secondary lung infections. These can be dangerous in elderly people and may require treatment with antibiotics and, possibly, admittance to hospital. In Britain, virus A is responsible for the majority of outbreaks.

intestinal obstruction and **intussusception**

Description: an obstruction of some part of the intestine or bowel,

preventing the passage of food material. Intussusception is an obstruction caused by one part of the bowel slipping inside another part beneath it, much as a telescope closes up.
Persons most commonly affected: all age groups and both sexes. Intussusception is more common in young children.
Organ or part of body involved: the small and large intestine or bowel.
Symptoms and indications: abdominal swelling and constipation, severe cramping pain that comes and goes, and characteristic vomiting. At first the vomit is normal but later it contains bile and is green, and later still resembles faeces (faecal vomiting). Symptoms of intussusception are similar, but a child passes a jelly-like blood-stained mucus. A person with these symptoms requires immediate, prompt medical treatment as a delay may be dangerous or even fatal. Nothing should be taken by mouth.
Treatment: involves admittance to hospital and, usually, surgery to remove the cause of the obstruction, or barium enema (intussusception). Recovery is usually good and complete in the case of intussusception, provided that the child receives prompt and early attention. Surgery to correct intestinal obstruction is also normally successful, especially when diagnosis and treatment begins early. However, a cure depends upon the underlying cause of the condition.
Causes and risk factors: intestinal obstruction has a number of causes, including the presence of a tumour pressing upon the area either within the bowel or in a near organ, scar tissue from previous lesions, infections or operations (adhesions), a swallowed object, e.g. a fruit stone or internal body such as a hard mass of faeces and a twisted bowel. There is a risk of abscess, perforation and PERITONITIS, which can prove fatal, particularly if treatment is delayed.

intussusception *see* INTESTINAL OBSTRUCTION

iritis
Description: inflammation of the iris, the coloured part of the eye, which is a muscular disc controlling the entry of light.
Persons most commonly affected: adults of both sexes, especially those aged under 60.
Organ or part of body involved: the iris.
Symptoms and indications: symptoms include eye pain, which may be severe, reddening and watering of the eye, sensitivity to light and blurring of vision. A person with symptoms of eye disorder should seek prompt medical advice.

irritable bowel syndrome

Treatment: consists of mydriatic eyedrops that dilate the pupil, and anti-inflammatory cortisone (steroid) eyedrops. Occasionally, steroid tablets may be prescribed. The eye should be rested as much as possible and the condition usually improves in one or two weeks.
Causes and risk factors: the cause may not be known but this condition is associated with SYPHILIS, viruses, TUBERCULOSIS, some disorders of the bowel, various forms of arthritis and some parasitic and fungal infestations and infections. There is a risk of permanent eye damage or the development of CATARACTs or GLAUCOMA.

irritable bowel syndrome or IBS
Description: (also known as spastic colon, irritable colitis or mucous colitis) a condition caused by abnormal muscular contractions (or increased motility), producing effects in the large and small intestine.
Persons most commonly affected: all age groups and both sexes.
Organ or part of body involved: bowel.
Symptoms and indications: symptoms include pain and discomfort in the abdomen, which changes location, disturbed bowel movements with diarrhoea, then normal movements or constipation, heartburn and a bloated feeling due to wind. These symptoms are produced without any signs of structural disorder or obvious cause. A person with these symptoms should seek medical advice. A series of tests are usually made to rule out other disorders (such as cancer) before the diagnosis is made.
Treatment: involves some drug therapy, including anticholinergic preparations to inhibit movement in the bowel. Also, drugs that reduce diarrhoea, such as codeine phosphate and Lomotil, may be prescribed. In addition, measures to reduce stress and anxiety and adjustments to the diet and lifestyle may prove helpful.
Causes and risk factors: the cause is usually not known but the condition sometimes develops after a gastrointestinal tract infection. Stress and anxiety are believed to be contributory factors and certain foods or drinks may make the symptoms worse in some people. If this is known to be the case, then these should obviously be avoided.

ischaemic heart disease *see* CORONARY ARTERY DISEASE

J

jaundice
Description: a condition characterised by the unusual presence of bile pigment (bilirubin) in the blood. The bile (produced in the liver and stored in the gall bladder) passes into the blood instead of the intestines and because of this there is a yellowing of the skin and the whites of the eyes. Jaundice is a symptom of an underlying cause, disease or disorder, rather than a disease in itself.

There are several types of jaundice: obstructive jaundice is due to bile not reaching the intestine because of an obstruction such as a GALLSTONE. Haemolytic jaundice is where red blood cells are destroyed by haemolysis, with the production of a yellow pigment in the blood. Hepatocellular jaundice occurs in liver diseases, such as HEPATITIS, which renders the liver incapable of using the bilirubin. Neonatal jaundice is quite common in newborn infants and is due to physiological immaturity of the liver. It usually only lasts for a few days.

Persons most commonly affected: all age groups and both sexes.
Organ or part of body involved: liver, gall bladder, bile ducts, blood circulation.
Symptoms and indications: the characteristic sign of jaundice is yellowing, first of the whites of the eyes and then the skin. The colour varies from a pale yellow to a bronze colour like a suntan. The urine may be dark and there may be a loss of appetite and a bitter taste in the mouth. The tongue may be furred and faeces may be pale and foul-smelling. The person may experience nausea and the skin may itch. There may be lethargy, a slow pulse rate and confusion. Jaundice should always be investigated so that the underlying cause or disorder can be treated. An affected person should seek medical advice.
Treatment: depends upon the nature of the causal illness or disorder. In general, the person requires admittance to hospital, bed rest and a diet high in protein and carbohydrates but very low in fat. Vitamin supplements may be needed. In severe cases of neonatal jaundice, the infant is exposed to blue light, which converts bilirubin to biliverdin, another (harmless) bile pigment.
Causes and risk factors: as indicated above, jaundice may be due

juvenile rheumatoid arthritis

to liver diseases such as HEPATITIS or obstruction of the bile ducts by GALLSTONES. Also, CIRRHOSIS OF THE LIVER, cancer of the pancreas or enlargement of glands close to the liver are causes of jaundice. Some infectious diseases, including MALARIA, TYPHOID FEVER and LEPTOSPIROSIS, cause jaundice. Many drugs and toxins that have adverse effects on the liver may cause jaundice, including snake venom and mercury. The risk of liver damage and jaundice increases with excess alcohol consumption.

juvenile rheumatoid arthritis *see* STILL'S DISEASE

K

kala-azar *see* LEISHMANIASIS

Kaposi's sarcoma
Description: a condition in which there are malignant skin tumours that form from the blood vessels. The disease is common in Africa, but less so in western countries. It does, however, occur in persons suffering from AIDS.
Persons most commonly affected: adults of both sexes and all age groups, especially children and young men. Persons with AIDS.
Organ or part of body involved: skin, especially of feet, ankles, hands and arms. It affects the gastrointestinal and respiratory tracts in AIDS patients, and also the lymph nodes.
Symptoms and indications: purple-coloured lumps due to tumours form on the feet and ankles and spread to arms and hands. In Aids patients the tumours form in the respiratory and gastrointestinal tracts and cause bleeding and anaemia. A person with symptoms of this disease requires medical treatment, which should start as early as possible.
Treatment: is in the form of radiotherapy, which is usually effective in mild cases of the disease. However, chemotherapy (anticancer drugs) is also required for those more severely affected in order to retard the growth and spread of the tumours.
Causes and risk factors: the cause is not known but this disease is a significant cause of death in some African countries. The form of the disease associated with AIDS is especially aggressive and the outlook for these patients is poor. Kaposi's sarcoma may occasionally accompany malignant LYMPHOMA, DIABETES and some other diseases.

Kawasaki disease (or mucocutaneous lymph node syndrome)

Description: a disease affecting young children, first reported in Japan but now widespread in other countries.

Persons most commonly affected: children of both sexes under five years but can occur in young adults.

Organ or part of body involved: lymph nodes, skin, coronary arteries of the heart.

Symptoms and indications: the disease usually passes through a number of stages, beginning with fever, tiredness, fretfulness and, sometimes, pains in the abdomen. A rash develops about one day later and after several days there may be conjunctivitis and changes to mucous membranes such as a red (strawberry) tongue and dry, cracked lips. Lymph glands in the neck are enlarged. During the first week of the illness the nails may become pale and there is reddening and hardening of the soles of the feet and palms of the hands. The skin may peel off revealing new skin underneath. Provided that the disease does not affect the coronary arteries (*see causes and risk factors*), recovery is normally good and complete within a few weeks. A child with this disease must receive medical treatment and monitoring because of the risk of coronary artery involvement, which occurs in 5–20% of all cases.

Treatment: there is no specific treatment but aspirin is usually prescribed for this disorder to reduce the risk of coronary artery disease. The child will require checks on the heart and coronary arteries for several months, including ECG and echocardiography.

Causes and risk factors: the cause of this disorder is not known and, as indicated above, the main danger arises from the risk of coronary artery and heart disease. There are fatalities in about 1–2% of cases, and these can occur some time after the original infection. The complications that can arise include inflammation of the coronary arteries, ANEURYSM, myocarditis (inflammation of the heart muscle), heart failure, THROMBOSIS, PERICARDITIS (inflammation of the membrane called the pericardium, which is a sac surrounding the heart), and heart rhythm disorders (arrhythmias). If these develop, then the appropriate treatment is necessary.

keratitis

Description: inflammation and/or infection of the cornea of the eye, which may arise from a number of different causes. (The cornea is the outermost, transparent exposed layer of the eye that lies over the iris and lens.)

Persons most commonly affected: all age groups and both sexes.

Organ or part of body involved: cornea of the eye.

Symptoms and indications: reddening, inflammation, watering and severe pain and blurring of vision. There may be a yellow discharge. A person with symptoms of keratitis should seek immediate medical treatment as the bacterial form can rapidly lead to a loss of sight.

Treatment: depends on the cause of the keratitis. If it is bacterial, the person requires admittance to hospital for intensive antibiotic therapy in the form of eyedrops and tablets. If the cause is a virus, antiviral eyedrops will be required. Other treatments include the use of artificial tears and wearing a patch to rest the eye until the condition clears. Some conditions may require corrective surgery. With prompt treatment at an early stage most forms of keratitis can be cured. However, there is a danger of permanent damage and loss of vision in some cases, especially if treatment is delayed.

Causes and risk factors: as indicated above, the cause may be a bacterial infection (usually staphylococcus, streptococcus, enterobacteria or pseudomonas) or a virus (often *herpes simplex*). Other causes include dry eyes (exposure keratitis, due to a failure of tear production and spread by blinking), paralysis of the facial nerve so that the eyelids are unable to blink, previous injury, and scarring of eyelids and protrusion of the eye so that the eyelids do not completely close. All these are likely to increase the risk of the development of exposure keratitis.

keratosis

Description: a condition or disease of the skin in which there is a thickening and overgrowth of the horny layer (called the stratum corneum) of the skin. There are two types: actinic keratosis, which is usually induced by prolonged exposure to sunlight and seborrhoeic keratosis, which develops to a certain extent in most people with increasing age.

Persons most commonly affected: adults of both sexes and all age groups. If sun-related, the age at which it develops depends upon the climate and degree of exposure to the sun.

Organ or part of body involved: skin.

Symptoms and indications: actinic keratosis – scaly patches of dry, reddish-brown skin, which are not painful and do not itch. Seborrhoeic keratosis – small, raised, yellow-brown warts or papules that vary in colour.

A person with symptoms of keratosis should seek medical advice. Actinic keratosis may be a precancerous condition and an affected person may require periodic skin check-ups.

Treatment: actinic keratosis – preventative and ongoing treatment is avoidance of overexposure to the sun. If only small areas of skin are affected, freezing with liquid nitrogen provides rapid and successful treatment (cryotherapy). For larger areas, treatment with topical preparations (creams, ointments or solutions) containing 5-fluorouracil is very effective but there are unpleasant side effects, in the form of burning, inflammation and scaling of the skin. These are uncomfortable and disfiguring while treatment lasts.

Seborrhoeic keratosis – the warts or papules are not harmful and can be left unless they are itchy, troublesome or unsightly. Methods of removal include cryosurgery (freezing with liquid nitrogen or carbon dioxide, 'dry ice') or chemocautery (surgical removal after an injection into the area of 1% lidocaine).

Causes and risk factors: as indicated above, actinic keratosis is caused by overexposure to sunlight and is more likely to occur in those who regularly sunbathe or who work outdoors. Seborrhoeic keratosis tends to affect most adults to a slight extent by the time they reach middle or older age, but the cause is not known.

kidney failure

Description: either a sudden failure of the kidneys to perform their usual function of eliminating waste products from the body (acute kidney failure) or a more slow and gradual development of this state (chronic kidney failure). Kidney failure is, in itself, caused by a wide range of diseases and disorders.

Persons most commonly affected: all age groups and both sexes.

Organ or part of body involved: kidney.

Symptoms and indications: acute kidney failure – symptoms include a reduction in the amount of urine produced and the urine contains blood and albumin (a protein made in the liver). There may be nausea, vomiting, diarrhoea and headaches and the person becomes lethargic and later collapses into unconsciousness. The skin may be intensely itchy, with bruising and bleeding. There may be convulsions. Symptoms develop due to electrolyte imbalances and acidosis caused by the failure of the regulatory function of the kidneys to filter the blood and eliminate waste products. The general state is called 'uraemia', which means an excess of urea in the blood. Other symptoms are likely to be present depending upon the cause of the acute kidney failure. (*See causes and risk factors*).

Chronic kidney failure – this may be well advanced before symptoms become apparent. These include itchy skin, fluid retention, tiredness and lethargy, pains, bleeding, ANAEMIA and HYPERTENSION. A person with symptoms of kidney failure requires immediate medical attention.

Treatment: depends upon the cause and degree of the kidney failure.

kidney stones

It may include medication and/or surgery to correct the underlying disease or disorder. Kidney dialysis and/or a transplant operation will be needed if the disorder cannot be treated.

Causes and risk factors: there are a variety of causes of kidney failure, including heart and artery diseases, severe urinary tract infections, congenital kidney disorders, accidental kidney damage, GLOMERULONEPHRITIS, abuse of certain drugs and chemicals, and others. Persons suffering from some diseases or disorders, such as GOUT and DIABETES, are more at risk of developing kidney failure, as are those who have only one kidney due to previous surgery.

kidney stones or calculi (*singular* calculus)

Description: deposits of hard material, varying in size, that may form and collect within the kidneys and pass into the ureters (the tubes that carry urine to the bladder). The deposits are composed of calcium phosphate, calcium oxalate, ammonium phosphate, calcium carbonate, uric acid or urates.

Persons most commonly affected: adults of both sexes aged over 30 years but more common in men than women. They affect about 2% of adults in Britain, especially those in sedentary occupations.

Organ or part of body involved: kidneys and ureters.

Symptoms and indications: severe stabbing pain in the back that comes and goes, nausea, and there may be slight amounts of blood in the urine (haematuria). A person with symptoms of kidney stones should seek medical advice.

Treatment: depends upon whether the stones are small enough to be passed spontaneously with the urine. Large stones require surgical removal or ultrasound treatment to break them up so that they can be passed naturally. A person with kidney stones should drink plenty of fluids to help them to be passed naturally. Stones may form due to a change in the acidity or alkalinity of the urine hence, preparations to alter this may be prescribed. If they are mainly of calcium, bendrofluazide may be prescribed. Dietary changes to avoid foods high in calcium or phosphorus may be advised.

Causes and risk factors: there are various causes or factors that favour the formation of kidney stones. These include a high level of calcium (hypercalcuria) in the urine, a change in the acidity or alkalinity of the urine, concentration of the urine, which may occur if too little fluid is drunk or if sweating is excessive as in a hot climate. Also, GOUT (uric acid stones), a family tendency, kidney infections, a diet deficient in vitamin A and an overactive parathyroid gland are all factors that may lead to the formation of stones. Persons with an inactive lifestyle are more at risk.

L

labyrinthitis
Description: inflammation and infection of the inner ear affecting the membranous labyrinth of the semicircular canals and associated structures and the central cavity of the cochlea. These are organs of hearing and balance.
Persons most commonly affected: adults of all age groups and both sexes.
Organ or part of body involved: inner ear.
Symptoms and indications: severe dizziness and nystagmus (involuntary, quick movements of the eyes from side to side, up and down or circular). Also, loss of hearing, nausea, vomiting, falling and complete loss of balance. This is a serious condition and the person requires immediate medical attention.
Treatment: depends on cause, but may involve surgery for drainage of fluid from the labyrinth or removal of infected bone cells from the mastoid process (a part of the temporal bone), which is called mastoidectomy. Intensive therapy with antibiotics or antiviral drugs may be required, possibly given intravenously. With prompt treatment, recovery of hearing and from symptoms is usually good but complications can arise (*see causes and rish factors*). The person should rest in bed until all symptoms have disappeared.
Causes and risk factors: the cause is usually a viral or bacterial infection of the inner ear or one from the middle ear that has spread. Labyrinthitis may follow a viral infection such as CHICKEN POX, MUMPS or MEASLES. If the infection is caused by bacteria (purulent labyrinthitis) there is a risk of MENINGITIS and intravenous antibiotics are then necessary.

laryngeal cancer
Description: malignant growth in the larynx (vocal cords and surrounding tissues).
Persons most commonly affected: adults of both sexes in middle age or older, especially men.
Organ or part of body involved: larynx.
Symptoms and indications: persistent hoarseness and sore throat, with pain or difficulty in swallowing and a feeling that there is something caught or an obstruction in the throat. The lymph glands in

laryngitis

the neck may also be enlarged and tender. Any person with hoarseness or sore throat that persists should seek medical advice.
Treatment: involves admittance to hospital for radiotherapy and possible removal of the larynx (laryngectomy). In the latter case, the person requires therapy and counselling to learn to communicate without the vocal cords. As with many cancers, the outlook is best if the cancer is caught early before it has spread.
Causes and risk factors: the cause is linked with smoking; hence, the best preventative measure is not to smoke. Risks also increase with overconsumption of alcohol. There is a danger that the cancer will spread to other parts of the body, eventually causing death.

laryngitis
Description: inflammation and/or infection of the mucous membrane that lines the larynx and vocal cords. There are two forms: acute laryngitis accompanies infections of the upper respiratory tract; chronic laryngitis may be due to recurrence of the acute form or to other factors (*see causes and risk factors*). The symptoms are as for acute laryngitis, but with more permanent changes in the vocal cords.
Persons most commonly affected: all age groups and both sexes.
Organ or part of body involved: larynx (the part of the air passage connecting the pharynx with the trachea [or windpipe], and also the organ producing vocal sounds). It is situated high up in the front of the neck.
Symptoms and indications: hoarseness and loss of the voice. There may be a sore throat and difficulty in swallowing or a feeling of a lump in the throat. The person may be feverish. Sometimes the loss of the voice is the only symptom and the person otherwise feels quite well. A person with persistent symptoms of laryngitis should seek medical advice (*see* LARYNGEAL CANCER).
Treatment: the best treatment is to completely rest the voice and inhalations of moisture-laden air (steam inhalation) are also helpful. Painkillers such as paracetamol may be used to relieve other symptoms. Recovery is usually good, within ten days to two weeks, although it may take some time for the complete range of the voice sounds (i.e. high singing notes) to return. Antibiotics are only effective if a bacterial infection is known to be present. Preventative measures include not smoking and not straining the voice, especially when the person has a cold or upper respiratory tract infection.
Causes and risk factors: the usual cause is a viral infection, although sometimes laryngitis is bacterial in origin. Allergies that produce respiratory symptoms, excessive straining or use of the voice as in shouting or singing and (rarely) cancer of the larynx may cause the

condition. Chronic laryngitis is often attributable to excessive smoking with the effects exacerbated by overcon-sumption of alcohol. Wise preventative measures are not to smoke and to drink alcohol in moderation.

Lassa fever
Description: a serious and highly contagious viral infection first reported from Lassa in Nigeria. Outbreaks tend to occur in some African countries, but imported cases have been reported in the UK and the USA.
Persons most commonly affected: all age groups and both sexes.
Organ or part of body involved: whole body and all body systems except the central nervous system.
Symptoms and indications: the incubation period for this disease is usually about ten days but may be shorter or longer. Early symptoms are less severe and include fever, headache, sore throat, chills, muscle pains and lethargy. Later, vomiting, loss of appetite and weight and severe pains in the chest tend to develop. The sore throat worsens and may show a yellow-white discharge from the tonsils and vomiting worsens, with severe abdominal pains. There may be swelling of neck, face and conjunctiva of the eyes, due to fluid collection, ringing in the ears, rash, bleeding, and blood pressure and heart rate changes. Fluid and electrolyte balances are disturbed. Death may follow rapidly, mortality being especially high among pregnant women or those who have just given birth (50%). A person who has returned from an African country where this disease is present should seek immediate medical advice.
Treatment: there is little that can be done to combat the virus itself, so treatment is aimed at alleviation of the symptoms. The correction of fluid and electrolyte imbalance is particularly important. One antiviral agent that appears to be promising and has been used in trials is ribavirin. The person must be kept in isolation and barrier methods of nursing have to be used.
Causes and risk factors: the cause of Lassa fever is an arena virus that is harboured and spread by rats. In Africa, most people are probably infected by contamination of food with rat urine, but person to person infection can occur via body waste, blood or saliva.

Legg-Calvé Perthes' disease
Description: a condition belonging to a group of disorders known as the osteochondroses. These affect the epiphyses, or heads of the long bones, which are separated from the main shaft of these bones in children and fuse and disappear when growth is complete. Legg-

Calvé Perthes' disease is the most common form of the osteochondroses and affects the epiphysis at the head of the femur (thigh bone) at the hip joint. There is localised death and degeneration of epiphyseal cells leading to a gradual weakening of the hip joint.
Persons most commonly affected: children between the ages of five and ten years, especially boys.
Organ or part of body involved: epiphysis at head of femur and hip joint, usually on one side.
Symptoms and indications: stiffness and pain in the region of the hip joint and leg, development of a peculiar lopsided gait or limp. Wasting of the thigh muscles. The symptoms develop gradually and slowly. A child with these symptoms requires medical treatment.
Treatment: involves prolonged orthopaedic care. The child may need to be confined to bed for a long period of time, with the use of traction, splints and plaster casts. Surgery may sometimes be needed. Once the child is allowed to use the leg, braces or crutches are likely to be needed for a period of time. The child requires additional help and support in coming to terms with a long period of immobilisation. Treatment may be needed for three or four years.
Causes and risk factors: the cause is unknown and may involve a number of different factors. There is a risk of further problems, particularly degenerative OSTEOARTHRITIS, in the affected joint in adult life.

legionnaire's disease (*Legionella pneumophilia bronchopneumonia*)
Description: an influenza-like illness that is a bacterial infection and a form of pneumonia. It was named after an outbreak in America in 1976 at the American Legion Convention.
Persons most commonly affected: all age groups and both sexes, especially men.
Organ or part of body involved: lungs, respiratory system.
Symptoms and indications: symptoms appear after a two-to-ten day incubation period and include fever, chills, headaches, muscular aches, cough and breathing problems that may progress to chest pains and PLEURISY. A person with these symptoms should seek medical advice as treatment should begin as soon as possible.
Treatment: is by means of antibiotic drugs, usually erythromycin and rifampicin. Bed rest and the taking of painkillers is helpful to relieve pain and chills. The illness can usually be cured if caught early but may prove fatal in some cases.
Causes and risk factors: the bacterium responsible is called *Legionella pneumophila* and is commonly found in water and soil. Static water provides ideal conditions for multiplication and inhalation of water

in aerosol form is the usual means of infection. Air-conditioning cooling towers are a particular source of infected water and the organism may be able to grow at the outlets of taps or showers. If the organism is found to be present, it is vital that infected water tanks, air-conditioning systems, etc, are cleaned and chlorinated.

leishmaniasis or kala-azar
Description: a common tropical and sub-tropical disease (in Africa, Asia, South America), caused by minute parasitic organisms, protozoa belonging to the genus *Leishmania*. These organisms are transmitted to human beings by the bites of sandflies. There are two types of the disease, visceral and cutaneous leishmaniasis, which are caused by different varieties of *Leishmania*.
Persons most commonly affected: all age groups and both sexes. Depending upon the country or region, one age group may be more affected than another.
Organ or part of body involved: visceral leishmaniasis – internal organs, liver, spleen, glands, bone marrow. Cutaneous leishmaniasis – skin, and in some cases, nose, throat and nasal passages.
Symptoms and indications: visceral leishmaniasis – the person may show symptoms quite rapidly or become gradually unwell. The symptoms are fever and general enlargement of glands and liver and spleen. If not treated, three quarters of those affected will eventually die.

Cutaneous leishmaniasis – skin ulcers, spreading to involve the nose and throat in some cases and countries (South America). There may be erosion of the nasal passages and cartilage in the nose.

A person who has recently travelled to an area where leishmaniasis is prevalent and who shows signs of illness should seek medical advice.
Treatment: the person requires bed rest and good nutrition and intake of fluids. Drugs used include sodium stibogluconate and other pentavalent antimony compounds and pentamidine. These are usually given intravenously but may produce side effects of vomiting and nausea. Recovery is normally good with treatment but fatalities occur in untreated cases.
Causes and risk factors: the cause of leishmaniasis is a number of species of *Leishmania*, which have sandflies as their secondary host and are transmitted to humans via the bite of these insects.

leptospirosis
Description: an acute infection caused by bacteria in the genus *Leptospira*. It is relatively uncommon but some cases occur each year in the UK.

Persons most commonly affected: all age groups and both sexes, especially males. However, adults in certain occupations (*see causes and risk factors*) are most at risk.

Organ or part of body involved: respiratory system and, in the more severe form, the liver, kidneys and central nervous system may be involved.

Symptoms and indications: symptoms in the early stages resemble those of influenza, including fever, headache, chills, aches and pains. The disease may involve the liver causing severe damage and serious jaundice, the central nervous system (meningitis) or the kidneys. A person with symptoms of leptospirosis, especially in an occupation where contact with the organism is a possibility, should seek immediate medical treatment.

Treatment: involves the taking of antibiotics, particularly penicillin, ampicillin or tetracyclines and these must be given as soon as possible. Intravenous doses will be needed in those patients who are seriously ill. As serious metabolic disturbance takes place in the severe form of the disease, the person requires intensive nursing and treatment to correct fluid and electrolyte imbalances. Preventative measures include informing workers about the disease, wearing of protective clothing and, particularly, covering up cuts and abrasions through which the organisms can enter. Bathing or swimming in static water that may be contaminated should be avoided. Also, recent trials suggest that doxycycline might prevent the infection from developing.

Causes and risk factors: the causal organisms are found in the urine of many animals, including dogs and rats. Farmers, sewage workers and veterinary workers are all at greater risk, due to the nature of their occupation. The organisms can enter through cuts in the skin but also via the mucous membranes of the mouth, nose and eyes. Hence some people are infected by swimming in contaminated water. Pregnant women are at risk of aborting the foetus if they become infected, even during recovery from the illness. One particular species of the organism, *L. icterohaemorrhagiae,* is transmitted by rats and is responsible for Weil's disease.

As early and less severe symptoms of the infection resemble a respiratory illness like mild influenza, there may be many more cases of the disease than are currently reported. Often medical help is only sought when the disease has advanced and the person has become more seriously ill.

leukaemia

Description: any one of a number of malignant diseases in which there is an uncontrolled proliferation of leucocytes (white blood cells) in the bone marrow. The cells fail to mature to adult cells and thus cannot function as part of the defence mechanism or immune system of the body in fighting infections. Leukaemia is described as acute or chronic forms. In addition, it is further classified by the predominant type of white blood cell involved e.g. acute lymphoblastic leukaemia (lymphoblasts), acute myeloblastic leukaemia (myeloblasts), etc.

Persons most commonly affected: depends upon the type of leukaemia. Acute lymphoblastic leukaemia mainly affects children, especially boys between the ages of two and five. Another form, chronic lymphocytic leukaemia, mainly affects people in middle or older age.

Organ or part of body involved: white blood cells, bone marrow, spleen, lymph glands, liver, eventually affecting the whole body if the disease is not checked.

Symptoms and indications: anaemia, pallor, fatigue, bruising easily and, occasionally, nosebleeds or bleeding from the gums or gastrointestinal tract. Also, enlargement of the spleen, lymph nodes and liver. A person with symptoms of leukaemia requires immediate medical treatment that should begin as soon as possible.

Treatment: involves chemotherapy with such drugs as methotrexate, vincristine, mercatopurine, cyclophosphamide and cortisone, in some cases, for other acute forms of leukaemia. Other types of leukaemia may be treated with busulphan, mercatopurine, cyclophosphamide or chlorambucil. Also, surgery in the form of a bone-marrow transplant or radiotherapy may be needed. The outlook for patients with leukaemia has improved dramatically over recent years. Although there is still no cure, both short- and long-term survival rates have continued to improve and the outlook is now much more optimistic, especially for children.

Causes and risk factors: the cause of leukaemia is unknown, although there is a suspected link, for some forms of the disease, with ionising radiation, viruses, toxic chemicals, such as benzene, and genetic factors.

lipoma

Description: a common type of benign tumour made up of fat cells.
Persons most commonly affected: adults of both sexes and all age groups, especially women.
Organ or part of body involved: subcutaneous layers beneath the skin surface or in other fibrous tissues.
Symptoms and indications: a lump develops, usually beneath the skin of the arms or upper body but can occur anywhere. It can be

moved about and is relatively soft and painless. A person should seek medical advice if concerned about a lipoma or if its characteristics undergo a change.
Treatment: lipomas are harmless and do not require any treatment unless disfiguring or troublesome in any way. In the latter case, they can be removed by surgery or liposuction.
Causes and risk factors: the cause is not known and there is little evidence of lipomas being in any way connected with malignancy.

listeriosis
Description: an infectious and contagious disease of animals that can be transmitted to man.
Persons most commonly affected: all age groups and both sexes. Newborn babies may acquire the infection from the placenta if the mother has the infection.
Organ or part of body involved: respiratory system and possibly affecting the central nervous system.
Symptoms and indications: early symptoms are similar to those of influenza, including fever, headache, aches and pains, chills, tiredness. However, it often causes inflammation of the central nervous system (especially MENINGITIS) and ENCEPHALITIS (or inflammation of the brain). The eyes may be inflamed and lymph glands and nodes are enlarged. A person with symptoms of listeriosis requires admittance to hospital for intensive antibiotic treatment.
Treatment: is by means of antibiotics, especially penicillin, given intravenously. This treatment is usually effective but elderly persons, the very young and pregnant women are most at risk and the disease can be fatal.
Causes and risk factors: the cause is the bacterium *Listeria monocytogenes*, which infects farm animals. People acquire the organism either through eating infected foods or directly through contact with infected animals (particularly abattoir workers, butchers, vets and farmers). The bacteria are able to grow and survive on food stored in a refrigerator. If the infection is contracted during pregnancy, it may result in abortion or damage to the foetus.

liver abscess
Description: a collection of pus in the liver, which may develop as a complication of some other disease or condition.
Persons most commonly affected: all age groups and both sexes.
Organ or part of body involved: liver.
Symptoms and indications: symptoms include fever, general malaise, nausea, severe pain in the abdomen and tenderness, especially in the

area of the liver. Pain may also be felt in the right shoulder and there may be pronounced shivering (rigor). The liver is greatly enlarged. There is loss of weight and appetite. A person with symptoms of liver inflammation or abscess requires immediate medical treatment.
Treatment: is by means of antibiotic drugs, including the nitroimidazole group, usually metronidazole, if the cause of the abscess is amoebic DYSENTERY. The person requires bed rest and adequate intake of fluids. With treatment, recovery is normally good but may take some time.
Causes and risk factors: the cause is usually amoebic dysentery and the abscess may develop some time after disease symptoms have disappeared. Further causes include inflammation in the liver due to other diseases or conditions or as a result of blood poisoning. It may be necessary for the abscess to be drained by aspiration of its contents through a needle under local anaesthetic. However, this is less likely to be performed than formerly and antibiotics are the usual first choice of treatment.

liver cancer
Description: uncontrolled proliferation of malignant cells in the liver, which may either be primary (HEPATOMA) or a secondary growth resulting from a cancer elsewhere in the body. Primary liver cancer is rare in western countries but more common in Africa and Asia.
Persons most commonly affected: adults of both sexes but more likely to occur in men aged 60 and over.
Organ or part of body involved: liver.
Symptoms and indications: enlargement of the liver with lumps that may be able to be felt externally. Malaise, severe loss of weight and appetite, fluid retention (oedema), JAUNDICE and abdominal pain. A person with symptoms of liver disease should seek immediate medical treatment.
Treatment: the condition is not considered to be curable but treatment with anticancer drugs or surgery may be needed. Other drugs to control symptoms, especially pain, will also be needed.
Causes and risk factors: secondary liver cancer may occur as a result of spread of a primary cancer elsewhere in the body (metastasis). Tumours involved include those of the breast, colon, lung, stomach and pancreas. Sometimes, the secondary growth is discovered before the primary tumour is located. (*See also* HEPATOMA OR HEPATOCELLULAR CARCINOMA.)

lockjaw *see* TETANUS

lung abscess

Description: a relatively uncommon condition in which there is inflammation and a collection of pus in one or more areas of a lung.
Persons most commonly affected: all age groups and both sexes.
Organ or part of body involved: lung.
Symptoms and indications: symptoms include fever, malaise and chills with sweating. The person may have a cough, producing sputum that may contain pus or blood and be foul-smelling. The person may have pain in the chest. If pus is coughed up, it indicates that the abscess has burst and is discharging into the lung or bronchial tube. A person with symptoms of a lung abscess requires prompt medical treatment.
Treatment: consists of taking antibiotic drugs to kill the bacteria causing the abscess. The organism may first need to be isolated (from the sputum) and grown in order to prescribe the most effective antibiotic. Several courses of antibiotics for quite a long period may be needed to clear up the abscess and prevent a recurrence of the infection. The person may be required to practise postural drainage to rid the lungs of the secretions. Occasionally surgery may be needed to drain the abscess of pus and enable healing to take place.
Causes and risk factors: the cause may be mechanical, i.e. a foreign body such as a small piece of food that finds its way down into the lung setting up inflammation and infection. Or, it may result from PNEUMONIA, blood poisoning or TUBERCULOSIS or a wound in the lung allowing bacteria to penetrate.

lung cancer

Description: uncontrolled growth of malignant cells in the lung.
Persons most commonly affected: adults of both sexes aged over 40 but especially men.
Organ or part of body involved: lung.
Symptoms and indications: severe, permanent cough producing sputum that may be flecked with blood. Wheezing, pain in chest and abnormal tiredness. Unexplained weight loss. Any person with a persistent cough or other symptoms of lung cancer should seek medical treatment as soon as possible.
Treatment: may involve chemotherapy, radiotherapy, or occasionally, surgery. Pain-relieving drugs may also be prescribed. Lung cancer is incurable although symptoms can be relieved.
Causes and risk factors: in almost all cases, the cause is smoking – usually direct smoking of cigarettes but also 'passive smoking'. It may be caused by breathing airborne pollutants, especially asbestos

dust, but smoking is widely recognised to be the main preventable reason for this disease. Hence the most obvious preventative measure is not to take up, or to stop, smoking. A smoker who gives up the habit, immediately lessens his or her chance of developing the disease. Lung cancer causes thousands of premature deaths each year, more than any other form of the disease.

lupus erythematosus and lupus vulgaris or discoid lupus erythematosus or DLE
Description: lupus describes a number of skin disorders of which there are two main kinds, lupus erythematosus and lupus vulgaris (rare). The two types are not related.
Persons most commonly affected: lupus erythematosus – women, particularly those in their 30s but can also affect men. Lupus vulgaris – young people of both sexes below the age of 20, but lasts throughout life.
Organ or part of body involved: lupus erythematosus (discoid) – skin, especially of face, but also neck, scalp, ears and arms. If it affects the scalp, it may cause bald patches to appear. There may be some mild inflammation and pain in the joints. Lupus vulgaris – skin, especially of face and neck but also mucous membranes within the mouth and nose.
Symptoms and indications: lupus erythematosus – round, raised patches of reddened skin that may merge at the fringes, when they are described as 'butterfly' lesions. They are unsightly and may cause scarring.

Lupus vulgaris – appearance of a small, yellow, transparent nodules that gradually proliferate and are called 'apple jelly' nodules. The skin becomes ulcerated and thickened and, if not treated, over a number of years can even be eaten away in places. The lesions leave considerable scarring. A person with symptoms of lupus should seek medical advice. Tests are needed to confirm the diagnosis.
Treatment: lupus erythematosus (discoid) – the condition is made worse by exposure to sunlight, hence this should be avoided as far as possible and sunscreen products may need to be used. The patches are treated with ointments and creams containing corticosteroids. Sometimes, local injection of the lesions with triamcinolone acetonide may be required. A daily oral dose of hydroxy-chloroquine (an antimalarial drug) may be prescribed, which helps to control the symptoms.

Lupus vulgaris – this is treated with antituberculous drugs and nodules may occasionally be surgically removed.
Causes and risk factors: lupus erythematosus (discoid) – the cause

Lyme disease

is unknown but it is thought to be an autoimmune disease. About 10% of patients with this disorder go on to develop SYSTEMIC LUPUS ERYTHEMATOSUS (SLE).

Lupus vulgaris – this is caused by the bacterium responsible for tuberculosis, *Mycobacterium tuberculosis*. It is a rare manifestation of tuberculosis and can be effectively prevented and treated.

Lyme disease

Description: an inflammatory disorder that produces a wide range of symptoms over a period of time.

Persons most commonly affected: all age groups and both sexes.

Organ or part of body involved: skin, joints, heart, central nervous system.

Symptoms and indications: the first symptoms in most affected persons is the development of a small, raised red bump or papule, usually on the buttock, thigh or under the arm, which spreads and may become quite large. Other skin lesions may then appear. Accompanying symptoms include fever and chills, fatigue, headache, muscle and neck aches and general malaise. Nausea, vomiting, sore throat, backache and enlargement of spleen and lymph glands may occur. Within weeks or months about half of those affected develop symptoms of ARTHRITIS, especially in the knee joint. This may persist and cause problems for years. Less commonly, within weeks or months of acquiring the disease, inflammation of the central nervous system, particularly aseptic MENINGITIS and BELL'S PALSY may occur. Also, inflammation and enlargement of the heart resulting in conduction disorders may rarely occur.

Lyme disease occurs in many countries, especially in the autumn. A person with symptoms of this disease or who has received a tick bite should seek medical advice.

Treatment: is by means of antibiotics, especially penicillins and erythromycin. If complications arise, these are treated with other appropriate drugs, including aspirin and other NSAIDs (non-steroidal anti-inflammatory drugs). Skin symptoms may respond and clear within two weeks with early antibiotic treatment. Other symptoms may persist and only slowly subside and may have a tendency to recur.

Causes and risk factors: the cause of Lyme disease is a spirochaete bacterium *Borrelia burgdorfen*, transmitted by ticks that are parasites of a variety of mammals including deer. The risk increases for those living in wooded or other areas where ticks may be present.

lymphoma or lymphosarcoma, non-Hodgkin's lymphoma

Description: a tumour, usually malignant, of the lymph glands and nodes.

Persons most commonly affected: all age groups and both sexes, especially elderly persons aged 60 to 70.

Organ or part of body involved: lymph system – glands, nodes, vessels and spleen.

Symptoms and indications: enlargement of lymph glands anywhere in the body; this may be most obvious in the armpit, groin and neck. The swellings are usually not painful. The person is tired, with general malaise and loss of appetite and weight. The spleen and liver become enlarged, with symptoms of JAUNDICE and ANAEMIA. A person with symptoms of lymphoma should seek immediate medical advice.

Treatment: is by means of radiotherapy and chemotherapy. The outlook depends upon the type of lymphoma, with some responding better than others.

Causes and risk factors: the cause is unknown but there may be a link with viruses in some cases. There are no known preventative measures but it is wise not to smoke.

M

malaria

Description: an infection caused by minute parasites in the blood and characterised by recurring bouts of fever. It cannot be contracted in the UK but infection can be acquired by those travelling abroad.

Persons most commonly affected: all age groups and both sexes.

Organ or part of body involved: blood (red blood corpuscles or cells), liver and central nervous system.

Symptoms and indications: depending upon the type of malarial parasite, symptoms develop from about one to four weeks after a bite by an infected mosquito. The person may feel somewhat unwell for one or two days before the onset of an attack, which typically passes through three stages, although these are not always apparent. The first stage (cold stage) is marked by extreme shivering and feeling very cold although the person has a high temperature. After about one hour, this is followed by the hot stage. The person is burning with fever, has a very high temperature, a headache, nausea, giddiness and pain, and may become delirious. The final, sweating stage is marked by

malaria

profuse perspiration and a fall in temperature. The aches and pains subside and the person, although weak, feels better. Depending upon the type of parasite, there is a lapse of a certain period of time (two or three days or a few hours) before the next attack.

There may be widespread destruction of red blood cells, especially with recurrent attacks, and if the disease becomes chronic the person may become severely anaemic. The person becomes jaundiced and the liver and spleen are enlarged. Usually over a few weeks, even without treatment, the number of parasites in the blood drops to a low level and no more attacks occur. However, they can become active again and multiply to produce further bouts of fever.

Any person returning from a country where malaria occurs, who develops these symptoms should seek immediate medical treatment.

Treatment: complete bed rest and adequate intake of fluids is important. There are various drugs used for the prevention of malaria, and it is necessary to consult a doctor to obtain a course of these before travelling to a country where the disease occurs. The drugs afford some degree of protection but are not totally effective and infection may still occur. Treatment involves the taking of various antimalarial drugs, especially chloroquinine, but may vary according to the area in which the infection was acquired. (The parasites have developed resistance to some of the drugs used in certain areas.) Treatment is normally effective for most forms of malaria. However, life-threatening complications can arise and some people may require intensive treatment in hospital.

Causes and risk factors: the cause of malaria is infection by any one of four types of protozoan organisms. These belong to the genus *Plasmodium* and are *P. falciparium, P. malariae, P. vivax* and *P. ovale*. These organisms complete some stage of their lifecycle within female *Anopheles* mosquitoes. The mosquito acquires the organisms by biting an infected person. It passes them on in its saliva when it bites an uninfected person. The parasite passes in the blood circulation to the liver and multiplies there. Eventually they return to the blood and occupy red blood cells, further enlarging and multiplying in the process. Finally, they rupture and destroy the red blood cells. The bouts of fever correspond with the rupturing of the red blood cells and the parasites that are released go on to invade new cells. In some type of malaria (*P. vivax* and *P. ovale*) the parasite persists within the liver. A person may die due to the high fever that can occur during a malarial attack. Also, the parasites may be so numerous as to block small blood vessels in the brain, which again can be fatal (cerebral malaria). A very dangerous complication is blackwater fever, characterised by high fever, severe ANAEMIA, great destruction of red blood cells and the presence of haemoglobin (the red blood pigment) in the urine. Malaria is likely to be more dangerous if treatment is inadequate and does not eradicate the organisms. Also in people who are poorly nourished or otherwise ill or run-down from some other cause.

Malta fever *see* BRUCELLOSIS

mastitis
Description: acute inflammation and infection of the breast. Cystic mastitis is another form that does not involve inflammation but the presence of cysts (thought to be caused by hormonal factors) that make the breasts lumpy.
Persons most commonly affected: breast-feeding mothers of any age, especially during the first two months of nursing.
Symptoms and indications: some discomfort and hardness in the breast is usually noticed first. If not treated, the whole breast may become swollen, hard, red and painful, especially when suckling the baby, and the mother may be feverish. A woman with symptoms of mastitis should seek immediate medical advice.
Treatment: is by means of antibiotics, especially penicillin as soon as possible to prevent the formation of an abscess. Pain relief can be used as directed by a doctor. The breasts should be kept well supported and clean but it is usually not necessary to stop breast-feeding. If an abscess forms, breast-feeding must be stopped on the affected side and, in severe cases, finished completely by giving hormones to halt the production of milk. The abscess needs to be surgically opened and drained and antibiotic treatment given. Milk production often stops naturally in women who develop a breast abscess. Preventative measures include keeping the breasts scrupulously clean with careful washing and drying and use of creams. This is especially important at the start of breast-feeding when cracked nipples are more likely to occur, as the skin is not accustomed to suckling. If cracked nipples occur a cream should be used, as recommended by a doctor.
Causes and risk factors: the usual cause is bacteria that gain access through cracks in the nipples; often staphylococcus or streptococcus organisms are involved.

measles
Description: an extremely infectious disease, characterised by the presence of a rash, and usually occurring in children in epidemics every two or three years.

Mediterranean fever

Persons most commonly affected: children of both sexes but can occur at any age in people not immunised or previously exposed to the infection.

Organ or part of body involved: skin and upper respiratory tract, eyes.

Symptoms and indications: after an incubation period of 10-15 days, the initial symptoms are those of a cold, with coughing, sneezing, red, watery eyes and high fever. It is at this stage that the disease is most infectious and spreads from one child to another in airborne droplets before measles has been diagnosed. This is the main factor responsible for the epidemic nature of the disease. Small red spots with a white centre (known as Koplik spots) in the mouth, on the inside of the cheeks. Then a characteristic rash develops on the skin, spreading from behind the ears and across the face and also affecting other areas. The small red spots may be grouped together in patches and the child's fever is usually at its height while these are developing. The spots and fever gradually decline and no marks are left upon the skin, most children making a good recovery. The infection is not, however, without risk and complications can arise (*see causes and risk factors*). A child with symptoms of measles should be seen by a doctor and the diagnosis confirmed.

Treatment: involves keeping the child at home and in bed while he or she is feverish and unwell. Plenty of fluids should be drunk and pain relief in a form designed for children may be given, as advised by the doctor. If the symptoms worsen, particularly if there is a very high temperature, earache or severe headache or any signs of breathing difficulties, the doctor should be called immediately. Preventative treatment in the form of a vaccine is available and protects children from the severe symptoms and complications of measles. It is normally advisable for all children to be immunised.

Causes and risk factors: the cause of measles is a virus and it is an unpleasant infection that makes the child feel quite ill. Complications can occur, especially PNEUMONIA and middle-ear infections that can result in DEAFNESS. Also, inflammation of the brain (ENCEPHALITIS) or MENINGITIS can occur as a result of measles, and the infection may prove fatal in some children.

Mediterranean fever *see* BRUCELLOSIS

melanoma
Description: any one of several extremely malignant tumours of the melanocytes, the cells in the skin that produce melanin. Melanomas are also found, although less commonly, in the mucous membranes

and in the eye. A highly malignant form can also arise from the pigmented cells of moles on the skin.
Persons most commonly affected: adults of all age groups, particularly white-skinned people and both sexes. It is rare in dark-skinned people. The incidence of malignant melanoma is increasing in the UK.
Organ or part of body involved: skin but may spread to other body organs, especially the liver and lymph nodes.
Symptoms and indications: appearance of a raised or flat, painless skin lesion that may be of a variety of colours and may bleed slightly. A person with a skin lesion or mole, especially one that is active and undergoing change, should seek immediate medical advice.
Treatment: if malignant melanoma is diagnosed early, treatment in the form of surgical removal of the lesion is highly successful and the condition can be cured. However, if the melanoma has spread, the outlook is less favourable. Treatment with radiotherapy and chemotherapy may be recommended in these cases. Preventative measures include, most importantly, protecting the skin from exposure to the sun. This involves wearing clothing and a hat to cover or shade the skin, avoiding the sun during the hottest part of the day and using sunscreen products. These measures are particularly important in young children and fair-skinned people. Sunbathing should be avoided as should exposure to ultraviolet light (i.e. the use of sun lamps, sun beds, etc).
Causes and risk factors: there is a link between the development of malignant melanoma and exposure to the sun, especially harmful ultraviolet radiation. The fact that the incidence of the condition is rising has been linked by some with the formation of holes in the ozone layer that screens the earth from UV radiation. Any person whose work or leisure activities involves excessive exposure to the sun runs an increased risk of developing this form of cancer. Hence it is wise to be aware of and practise the preventative measures outlined above.

Ménière's disease
Description: a disease first described by the Frenchman, Prosper Ménière in 1861, which affects the inner ear causing a range of symptoms.
Persons most commonly affected: both sexes in middle age but slightly more common in men.
Organ or part of body involved: the membranous labyrinth of the inner ear, usually affecting one side only.
Symptoms and indications: this usually begins with some hearing

loss in one ear, followed after a period of months by a severe attack of giddiness or vertigo. This occurs suddenly, often waking the person up from sleep at night, and is accompanied by ringing in the ear (tinnitus). This is usually followed by vomiting and sweating. The symptoms usually subside in a few hours but the person is unsteady with loss of balance for some days afterwards. Another attack may follow in about one week or after some months. With each attack, the loss of hearing becomes worse until the person is completely deaf in the affected ear. A person with symptoms of Ménière's disease should seek medical advice.

Treatment: involves a variety of different drugs to control symptoms and also, possibly, surgery. An affected person should rest in bed until symptoms have subsided. Diuretic drugs to prevent fluid accumulation may be prescribed. No method of treatment is completely successful but some symptoms can be relieved.

Causes and risk factors: the cause is unknown but the symptoms are due to an overaccumulation of fluid in the labyrinth of the inner ear. It has been suggested that this may be an allergic reaction or due to spasm of tiny blood vessels supplying the inner ear.

meningitis

Description: inflammation of the meninges (membranes) of the brain (cerebral meningitis) or spinal cord (spinal meningitis) or the disease may affect both regions. Meningitis may affect the dura mater membrane, the outermost layer or meninx, in which case it is known as pachymeningitis. Or, it often results as a secondary infection due to the presence of disease elsewhere, as in the case of tuberculous and syphilitic meningitis. Meningitis that affects the other two membranes (the piaarachnoid membranes) is known as leptomeningitis, which is more common and may be either a primary or a secondary infection. Meningitis is also classified according to its causal organism (viral or bacterial).

Persons most commonly affected: all age groups and both sexes.

Organ or part of body involved: central nervous system.

Symptoms and indications: the symptoms include a severe headache, sensitivity to light and sound, muscle rigidity, especially affecting the neck, Kernig's sign (an inability to straighten the legs at the knees when the thighs are at right angles to the body), vomiting, confusion and coma, leading to death. These are caused by inflammation of the meninges and by a rise in intracranial pressure. One of the features of meningitis is that there is a change in the constituents and appearance of the cerebrospinal fluid and the infective organism can usually be isolated from it and identified. One of the most feared aspects of (bacterial) meningitis is that the onset of symptoms can be very rapid and death can also follow swiftly. A person with symptoms of meningitis requires admittance to hospital for urgent medical treatment.

Treatment: depends upon the cause of the meningitis, which is established by analysis of the cerebrospinal fluid. If the cause is a virus, the disease is usually less severe but may still prove fatal in some cases. Mild cases may recover spontaneously with bed rest in a darkened room. Some cases require treatment by means of antiviral drugs, such as acyclovir, given intravenously. If the cause is a fungal or yeast infection, the drug amphotericin B is normally given intravenously. Various bacteria may cause meningitis, especially those responsible for TUBERCULOSIS, PNEUMONIA and SYPHILIS. Treatment is by means of intensive doses of appropriate antibiotics and sulphonamide drugs given intravenously. The person requires additional treatment to correct dehydration and electrolyte disturbances and to lower fever.

Causes and risk factors: three types of bacteria are responsible for most cases of bacterial meningitis. These are *Haemophilus influenzae* type b, *Neisseria meningitidis* (meningococcus) and *Streptococcus pneumoniae* (pneumococcus). Meningococcus occurs in the nose and throat of about 5% of the population, who are carriers of the organism but rarely become ill themselves. Meningococcal meningitis is the most common form of the disease in children aged one year or under. Pneumococcal meningitis is the most common type in adults. In general, the very young and the very old are most at risk from meningitis but modern treatments and drug therapy have improved the outlook for recovery considerably.

mesothelioma

Description: a usually malignant tumour of the pleura of the chest cavity (a membrane that covers the lungs and inside of the chest wall). It may also affect the pericardium (the membrane surrounding the heart) or the peritoneum (the membrane lining the abdominal cavity).

Persons most commonly affected: men in middle age who have previously worked with asbestos but can affect adults of either sex.

Organ or part of body involved: lungs and lining membranes.

Symptoms and indications: early indications include breathlessness on exercise, and there may be chest pain and a cough and symptoms of bronchitis. The breathlessness continues to get worse, ultimately leading to respiratory failure and death as the cancer spreads. A person with symptoms of breathlessness, persistent cough, etc, should seek early medical advice.

Treatment: most mesotheliomas are in sites that are inoperable, although occasionally surgery may be possible. Chemotherapy and radiotherapy may be used, although success is limited. Treatment is mainly aimed at relieving symptoms and easing breathing difficulties.

Causes and risk factors: the cause of malignant mesothelioma is usually previous exposure to asbestos dust, especially the form called crocidolite. Even a brief period of exposure of as little as six months to two years may be sufficient to cause problems in later life. Less common, benign mesothelioma of the pleura is not related to asbestos dust. The risk of developing all forms of lung cancer is greatly increased in persons who smoke cigarettes. Preventative measures for those who have to work with asbestos include dust suppression and the wearing of protective clothing. *See also* ASBESTOSIS.

methahaemoglobinaemia

Description: the presence in the blood of an excess of methahaemoglobin. Methahaemoglobin is derived from the blood pigment haemoglobin, and is formed when the iron this contains is oxidised from ferrous to ferric form. Methahaemoglobin cannot combine with oxygen in the lungs and so is unable to carry this in the blood circulation to the body tissues. There are two types of methahaemoglobinaemia, hereditary and toxic. A third form, infantile methahaemoglobinaemia, may rarely occur in bottle-fed babies due to high level of nitrates in the water used to make the baby's feed.

Persons most commonly affected: all age groups and both sexes.

Organ or part of body involved: blood circulation – affecting all body systems.

Symptoms and indications: a blue tinge to the lips, tips of the ears, cheeks and nails and then the whole of the skin (cyanosis), tiredness, headache, sickness and nausea, giddiness and breathlessness. A person with these symptoms should seek immediate medical treatment.

Treatment: for the toxic form, the drug that is suspected to have caused the condition should be immediately stopped, if the symptoms are severe. The person may require ascorbic acid (vitamin C) or methylene blue and these are used to treat the inherited form of the condition.

Causes and risk factors: the cause of the inherited form is an abnormality of the haemoglobin molecule in the blood. The toxic form is caused by certain drugs that cause the iron atoms in the haemoglobin molecules to become oxidised. These include sulphonamides, phenacetin, acetanilide, benzocaine and prilocaine (local anaesthetics), polyphenols and dinitrophenol. An excess of nitrates in some foods, e.g. spinach and carrots, and bakery products containing excess nitrobenzene may also cause the formation of methahaemoglobin in the blood. Serious cases of the infantile form of the condition have mainly affected people with a private water supply. Guidelines exist to ensure that if public water supplies are likely to exceed the recommended safety levels for nitrate, alternative arrangements can be made.

migraine
Description: a very severe, throbbing headache, usually on one side of the head, and often accompanied by other symptoms.
Persons most commonly affected: adolescents and adults of both sexes but especially premenopausal women.
Organ or part of body involved: head, eyes, gastrointestinal tract.
Symptoms and indications: early symptoms of a migraine attack may be nausea and disturbance of vision in the form of seeing flickering bright lights (the aura of migraine). A severe, throbbing pain develops, often sited over one eye, nausea continues and there may be vomiting. The person is sensitive to light and sound, which make the condition worse.
Treatment: consists of rest in bed in a darkened, quiet room until the symptoms subside (up to 24 hours), and taking pain-relieving drugs. Other drugs that may be prescribed are ergotamine tartrate and metoclopramide. An affected person may have to experiment to find which pain-relieving drugs are the most helpful. Usually, they are most effective if taken during the period when an attack is felt to be coming on.
Causes and risk factors: the cause is unknown but is thought to involve constriction followed by dilation of blood vessels in the brain and an outpouring of fluid into surrounding tissues. Migraine is a common condition and seems to be triggered by any one or several of a number of factors. These include anxiety, fatigue, watching television or video screens, loud noises, flickering lights (e.g. strobe lights) and some foods such as cheese and chocolate, and alcoholic drinks. There may be an inherited tendency for migraine and the most common time of onset is puberty. In women, attacks may no longer occur after the menopause.

mitral incompetence or mitral regurgitation
Description: a condition in which the mitral valve of the heart is defective and allows blood to leak back from the left ventricle (larger,

mitral stenosis

lower chamber) into the left atrium (smaller, upper chamber). It may be a congenital condition or result from disease of the valve. The mitral valve, formerly known as the bicuspid valve, is located between the atrium and ventricle of the left side of the heart, attached to the walls at the opening between the two. It has two cusps or flaps that normally allow blood to pass into the ventricle from the atrium but prevent any backflow.

Persons most commonly affected: adults of both sexes in middle or older age groups, or newborn babies if a congenital condition.

Organ or part of body involved: mitral valve of heart.

Symptoms and indications: if mild, there may be few or no symptoms. In more severe cases, there is breathlessness, especially at night, wheezing, changes in heartbeat rhythm (ATRIAL FIBRILLATION) and a tendency for clots to form (EMBOLISM). The left ventricle is forced to work harder and enlarges but eventually may be unable to cope and this can result in left-sided heart failure. A person with symptoms of mitral valve disease should seek medical advice.

Treatment: a person with mild or moderate mitral incompetence should not undertake hard physical exercise. Treatment with antibiotics may be required to prevent endocarditis (inflammation of the endocardium, a membrane lining the heart, and heart valves and muscle). Intensive antibiotic treatment may be needed before dental work is carried out. If the cause of the condition is RHEUMATIC FEVER, then daily doses of penicillin may be needed to prevent a flare-up of the condition, risking further damage to the mitral valve. In more severe cases, surgery to replace the defective valve may be required (mitral prosthesis).

Causes and risk factors: as indicated above, the cause may be a congenital abnormality or due to scarring and damage to the valve caused by rheumatic fever. Also, heart disease, a previous heart attack, infection or inflammation may be responsible for mitral valve incompetence. *See also* MITRAL STENOSIS.

mitral stenosis

Description: a condition in which the opening between the left atrium (smaller, upper chamber of the heart) and left ventricle (lower, larger chamber of the heart) is narrowed, due to scarring and adhesion of the mitral valve. The mitral valve, formerly known as the bicuspid valve, is located between the atrium and ventricle of the left side of the heart, attached to the walls at the opening between the two. It has two cusps or flaps that normally allow blood to pass into the ventricle from the atrium, but prevent any backflow.

Persons most commonly affected: adults of both sexes between the

ages of 30 and 40 who have previously (in childhood) had RHEUMATIC FEVER.
Organ or part of body involved: mitral valve of heart.
Symptoms and indications: the condition may be symptomless, even in patients with quite considerable mitral valve stenosis. Symptoms, when present, are similar to those found in MITRAL INCOMPETENCE but there is also a diastolic murmur. (Diastole is the point in the cycle of heart contraction when the heart relaxes between contractions and the ventricles fill with blood.) A person with symptoms of mitral stenosis should seek medical advice.
Treatment: various drugs may be prescribed for those patients with a mild or moderate degree of mitral stenosis, in order to manage the condition. These include calcium antagonists or betablockers, digitalis, anticoagulants, warfarin and aspirin. In more severe forms of the disease, the condition may be treated surgically by widening the stenosis (mitral valvotomy) or by valve replacement (mitral prosthesis).
Causes and risk factors: the cause of this condition is almost always previous rheumatic fever and it may be many years before the damage to the mitral valve becomes apparent (10–20 years), and symptoms are noticed. The cause may occasionally be congenital but an affected infant does not usually survive.

moniliasis *see* CANDIDIASIS

mortification *see* GANGRENE

mucotaneous lymph node syndrome *see* KAWASAKI DISEASE

multiple sclerosis (MS)
Description: a disease of the brain and spinal cord, which affects the myelin sheaths (protein and phospholipid coverings) of nerves and disrupts their function.
Persons most commonly affected: adults of both sexes in younger age group between the ages of 20 and 40.
Organ or part of body involved: the brain and spinal cord (the central nervous system).
Symptoms and indications: the disease is characterised by the presence of patches of hardened (sclerotic) connective tissue irregularly scattered through the brain and spinal cord. At first the fatty part of the nerve sheaths breaks down and is absorbed, leaving bare nerve fibres, and then connective tissue is laid down. Symptoms depend upon the site of the patches in the central nervous system and the disease is characterised by periods of progression and remission.

mumps

However, they include unsteady gait and apparent clumsiness, tremor of the limbs, involuntary eye movements, speech disorders, loss of bladder and bowel control, paralysis and male impotence. A particular reflex sign, known as Babinski sign, is shown when the sole of the foot is firmly stroked. This is an abnormal reaction of the toes (the large toe curls upwards and the other toes spread outwards, whereas normally all the toes curve downwards) that is exhibited by people with multiple sclerosis. A person with symptoms of multiple sclerosis should seek medical advice.

Treatment: there is no specific treatment and since the progress of the disease is marked by periods of remission (which may last for months or even years), followed by relapse, the effectiveness of drugs is difficult to determine. Prednesone, dexamethasone and corticosteroids may be prescribed during periods when the symptoms are active. The affected person should lead as normal and active a life as possible but avoid stress and becoming overtired. Massage and physiotherapy are helpful, as are all physical and mental activities that help the person to maintain an optimistic outlook on life.

Causes and risk factors: the cause is unknown but is the subject of ongoing research. It is not clear whether there is a hereditary factor involved or, possibly, infection by a slow virus may be implicated. There may be some abnormality in the immune system that makes certain people susceptible or multiple sclerosis may be an autoimmune disorder.

mumps

Description: an inflammatory and infectious disease of childhood caused by a virus.

Persons most commonly affected: children of both sexes between the ages of 5 and 15 but can occur in older age groups.

Organ or part of body involved: parotid salivary glands, other salivary glands and, possibly, the pancreas, breasts, testes, ovaries, meninges of the brain and spinal cord.

Symptoms and indications: the incubation period, following infection, is two to three weeks before symptoms start to appear. These include feverishness, headache, sore throat and vomiting before, or along with, a swelling of the parotid gland on one side of the face. (The parotid glands are a pair of salivary glands, one situated in front of each ear and opening inside on the cheek near the second last molar of the upper jaw.) The swelling may be confined to one side or spread to the other side of the face, and may also go on to include the submaxillary and sublingual salivary glands beneath the jaw. Generally after a few days, the swelling subsides and the child recovers but remains infectious until the glands have returned to normal. If a child has symptoms of mumps it is advisable to consult a doctor.

Treatment: there is no specific treatment, other than keeping the child isolated from others until no longer infectious, and in bed while the symptoms are at their height. Pain relief suitable for children may be given, as advised by a doctor, and the child should be encouraged to drink plenty of fluids. However, acidic foods and drinks (fruit juices, etc) should be avoided. Food should be soft, to reduce the pain of chewing and swallowing. Complications may arise, especially in adults and young people past puberty. About 20% of males develop inflammation of the testes (orchitis) which, in rare cases, can cause sterility. The testes may need to be supported and ice packs applied to relieve pain and, occasionally, corticosteroid drugs may be prescribed by the doctor. A smaller proportion of females develop inflammation of the ovaries (oophoritis), which is generally treated with appropriate pain relief. PANCREATITIS (inflammation of the pancreas) may occur, causing vomiting and nausea. If this is severe, the patient may become dehydrated and require salt and dextrose solutions by intravenous drip to restore fluid and electrolyte balance. Also, inflammation of the brain and meninges (membranes) or meningoencephalitis, may arise as a complication of mumps, requiring appropriate treatment in hospital.

Preventative treatment for mumps is in the form of the MMR (measles, mumps, rubella) vaccine which, in the UK, is routinely offered to children usually in their second year.

Causes and risk factors: the cause is a virus affecting the salivary glands.

muscular dystrophy or myopathy

Description: any one of a group of diseases that involve wasting of muscles and in which a hereditary factor is involved. The disease is classified according to the groups of muscles that it affects and the age at which it first appears. The commonest form is Duchenne muscular dystrophy, which is a sex-linked, recessive disorder. (It is carried on the X chromosome and affects males because they have the sex chromosomes XY, females being XX.) The genes responsible are recessive, but in males there is no other X chromosome to mask them and so they are able to be expressed and cause the disorder.) The mother is the carrier but has no symptoms of the disease herself; however, half of her sons are likely to be affected.

Persons most commonly affected: (Duchenne muscular dystrophy) boys between the ages of three and seven years.

Organ or part of body involved: muscles, usually attacking the pelvic girdle first (hips) and the shoulder girdle.

Symptoms and indications: the disease causes muscle fibres to degenerate and be replaced by fatty and fibrous tissue. Early symptoms are a peculiar waddling gait, numerous falls, difficulty in standing up and going up and down stairs. The spine curves inwards, a condition known as lordosis, and the child walks on his toes rather than placing the heel down first. The muscles appear large and firm but this is due to the internal changes that are taking place. Muscles become progressively weaker and usually the child is confined to a wheelchair by about the age of 12. Some other forms of muscular dystrophy are, however, less severe. A child with muscular dystrophy requires ongoing support and therapy.

Treatment: there is no specific drug treatment at present although trials on the corticosteroid drug prednisone are being carried out. Therapy is aimed at keeping the child as physically and mentally active as possible. Methods used include physiotherapy, massage and orthopaedic measures. There is no cure for this disorder, and the outlook depends upon the type of disease, discovered by tests (muscle biopsy and electromyography).

Causes and risk factors: the cause is a genetic mutation resulting in a lack of a protein called dystrophin, which is essential for the normal functioning of muscle cells. In the severest form, Duchenne muscular dystrophy, serious life-threatening complications can arise, especially chest and other infections, such as pneumonia. Most children also develop heart abnormalities. In other types of muscular dystrophy, degrees of disability and complications may be less severe. Persons with a family history of the more severe forms of muscular dystrophy should seek genetic counselling.

myalgic encephalomyelitis (ME)

Description: a disorder that has been the subject of much controversy, and is characterised by extreme tiredness and certain other symptoms. It appears to follow on from viral infections such as influenza and those affecting the gut; hence, it is also called postviral fatigue syndrome.

Persons most commonly affected: all age groups and both sexes.

Organ or part of body involved: whole body – physical and psychological effects.

Symptoms and indications: symptoms include muscular pain, extreme weariness and fatigue, depression, loss of memory and concentration and panic attacks. There are no physical signs of disease.

Treatment: there is no specific cure or treatment but rest is usually essential as the affected person has very little energy. Recovery may be prolonged and the person may only slowly return to normal after months or even longer.
Causes and risk factors: the cause is not understood but there appears to be a link with infection by certain viruses, the enteroviruses. An enterovirus is one that enters via the gut, where it multiplies and goes on to attack the central nervous system.

myasthenia gravis
Description: a serious and chronic disorder characterised by great muscular weakness and fatigue.
Persons most commonly affected: young people and young adults, especially women. Males usually develop the disease after the age of 40.
Organ or part of body involved: muscles – skeletal muscles and those for breathing and swallowing, etc.
Symptoms and indications: muscle weakness that may be noticed in the face leading to 'flatness' of expression and drooping of eyelids, swallowing and breathing difficulties and speech disorder. There may be flare-ups of symptoms, followed by periods of improvement. There is no wasting of the muscles, only weakness. A person with symptoms of myasthenia gravis should seek medical advice and requires referral to a skilled specialist in this disorder.
Treatment: is by means of various kinds of drugs. These include anticholinesterase drugs, which inhibit the action of the enzyme, cholinesterase. This is the enzyme that removes excess acetylcholine (a chemical substance that is a neurotransmitter and transmits nerve impulses to the muscles). Anticholinesterase drugs, e.g. pyridostigmine, increase the amount of acetylcholine available to transmit nerve impulses, so that muscles can continue to contract. Other drugs used are immunosuppressives, which suppress the production of antibodies. Two types that are used are azathioprine and corticosteroids but these may need to be taken for some time before an improvement can be discerned. Rest and avoidance of any unnecessary exertion is very important in myasthenia gravis in order to conserve muscle strength. Treatment may also involve removal of a whole or part of the thymus gland (thymectomy) (*see causes and risk factors*) which is helpful for many persons with this disease.
Causes and risk factors: myasthenia gravis is believed to be an autoimmune disorder, i.e. a failure of the immune system, in which the body develops antibodies that attack its own tissues. For reasons that are not understood, the immune system loses the ability to distinguish between 'self' and 'non-self'. In this case, the antibodies

produced interfere with acetylcholine receptors in the nerve endings of the muscles, causing a reduction in their number or rendering them ineffective. The thymus gland is thought to be the site of production of the acetylcholine receptors. Some patients with myasthenia gravis are found to have a tumour of the thymus gland and the condition goes into remission if this is removed. There is a risk of myasthenic crisis, when symptoms of muscular weakness (especially involving the respiratory muscles) become particularly acute. This can occur during the course of drug treatment and may be life-threatening, causing serious respiratory distress. If this occurs, the person requires assisted ventilation in an intensive care unit.

Myasthenia gravis cannot be cured but symptoms can be managed and controlled.

myeloma or multiple myeloma or myelomatosis

Description: a malignant disease of the bone marrow in which tumours are present in more than one bone at the same time. Characteristically, when the bones are X-rayed, they appear to have holes in them due to the presence of typical deposits. The bone marrow contains an abnormal quantity of malignant plasma cells. The blood often contains abnormal protein (an immunoglobulin), which is usually produced to combat infection. An unusual amount of protein may also be present in the urine.

Persons most commonly affected: both sexes but more common in persons over 40 years of age.

Organ or part of body involved: bone marrow especially of ribs, pelvis, skull and spine.

Symptoms and indications: the patient may suffer from bone pain that can be severe and abnormal tiredness due to ANAEMIA. He or she may be subject to recurrent bacterial infections, especially of the respiratory tract, e.g. pneumococcal pneumonia. There may be kidney failure and the weakened bones are susceptible to fractures, or vertebrae may collapse, causing spinal cord damage and paralysis. A person with symptoms of myeloma requires immediate medical treatment.

Treatment: involves radiotherapy, chemotherapy and the use of painkilling drugs and antibiotics to fight infections. The person should remain as active as possible and should drink plenty of fluids. The use of bone-marrow transplants for this disease is under investigation in some hospitals.

Causes and risk factors: the cause is not known and the disease is not considered curable. However, symptoms can be relieved and a majority of patients show improvements with treatment.

Myelomatosis is the process of production of myeloma in the bone marrow.

myocardial infarction *see* CORONARY THROMBOSIS

myxoedema

Description: a common disease caused by underactivity of the thyroid gland, known as hypothyroidism, which may arise from a variety of different causes.

Persons most commonly affected: adults of both sexes between the ages of 30 and 60 years but more common in women.

Organ or part of body involved: thyroid gland – affecting the metabolism of the whole body.

Symptoms and indications: myxoedema affects both physical and intellectual abilities. There is intellectual impairment, with slow speech, mental dullness and lethargy. Physical symptoms include a characteristic development of a dry, yellow, coarse skin and swelling of subcutaneous tissue (beneath the skin). Also, weight gain and constipation, thinning of hair, which becomes brittle, with bald patches appearing, and pains in the muscles. Some deafness in the middle ear and CARPAL TUNNEL SYNDROME may occur. A person with symptoms of myxoedema should seek medical advice.

Treatment: the symptoms are caused by a lack of the thyroid hormones thyroxine and triodothyronine, which control metabolic processes in the body. Treatment is in the form of hormone replacement therapy with thyroxine. A small dose is given each day at first, and is gradually increased as necessary.

Causes and risk factors: there are various causes for underactivity of the thyroid gland, including goitre, and congenital factors such as rare enzyme deficiencies and cretinism. The most usual cause is an autoimmune disorder, chronic thyroiditis, in which the thyroid gland becomes fibrous and shrinks and has very little or no functional ability. Also, the condition may arise due to previous drug treatment or surgery for the opposite condition, an overactive thyroid gland (HYPERTHYROIDISM). Some of these causes are primary and others are secondary, i.e. the condition results from another disorder or disturbance.

A rare, life-threatening complication may arise, which is myxoedema coma, requiring immediate emergency medical treatment. It tends to occur in patients with a long medical history of hypothyroidism and is precipitated by a variety of factors including chilling or physical trauma, infections and treatment with drugs that act on the central nervous system.

N

narcolepsy

Description: a rare condition in which a person has a tendency to fall asleep a few times each day for several minutes or hours.
Persons most commonly affected: all age groups and both sexes but continues throughout life.
Organ or part of body involved: central nervous system.
Symptoms and indications: falling asleep for several minutes or longer (usually about a quarter of an hour). These may occur at times likely to induce sleep e.g. in a warm, quiet room after a meal, but also on other occasions, such as during a conversation. The person is easily woken and feels refreshed and the 'attacks' of sleep may occur several times in a day. They may occur during laughter or when the person is carrying out routine, monotonous activity. Eventually, after a period of time that may be years later, the condition becomes associated with attacks of cataplexy (a condition in which there are transient bouts of muscle weakness or momentary paralysis). A person with symptoms of narcolepsy should seek medical advice.
Treatment: drugs of the amphetamine type (dexamphetamine) may be prescribed to be taken on special occasions when an attack would be particularly inappropriate or embarrassing. For cataplexy, the drugs clomipramine or imipramine are usually prescribed. A person with narcolepsy may have to avoid risky activities, such as driving, or hazardous sports. If an attack is triggered by laughter or monotonous activity, then these should be avoided as much as possible.
Causes and risk factors: the disorder is present for life and the cause is unknown, although there is a tendency for narcolepsy to run in families. Recent research suggests that narcolepsy is a disorder related to the immune system.

narrow-angle glaucoma *see* GLAUCOMA

nephrotic syndrome

Description: a disorder of the kidneys in which there is an excess of protein in the urine, low levels of albumin in the blood and swelling of the tissues due to considerable fluid retention or oedema. There are high levels of cholesterol in the blood. Nephrotic syndrome

has a number of different causes and may be a primary or secondary disorder.
Persons most commonly affected: all age groups and both sexes. In children it is most common between the ages of one and five and in boys rather than girls.
Organ or part of body involved: kidneys.
Symptoms and indications: an early symptom is production of frothy urine. Oedema or fluid retention occurs, which may be localised e.g. in the knees, eyes, ankles, chest (where it can cause breathing difficulties) or abdomen (where it may cause pain). Frequently, the site may change, involving the eyelids first thing in the morning and then the ankles once the person has got up and walked about. There is a loss of appetite and weight, muscle wastage and general malaise and weakness. There is a reduction in the amount of urine produced and some patients develop kidney failure. A person with symptoms of nephrotic syndrome should seek medical advice.
Treatment: depends upon the underlying cause of the nephrotic syndrome and whether it is primary or secondary (i.e. arising out of another disorder). If the underlying disorder is treatable, then the outlook is generally favourable and the condition can be controlled. These varieties of nephrotic syndrome usually respond well to treatment with corticosteroid drugs e.g. prednisone but there may be a tendency for relapses to occur. Other types of nephrotic syndrome, which respond less well to corticosteroids alone, may be treated with prednisone and a cytotoxic drug on alternate days in order to control the condition. Some patients with types of nephrotic syndrome that do not respond to drug treatment go on to develop KIDNEY FAILURE, which requires dialysis or organ transplant. Patients with nephrotic syndrome often require a special diet low in salt and saturated fats.
Causes and risk factors: there are a number of different causes and diseases with which the syndrome is associated. These include GLOMERULONEPHRITIS, DIABETES MELLITUS, cancers such as LYMPHOMAS and LEUKAEMIAS, SYSTEMIC LUPUS ERYTHEMATOSUS, autoimmune disorders, infections including HIV and syphilis and certain drugs and naturally occurring toxins e.g. snake venom. Some types have a hereditary factor involved. A number of complications can arise accompanying this disorder, including kidney failure, heart and central nervous system disorders, THROMBOSIS, HYPERTENSION, susceptibility to recurrent infections including PERITONITIS and a tendency for relapses to occur.

neuralgia
Description: this strictly describes pain in some part, or the whole,

of a nerve without there being any physical change in that nerve. However, neuralgia is used more widely to describe any pain in a nerve or its branches, whatever the cause. It occurs in several forms and is named accordingly; trigeminal neuralgia affects the face and intercostal neuralgia the ribs. *See also* SCIATICA.

Persons most commonly affected: intercostal neuralgia: adults of both sexes, but more common in women over 50 years, especially in persons who are already in poor health. Trigeminal neuralgia: adults of both sexes.

Organ or part of body involved: any nerve or its branches, usually the trigeminal (facial) nerve, nerves that arise from the spinal cord and run between the ribs (intercostal) and the sciatic nerve.

Symptoms and indications: intercostal neuralgia; pain, usually on the left side, especially where the nerve leaves the spine in the back and in the front where it branches into the skin. The pain may come in intense bursts and may occur more often at a particular time of the day or night. There may be other symptoms, such as tingling, numbness or paralysis, and loss of appetite and muscle wastage.

Trigeminal neuralgia (tic douloureux) usually on one side of the face; severe pain of a burning or cutting nature, which may be constant or spasmodic and may be provoked by simple actions such as eating or by heat or cold. The skin of the face may become inflamed and the eye on the affected side red and watery. The condition is very debilitating in that the pain can be so intense as to interfere with sleeping and eating. Hence, the person may suffer from loss of appetite and weight.

A person with symptoms of neuralgia should seek medical advice.

Treatment: various treatments may be tried according to the type of neuralgia. Externally, heat in the form of a hot bath or rubbing in liniment (ABC liniment containing aconite, belladonna and chloroform) may be helpful and also, diathermy and the application of blisters (button cautery). Drugs used include pain-relieving analgesics, with carbamazepine being especially effective in the treatment of trigeminal neuralgia. If other treatments prove ineffective, injections to freeze the nerve or surgery to destroy a whole or a part of it may become necessary.

Causes and risk factors: sometimes the cause of neuralgia may be inflammation or pressure on the nerve but often the cause cannot be discovered. Neuralgia attacks tend to recur from time to time in an affected person, especially if the overall state of health is low.

neuritis

Description: inflammation of and degeneration of one or more nerves,

which may be localised (localised neuritis) or widespread, when it is known as polyneuritis, multiple neuritis or peripheral neuritis.
Persons most commonly affected: adults of both sexes and all age groups. Polyneuritis, if caused by alcohol, is more common in women than in men.
Organ or part of body involved: nerves.
Symptoms and indications: localised neuritis: symptoms depend upon whether the nerve involved is sensory (i.e. carrying sensations to the central nervous system) or motor (carrying electrical impulses from the central nervous system to a muscle to make it contract). If a sensory nerve is involved the main symptom is pain, as in NEURALGIA. If a motor nerve is involved, the main symptom is a degree of paralysis of the muscle that is supplied by that nerve. The overlying skin may become shiny or ulcerated, the nails ridged or pitted, and OSTEOPOROSIS may develop.

Polyneuritis: symptoms are often slow to develop and generally vague but include tingling, numbness and pains in the limbs, hands and feet, a peculiar stepping gait and drooping wrists, and there may be breathing difficulties and effects on the heart.

A person with symptoms of neuritis should seek medical advice.
Treatment: for localised neuritis, depends upon the cause but is, in general, the same as that for neuralgia. Treatment of polyneuritis primarily involves identifying the cause and/or removing the toxin that is affecting the nerves. Rest in bed, massage and physiotherapy, and electrical treatments are all used to preserve and then strengthen weakened nerves and muscles.
Causes and risk factors: the cause of localised neuritis may be an infection e.g. DIPHTHERIA, injury or other disease, such as DIABETES MELLITUS. Polyneuritis may be caused by a nutritional deficiency e.g. beriberi, which results from a lack of thiamine (vitamin B_{12}), metabolic disease or disorder e.g. DIABETES MELLITUS, hypothyroidism (MYXOEDEMA) and PORPHYRIA, infectious disease, autoimmune disorder, cancer or long-term ingestion or exposure to a toxin such as lead, mercury, many solvents and alcohol. *See also* GUILLAIN-BARRÉ SYNDROME.

non-Hodgkin's lymphoma *see* LYMPHOMA

non-specific urethritis (NSU)
Description: sexually transmitted inflammation and infection of the urethra, caused by various types of microorganism.
Persons most commonly affected: sexually active adults of both sexes.

non-specific urethritis

Organ or part of body involved: urethra, pelvic organs, cervix, possibly pharynx and anus.

Symptoms and indications: men: discomfort and pain in the urethra, mild pain on urination, increased frequency of urination and slight or more profuse discharge. The urethra is red and inflamed. Symptoms vary from mild to more severe. Women: there may be few or no symptoms but, if they do occur, include pain on urination, frequency of urination and pain in the pelvic region. Also vaginal discharge, which may be yellowish and thick, and pain during sexual intercourse.

A person with symptoms of non-specific urethritis should seek medical advice. The affected person and his or her sexual partner require treatment.

Treatment: diagnosis requires bacteriological examination of urethral sample or urine to exclude other causes of infection, such as GONORRHOEA. Treatment is by means of antibiotics including tetracycline, doxycycline or erythromycin, usually for one week, but longer if infection persists or if complications arise (*see causes and risk factors*). Patients should refrain from sexual intercourse and are usually given a follow-up examination to ensure that the infection has cleared.

Causes and risk factors: the microorganisms commonly responsible for the infection are chlamydia trachomatis and ureaplasma urealyticum but the causal organism is not always known. In both men and women, if there has been anal or oral sexual activity, inflammation of the anus (proctitis) and pharynx (throat – PHARYNGITIS) can occur. In men there may be inflammation of the sperm ducts in the testes (epidymitis), producing symptoms of pain, feverishness and swelling, and also narrowing or stricture of the urethra. In women, there may be inflammation or the development of cysts on the Bartholin's glands (secretory vaginal glands), inflammation of the Fallopian tubes (salpingitis) and perihepatitis. These complications can cause sterility or increased risk of ectopic pregnancy and even death in some cases. A serious complication that can arise, especially in men, is REITER'S SYNDROME (an arthritic disorder with CONJUNCTIVITIS, inflammation of the uveal tract of the eye and urethritis). A newborn baby may acquire an infection of the eye (called ophthalmia neonatorum) during passage through the birth canal if the mother has non-specific urethritis. This is treated with antibiotic (chlortetracycline) eye ointment.

O

oesophageal cancer or cancer of the oesophagus

Description: a malignant growth of abnormal cells in the oesophagus (gullet – the tube that takes food from the mouth to the stomach). It most frequently occurs at the lower end of the tube near the opening into the stomach.

Persons most commonly affected: adults of both sexes, especially men, in middle or older age.

Organ or part of body involved: oesophagus.

Symptoms and indications: symptoms include difficulty in passing food from the oesophagus into the stomach, which gradually becomes worse. Loss of weight, weakness and tiredness, swelling of lymph glands in the neck. A person with symptoms of oesophageal cancer should seek medical advice.

Treatment: involves admittance to hospital for radiotherapy, surgery and chemotherapy. The person may require food in liquid form or in extreme cases an operation to introduce food directly into the stomach (gastrostomy).

Causes and risk factors: the cause is not known but it is wise not to smoke.

oesophageal stricture

Description: a narrowing of the oesophagus (or gullet) which may arise for a number of different reasons and causes difficulty in the passage of food.

Persons most commonly affected: adults of all age groups and both sexes.

Organ or part of body involved: oesophagus.

Symptoms and indications: discomfort and pain in swallowing and regurgitation of (undigested) food back into the mouth, weight loss and weakness. A person with symptoms of oesophageal stricture should seek medical advice.

Treatment: depends upon the cause and extent of the stricture. The aim of treatment is to enlarge the opening so that food can pass down into the stomach. Treatment may involve dilation by means of special instruments, surgery or radiotherapy, if the cause of the stricture is cancer.

Causes and risk factors: causes of oesophageal stricture include

open-angle glaucoma

scarring from a previous injury (due to infection or swallowing of a drink that is too hot or corrosive substance), cancer and some serious nerve diseases. Also, a condition known as cardiospasm in which the cardiac sphincter (a ring of muscle located at the lower end of the oesophagus) fails to relax when food is swallowed to allow its passage into the stomach. Treatment consists of passing special instruments called bougies down the oesophagus to widen the opening, before a meal is eaten. The treatment is tedious as it may be needed for several months, but it is usually ultimately successful.

open-angle glaucoma *see* GLAUCOMA

Osgood-Schlatter's disease
Description: a condition belonging to a group of disorders known as the osteochondroses. These affect the epiphyses, or heads of the long bones, which are separated from the main shaft of these bones in children, and fuse and disappear when growth is complete. Osgood-Schlatter's disease affects the tibial tubercle (a bony nodule) of the knee.
Persons most commonly affected: children, especially boys, between the ages of 10 and 15.
Organ or part of body involved: knee.
Symptoms and indications: swelling, warmth, tenderness and pain in the knee, especially when the leg is straightened. A child with these symptoms should see a doctor.
Treatment: resting the affected leg, and avoidance of activities that are liable to stress the knee, especially sports, are necessary until recovery takes place. Rarely, some surgical procedures, injections of hydrocortisone into the knee or encasing the leg in plaster, may be required. Painkillers suitable for children may be recommended by the doctor.
Causes and risk factors: the cause is believed to be excessive stress on the tibial tubercle, which may be pulled out of line, caused by overuse of the quadriceps muscle. This is often due to excessive participation in vigorous sporting activities. Sports can be cautiously resumed once the knee has recovered completely.

osteitis deformans *see* PAGET'S DISEASE OF BONE

osteoarthritis
Description: an imprecise term generally describing a form of arthritis involving joint cartilage with accompanying changes in the associated bone. It usually involves the loss of cartilage and the

development of osteophytes (bony spurs or projecting knobs) at the bone margins. Osteoarthritis is a painful condition affecting the function of the affected joint.
Persons most commonly affected: adults of both sexes aged over 45. All persons are affected by changes in the joints with advancing years but not all have serious or disabling symptoms.
Organ or part of body involved: joints, especially toes, fingers, ankles, knees, hips and spine.
Symptoms and indications: stiffness and pain in affected joints. The aching may be weather-affected and worse when it is cold and damp. There is a loss of dexterity and movement in the affected joint. There may be a cracking or grating sound with movement and the joint may show signs of swelling. Persons with symptoms of osteoarthritis should seek medical advice.
Treatment: is aimed at maintaining movement and relieving pain. Analgesics may be prescribed and, possibly, non-steroidal anti-inflammatory drugs for acute phases of osteoarthritis. Surgery to replace the affected joint may ultimately be required.
Causes and risk factors: there are a variety of causes including overuse and stress of the joints, injury and natural processes of ageing. Some occupations are likely to pose a greater risk, e.g. certain sports, ballet and dance or other activities that put joints under stress.

osteogenesis imperfecta or brittle bone disease
Description: an uncommon hereditary disease that results in the bones being unusually fragile and brittle. There are several forms but that which affects newborn babies (osteogenesis imperfecta congenita) is the most severe. The form that is usually diagnosed slightly later (osteogenesis imperfecta tarda) is usually somewhat less severe.
Persons most commonly affected: children of both sexes. Babies born with this condition may not survive.
Organ or part of body involved: skeleton.
Symptoms and indications: symptoms include fractures that occur with the slightest degree of trauma, joints that are unusually mobile, transparent teeth and bluish sclera (eyeballs that normally appear white). In addition there may be DEAFNESS and dwarfism, as the bones are so severely affected. Symptoms range from very severe to relatively mild and in the latter form, often become apparent when the child starts to walk. A parent who is concerned about the development of a child should always seek medical advice.
Treatment: there is no effective medical treatment or cure for this condition. The child requires orthopaedic support to limit the adverse

osteomyelitis

effects of brittle bone disease and other measures to encourage life to be as normal as possible.

Causes and risk factors: the cause is an inherited abnormality of collagen (a protein substance that is widely found in large amounts in the body in connective tissue, tendons, skin, cartilage, bone and ligaments).

osteomyelitis

Description: inflammation and infection of bone marrow and bone, which may be an acute or chronic condition.

Persons most commonly affected: both sexes and all age groups. In children, it more commonly occurs in those aged 5 to 14.

Organ or part of body involved: bones. The infection may be localised or more general. In children, it usually occurs in the long bones of the arms and legs, and in adults, in the spine or pelvis.

Symptoms and indications: symptoms include worsening pain in the affected bone, swelling, fever and muscle spasm, redness and warmth. The pain is usually increased when a nearby joint is moved. A person with symptoms of osteomyelitis requires immediate medical attention.

Treatment: may require admittance to hospital for high doses of antibiotics, which may need to be delivered intravenously. Bed rest is needed until the infection has cleared and symptoms have subsided. Antibiotics are likely to be needed for several weeks. Appropriate pain relief is normally prescribed by the doctor.

Causes and risk factors: the infection is usually caused by staphylococcal bacteria, which enter the bone via the bloodstream following injury or surgery or an infection elsewhere, such as a BOIL. Sometimes after an acute attack, chronic myelitis may develop with a periodic flare-up of symptoms. This may be due to bits of dead bone or sequestra that have been left behind, perhaps after injury, which are sites of irritation and infection.

osteoporosis

Description: a loss of bone tissue, due to it being resorbed, resulting in bones that become particularly brittle and likely to fracture.

Persons most commonly affected: loss of bone density is a feature of ageing and affects older people of both sexes. However, problems mainly occur in postmenopausal women, especially those with a small frame.

Organ or part of body involved: bones.

Symptoms and indications: there may be few symptoms but those that may occur include backache, loss of height and deformation of the spine. Also, bones that fracture easily with minor falls. Persons with symptoms of osteoporosis should seek medical advice.

Treatment: is mainly preventative and for women, hormone replacement therapy in the form of oestrogen after the menopause, is effective, especially in the first few years. A good diet that is high in calcium is also essential. Calcium and vitamin D supplements may be prescribed. Remaining active and taking regular exercise, particularly walking, is helpful in maintaining the condition and strength of the bones.

Causes and risk factors: the cause in women appears to be related to the decline in oestrogen levels after the menopause, or if the ovaries have been removed due to disease. Patients with CUSHING'S SYNDROME or who have had prolonged treatment with corticosteroid drugs are also at risk of osteoporosis, as are women who have undergone radiotherapy for ovarian cancer. Those with poor nutrition and especially a low calcium intake are more at risk of developing osteoporosis. The main complications that arise, and can be life-threatening in the elderly, are bone fractures, which occur easily. Eliminating the risks to minimise the the possibility of accidents in the home are important for elderly persons with osteoporosis.

osteosarcoma

Description: the commonest and most malignant form of bone tumour.

Persons most commonly affected: older children of both sexes and young adults (ages 10 to 20).

Organ or part of body involved: bones. About half affect the femur near the knee and others may occur in the long bones of the arm. Secondary tumours (metastases) commonly occur, especially in the lungs.

Symptoms and indications: symptoms include pain and swelling around the site of the tumour. A person with symptoms of osteosarcoma should seek immediate medical advice.

Treatment: involves admittance to hospital for chemotherapy and surgery. Formerly, amputation of the limb was standard treatment but newer surgical techniques often enable the tumour to be removed and the limb reconstructed. Radiotherapy may also be needed.

Causes and risk factors: the cause is not known and this is a serious and life-threatening disease. Much research is being carried out into treatment regimes and control of symptoms to improve the outlook and quality of life of patients.

otitis externa

Description: an infection of the outer ear.
Persons most commonly affected: all ages and both sexes.
Organ or part of body involved: ear.
Symptoms and indications: pain, discharge from the outside of the ear and itching.
Treatment: usually, syringing with warm saline (salt solution) and packing with a soothing lotion are all that is required. The application of mild heat may help relieve the pain.
Causes and risk factors: this infection is most common in hot countries, but it may happen anywhere. It can be caused by scratching the ear with dirty fingers, or by the use of a badly cleaned, ill-fitting hearing-aid earpiece. It sometimes occurs after swimming in chlorinated water.

otitis media

Description: an infection of the middle ear.
Persons most commonly affected: both sexes and all ages, but mostly children.
Organ or part of body involved: ear.
Symptoms and indications: the patient complains of earache. In small babies, this may be shown by frequent rubbing of the affected ear. They are often feverish, and there may be partial deafness, or sometimes tinnitus (a ringing or buzzing sound in the ear, with no real source).
Treatment: antibiotics are prescribed, and sometimes external heat (for example, a hot-water bottle) may help to reduce the pain. In exceptional cases, if the antibiotics do not give fast relief, it may be necessary to make an incision in the eardrum, in order to allow pus to escape. This relieves the pressure in the ear, and therefore reduces the pain.
Causes and risk factors: otitis media often develops as a result of a cold or SINUSITIS, when infection spreads from the nasal passages via the Eustachian tubes that connect them with the middle ear. It can also follow jumping or diving into water without holding the nose, when infection can be forced into the ear by the same route. It is very important for the doctor to follow up the course of the infection, as repeated infections or incomplete clearance of the infection may lead to secretory otitis media, which is the main cause of glue ear in children, which is itself a cause of DEAFNESS. *See also* MÉNIÈRE'S DISEASE, MEASLES

otosclerosis

Description: a hereditary disorder in which abnormal bone is

deposited in the middle ear, which fixes the stapes (one of the three small bones in the ear). The stapes can no longer vibrate and transmit sound waves, resulting in loss of hearing.
Persons most commonly affected: usually becomes apparent in young people aged 15 to 30 and is more common in women.
Organ or part of body involved: bones of the middle ear.
Symptoms and indications: progressive loss of hearing and tinnitus (ringing in the ears). A person experiencing these symptoms should seek medical advice.
Treatment: involves admittance to hospital for microsurgery to remove the stapes and to fit an artificial replacement. The loss of hearing can usually be, at least partially, restored by this procedure. Some patients may require a hearing aid.
Causes and risk factors: the cause is a dominant genetic factor that affects about 10% of white people although not all develop a loss of hearing. In pregnancy, the course of the disease may accelerate rapidly and become apparent for the first time.

ovarian cyst

Description: a growth in the form of a sac, filled with fluid or other more solid material, that develops in the ovary and is nearly always nonmalignant.
Persons most commonly affected: women of all age groups.
Organ or part of body involved: ovary.
Symptoms and indications: often there are no symptoms until the cyst has grown to a large size and exerts pressure on nearby organs. Symptoms that can occur include abdominal pain, interference with bladder function or pain on urination, painful sexual intercourse and vaginal discharge. A person with these symptoms should seek immediate medical advice.
Treatment: usually involves admittance to hospital for surgical removal of the affected ovary, and this is most successful if carried out at an early stage, before the cyst has grown too large. In other cases, the cyst itself may be removed or drained.
Causes and risk factors: the cause is hormonal and ovarian cysts may be triggered by hormonal changes during pregnancy. If an ovarian cyst grows too large it may form adhesions (bands of tissue) that attach to other pelvic organs causing a range of symptoms. Surgery tends to be less successful if this occurs. Ovarian cysts vary in their nature. There is a danger of rupture in thinner-walled types, or twisting, which causes severe pain, fever and vomiting, requiring emergency surgery. This is a life-threatening situation that can cause death due to PERITONITIS or haemorrhage within the abdomen.

ovarian tumours

Description: a solid tumour in the ovary, which may be either benign or malignant.
Persons most commonly affected: women of all ages but more common in those between 45 and 65.
Organ or part of body involved: ovary, often one but possibly both.
Symptoms and indications: the tumour usually produces few symptoms until it has grown to a relatively large size. The symptoms of malignancy include abdominal discomfort and pain, digestive upset and, later, more severe pain and ANAEMIA, a hard mass that can be felt, deepening of the voice and hair growth. A woman with any symptoms, however vague, of ovarian tumour should seek immediate medical advice.
Treatment: involves admittance to hospital and surgery to remove the tumour or, usually, the ovary and Fallopian tube. In some cases of malignancy, hysterectomy may be required. Chemotherapy and/or radiotherapy are likely to be needed if the tumour is cancerous. There may be a need for more than one type of anticancer (cytotoxic) drug to be taken.
Causes and risk factors: the cause is not known. The outcome may be fatal if the cancer spreads to other parts of the body and secondary growths occur.

overactive thyroid gland *see* HYPERTHYROIDISM

oxyurisis *see* THREADWORMS

P

Paget's disease of bone or osteitis deformans

Description: a chronic disease, particularly affecting the long bones, skull and spine, which results in the bones becoming thickened, disorganised, soft and weak.
Persons most commonly affected: adults of both sexes over the age of 40 but more common in men.
Organ or part of body involved: bones, especially of the limbs, skull and spine.
Symptoms and indications: symptoms include bone pain, which is of an aching nature and can be very severe, especially at night. Also, the bones become enlarged and deformed and movement is impaired.

The skull may become enlarged, nerves compressed and damaged (especially if the spine is involved), causing some degree of paralysis. There may be bowing of the spine or legs and the bones are liable to fracture. The person may experience headaches and loss of hearing. The symptoms may be vague or absent in the early stages of the disease, which tends to progress in active phases with quiescent periods in between. A person with symptoms of Paget's disease should seek medical advice.
Treatment: there is no cure for the disease and treatment is aimed at the relief of pain. Various drugs may be used, including salicylates, non-steroidal anti-inflammatory drugs, calcitonin and diphosphonates. Some patients may require orthopaedic surgery and devices to increase mobility. Heat in the form of hot baths, heating pads, etc, are helpful in the relief of pain and bed rest is necessary during the acute phases of the disease.
Causes and risk factors: the cause is not known but is more likely in those with a family history of the disease. Various complications can arise, including compression of the brain by the enlargement of the skull, HYPERTENSION and heart disease. Paget's disease may be misdiagnosed as secondary bone cancer (especially from primary breast or prostate gland cancer) or an overactive parathyroid gland (hyperparathyroidism).

pancreatic cancer or cancer of the pancreas
Description: an abnormal malignant proliferation of cells in the pancreas, which is an increasingly common type of cancer in Britain.
Persons most commonly affected: adults of both sexes in middle or older age but more common in men.
Organ or part of body involved: pancreas (a gland located behind the stomach between the duodenum and spleen, which produces digestive enzymes and the hormone insulin).
Symptoms and indications: in the early stages there may be few or no symptoms and by the time they appear, the cancer may have spread to the lymph nodes, lungs or liver. Symptoms include abdominal pain that radiates to the back and lessens if the person bends forward, JAUNDICE, loss of weight, and haemorrhage (bleeding) in the gastrointestinal tract. The jaundice often causes severe itching of the skin. A person with symptoms of cancer of the pancreas should seek immediate medical treatment.
Treatment: involves admittance to hospital for chemotherapy, radiotherapy and, possibly, surgery. In addition, pain-relieving drugs, pancreatic enzymes and preparations to relieve itching may be needed. Insulin may also be needed.

Causes and risk factors: the cause is not known but the risk increases in those who have chronic PANCREATITIS, DIABETES MELLITUS, excessive consumption of alcohol and smoking. The condition is incurable but symptoms can be relieved.

pancreatitis

Description: inflammation of the pancreas, which can arise from a variety of causes and may be either acute or chronic.
Persons most commonly affected: adults of all age groups and both sexes.
Organ or part of body involved: pancreas.
Symptoms and indications: acute pancreatitis; very severe abdominal pain, fever, sweating, vomiting, which may lead to SHOCK and collapse. This is a life-threatening disorder and the patient requires immediate emergency medical treatment in hospital. Chronic pancreatitis: symptoms include pain that varies in intensity and may last for one day or several days with repeated attacks over a period of time. The function of the pancreas in secreting important digestive enzymes may be impaired and abnormal fatty stools are produced. Also, the cells that secrete the hormone insulin become ineffective and the person is likely to develop DIABETES MELLITUS. A person with symptoms of chronic pancreatitis should seek immediate medical attention.
Treatment: for acute pancreatitis, admittance to an intensive care unit is necessary. The person has to be maintained in a fasting state and requires various solutions given intravenously. Usually, the person has a nasogastric tube (a tube through the nose into the stomach) through which antacids can be given to neutralise stomach acid and prevent the possible development of ulcers. The patient may need to be starved for two to four weeks and other body systems and functions (e.g. heart) require careful monitoring. For less severe cases, fasting is still likely to be needed and fluids may be required intravenously. Various painkillers may be prescribed along with other drugs, such as pancreatic enzymes. Depending upon the cause of the pancreatitis, some surgery may be needed. In all cases of pancreatitis, alcohol must be avoided.
Causes and risk factors: causes include excess consumption of alcohol, GALLSTONES and disease of the gall bladder and bile duct. Also, injury and disease of the pancreas, such as cancer, and as a complication of surgery (especially of the stomach, gall bladder and bile ducts) or other metabolic diseases and disorders. Hereditary factors may be involved in some people or it may arise as a complication of an infection e.g. MUMPS. The risk of developing pancreatitis

increases with abuse of alcohol and with the taking of certain drugs, especially chlorothiazide, sulphasalazine, azathioprine, valproic acid and furosemide. Abuse of alcohol over a prolonged period is responsible for many cases of the disease.

Parkinson's disease or Parkinsonism

Description: a progressive condition occurring in mid to later life, due to a degenerative change in a part of the brain. It results in a rigidity of muscles and tremor when resting and unsteadiness in walking.

Persons most commonly affected: elderly adults of both sexes but more common in men.

Organ or part of body involved: part of the brain (ganglia located at the base of the cerebrum) that controls certain muscle movements.

Symptoms and indications: early symptoms include a fixed expression of the face and lack of blinking, resulting in a mask-like look, tremor of the hand when sitting still, which reduces with movement and does not occur when the person is sleeping. This may also affect the arms and legs. Movements eventually become slow, and there is a loss of the postural reflexes that help to maintain the person in an upright position. The person develops a typical shuffling gait and the body stoops. There is a tendency to fall forward or backwards or to break into a run to prevent falling. Voice and speech may be affected and there may be difficulty in swallowing. A person with symptoms of Parkinson's disease should seek medical advice.

Treatment: the condition cannot be cured but symptoms can be managed and relieved by means of various drugs, the most important of which is levodopa (a precursor of 'dopamine' – *see causes and risk factors*). The drugs used in the treatment of Parkinson's disease must be individually tailored to the needs of each patient and are administered under specialist medical care. Side effects from drug treatment may occur and should be immediately reported to the doctor. Also, the patient's response to the drugs may vary over a period of time and treatment requires monitoring and possible alteration with time.

Causes and risk factors: the cause is believed to be a degenerative change in the basal ganglia of the brain, resulting in a deficiency of the naturally occurring substance, dopamine, which transmits nerve impulses. However, in some cases, it may result from a lack of other 'neurotransmitters' (chemical substances that are naturally present in the body). Parkinson's disease also arises as a result of the taking of certain (neuroleptic) drugs, e.g. phenothiazine tranquillisers and reserpine. Parkinson's disease may arise after inflammation of the

pelvic inflammatory disease

brain (ENCEPHALITIS), brain tumours, injuries or degenerative diseases, ingestion of manganese or carbon monoxide and HYDROCEPHALUS. Drug abusers may develop Parkinson's disease from injecting a form of heroin.

pelvic inflammatory disease (PID)
Description: any acute or chronic inflammation and infection of the female reproductive organs.
Persons most commonly affected: women of all age groups; the most common form affects those who are sexually active under the age of 35.
Organ or part of body involved: ovaries, Fallopian tubes, cervix.
Symptoms and indications: symptoms may be slight or severe. These include pain, which often increases in severity and usually starts during menstruation, malaise and fever, foul-smelling vaginal discharge, abnormal bleeding, pain during intercourse and vomiting. If an abscess develops, this can be felt as a soft, movable mass. Rupture of such an abscess produces severe symptoms of pain, shock and collapse and is a life-threatening condition requiring emergency medical treatment. A person with any symptoms of pelvic inflammatory disease should immediately seek medical treatment.
Treatment: often involves admittance to hospital for antibiotics given at first intravenously and then by mouth for two to four weeks. Surgery may be necessary in some cases. Recovery is normally good if caught and treated early but may take several weeks, according to severity of symptoms.
Causes and risk factors: the cause is a bacterial infection, especially chlamydia trachomatis or NEISSERIA GONORRHOEAE, contracted through sexual intercourse. However, infection elsewhere e.g. in the appendix, which spreads either directly or via the blood circulation, caused by other organisms, is sometimes responsible. Women are more at risk after childbirth, abortion or surgery involving reproductive organs. Also, women who have an intrauterine contraceptive device (IUD) are more likely to develop the infection. There is a risk of permanent sterility if the disease is not diagnosed and treated at an early stage.

pemphigus
Description: a group of disorders, known as bullous diseases, including a serious but rare disease of the skin and mucous membranes, pemphigus vulgaris. It is locally common in some countries, particularly Brazil and parts of South America.
Persons most commonly affected: adults of both sexes in middle and older age.

Organ or part of body involved: skin and mucous membranes with possible systemic (whole body) involvement.

Symptoms and indications: there is the development of bullae, which are thin-walled blisters containing clear fluid, and usually these occur first in the mouth and later on the skin. These rupture and leave raw and painful areas that render the person susceptible to serious infection. There is a loss of weight, malaise and weakness. A person with symptoms of pemphigus requires immediate medical treatment.

Treatment: is aimed at prevention of the development of new blisters. In all but mild cases, admittance to hospital is necessary for large doses of corticosteroid drugs such as prednisone. Long-term maintenance doses of these drugs, and others such as cyclophosphamide, methotrexate and azathioprine are often needed to prevent a relapse, but there is a risk of side effects. If complications arise in the form of other infections these require appropriate antibiotic treatment.

Causes and risk factors: pemphigus is an autoimmune disorder (i.e. one in which the body's immune system fails to recognise 'self' and 'non-self' and produces antibodies that attack its own tissues). Characteristically, the blood serum and skin contains IgG antibodies or 'ABs' and the amount of these may be related to the severity of the symptoms produced.

peptic ulcer *see* STOMACH ULCER

periarteritis nodosa *see* POLYARTERITIS NODOSA

pericarditis

Description: inflammation of the pericardium, the smooth membranous sac surrounding the heart.

Persons most commonly affected: all age groups and both sexes.

Organ or part of body involved: pericardium.

Symptoms and indications: pain in the chest, which varies in severity and worsens with movement. The inflammation causes roughening of the sac and the pain results from the heart rubbing against it as it contracts. The rubbing can be heard as a scratching noise through a stethoscope and is called pericardial or friction rub. The person is feverish and breathing is rapid and shallow. Fluid may collect within the pericardial sac and this is called pericardial effusion. The resultant pressure that this exerts on the heart may cause blood pressure to fall and failure of the circulation. Chronic constrictive pericarditis – an uncommon condition in which there is a thickening of the pericardium – produces symptoms similar to those of heart failure. There is oedema and collections of fluid in the peritoneal cavity (ascites),

which may cause the abdomen to swell. A person with symptoms of pericarditis should seek medical treatment.
Treatment: depends upon the underlying cause, but will normally require admittance to hospital. Pericardial fluid needs to be drawn off or aspirated by means of a needle inserted through the chest wall. Surgery may be required in some cases, e.g. in chronic constrictive pericarditis to remove the pericardium. Pain-relieving drugs are likely to be prescribed but other medication depends upon the cause of the condition.
Causes and risk factors: a common cause is infection by a virus but also pericarditis may result from RHEUMATIC FEVER, TUBERCULOSIS, cancer, LUPUS ERYTHEMATOSUS and kidney failure. Other causes can be a complication resulting from chest or heart injury or surgery or heart attack.

peritonitis

Description: inflammation and, usually, infection of the peritoneum, a serous membrane (one lining a large cavity in the body) that lines the abdominal cavity. It may be acute or chronic (rare), localised or general. Acute, general peritonitis is the most dangerous form.
Persons most commonly affected: all age groups and both sexes.
Organ or part of body involved: peritoneum.
Symptoms and indications: pain in the abdomen, which usually rapidly becomes severe. There is shivering, chills and high fever, and the skin is hot. The abdomen swells and the muscles become rigid. Breathing is shallow and rapid, blood pressure falls and heartbeat rate rises. The symptoms may lead to shock and collapse and can prove rapidly fatal. A person with symptoms of peritonitis needs immediate emergency medical treatment in hospital.
Treatment: the underlying cause of the peritonitis must be identified and treated and this may involve surgery. Antibiotics are required to fight infection and fluids and nourishment are given intravenously. Recovery is likely, providing treatment begins at an early stage.
Causes and risk factors: the cause is usually bacterial infection, the organisms responsible gaining access either from an external wound (especially a deep stab wound) or from perforation of any of the digestive organs within the abdomen. Hence, inflammation of the stomach, gall bladder and bile duct (GALLSTONES), bowels (obstruction or twisting), HERNIA (which may become strangulated), ulcers in the digestive tract that may rupture, APPENDICITIS, ECTOPIC PREGNANCY, PELVIC INFLAMMATORY DISEASE, PANCREATITIS, abscesses or cysts e.g. in the ovaries or Fallopian tubes, and infection following abdominal surgery all carry a potential risk of peritonitis. A form

known as puerperal fever may occur in the first two days after childbirth, but is rarely serious, provided that the mother has access to hygienic conditions and good medical care. The chronic form of peritonitis is normally the result of TUBERCULOSIS. A variety of bacteria can cause peritonitis, particularly *E. coli*, which is normally present in the gut, staphylococci and streptococci.

Adhesions or scar tissue may form as a result of peritonitis, causing symptoms and problems later on.

pernicious anaemia

Description: a type of anaemia due to a deficiency in vitamin B_{12}.
Persons most commonly affected: all age groups and both sexes, depending upon underlying cause. More common in elderly persons.
Organ or part of body involved: blood, bone marrow, peripheral nerves, spinal cord.
Symptoms and indications: symptoms include weight loss, a burning feeling in the tongue, ANAEMIA that becomes progressively worse, leading to pallor, diarrhoea and constipation, numbness or tingling in the fingers and toes, fever and malaise. If the spinal cord is affected (rare), there may be unsteadiness, disorders of movement and spasticity. Persons with symptoms of pernicious anaemia should seek medical advice.
Treatment: consists of regular injections (once a month) of vitamin B_{12}.
Causes and risk factors: in pernicious anaemia, there is a failure to produce the substance (intrinsic factor) that enables vitamin B_{12} to be absorbed from the bowel. Or, the symptoms may arise from a dietary lack of this vitamin, vegans being at particular risk. The failure to produce sufficient intrinsic factor may be an autoimmune disorder (one in which the body fails to recognise 'self' and 'nonself' and produces antibodies that destroy its own tissues). In this case, the parietal cells in the stomach, which secrete the intrinsic factor (the carrier protein for vitamin B_{12} that enables it to be absorbed in the small intestine), are attacked and rendered ineffective. GASTRITIS, removal of part of the stomach (gastrectomy) or small intestine, ILEITIS (inflammation and infection of the ileum, where absorption of vitamin B_{12} takes place), enteritis, PANCREATITIS, malabsorption syndrome, COELIAC DISEASE, SPRUE, parasitic infestation, some other disorders and congenital factors may all be responsible for vitamin B_{12} deficiency. The deficiency of vitamin B_{12} in the body causes a lack of red blood cell production and the presence of abnormal large cells (megaloblasts) in the bone marrow. Before the discovery of vitamin B_{12} and its role in the body,

pernicious anaemia invariably resulted in the death of the sufferer but the condition can now be successfully treated.

pertussis *see* WHOOPING COUGH

phaeochromocytoma
Description: a tumour of the adrenal gland (one of a pair of 'endocrine' or hormone-secreting glands each situated above a kidney). The tumour is normally benign and usually located in the inner part of the gland, the medulla. The tumour is usually a few centimetres in diameter but, occasionally, can be of a much greater size and weight.
Persons most commonly affected: all age groups and both sexes but especially in adults aged 30 to 50.
Organ or part of body involved: one or both adrenal glands.
Symptoms and indications: symptoms include hypertension, headaches, vomiting and nausea, weight loss, palpitations, clammy skin, anxiety and nervousness, rapid heartbeat (tachycardia) rate, disturbance of vision, hypotension on rising, fainting and sweating. Some or all of these symptoms may be present more or less frequently, i.e. each day or every few weeks. A person with symptoms of phaeochromocytoma should seek immediate medical advice.
Treatment: analysis of urine samples for the presence of catecholamines (the breakdown products of adrenal gland hormones) confirms the diagnosis. Treatment involves admittance to hospital and, usually, monitoring of the patient's condition, along with drugs to block hormone secretions for a few days before surgery to remove the tumour. Surgery is usually effective.
Causes and risk factors: the presence of the tumour causes excess production of the hormones noradrenaline and adrenaline, producing the symptoms described above. The cause is unknown, although there may be a connection with some other types of disorder. The high blood pressure that is the main feature of phaeochromocytoma carries a risk of death through stroke or heart disease.

pharyngitis
Description: inflammation and infection of the pharynx or throat.
Persons most commonly affected: all age groups and both sexes except young babies.
Organ or part of body involved: throat and tonsils.
Symptoms and indications: symptoms include a sore throat, difficult, painful swallowing, a feeling of a lump in the throat and possibly fever and swollen glands. The throat may look red and inflamed or be covered by a grey-coloured membrane with pus discharge. A

person with symptoms of pharyngitis should seek medical advice.
Treatment: involves bed rest, and plenty of fluids should be drunk. Liquid foods may be needed if swallowing is painful. Appropriate pain relief may be prescribed by the doctor and antibiotics, if the pharyngitis is caused by bacteria. Penicillin is given for streptococcal pharyngitis to prevent the possible complication of RHEUMATIC FEVER. Pharyngitis caused by a virus usually clears up with bed rest and supportive measures.
Causes and risk factors: the cause may be a virus or various bacteria, especially species of the streptococcus genus, *Chlamydia pneumoniae* or *Mycoplasma pneumoniae*.

pituitary gland tumour

Description: a benign or malignant abnormal growth of cells in the pituitary gland. The pituitary is a small, but very important endocrine (hormone-secreting) gland situated at the base of the brain. The hormones it produces control the activity of other endocrine glands. A malignant tumour of the pituitary gland does not usually spread.
Persons most commonly affected: all age groups and both sexes but more common in adults aged 30 to 50.
Organ or part of body involved: pituitary gland.
Symptoms and indications: in children, there are likely to be effects on growth, which is either accelerated (gigantism) or retarded (dwarfism). (The tumour may cause either an overproduction or an underproduction of growth hormone). The tumour may affect the production of gonadotrophic hormones, which stimulate the testes and ovaries to produce their hormones. In this case, puberty does not take place or, at a later stage, there is an absence of menstruation in females and depression of libido in both sexes.

In adults, if the tumour causes an excessive production of growth hormone, a condition known as acromegaly occurs in which there is abnormal enlargement of hands, feet, ears and face. There may be hypothyroidism (MYXOEDEMA), CUSHING'S SYNDROME and a form of diabetes (DIABETES INSIPIDUS). The person may experience fits, gastrointestinal upset, headaches and vision disturbance, if the tumour exerts pressure on the nerves supplying the eye. A person with symptoms of a pituitary gland tumour should seek medical advice.
Treatment: involves admittance to hospital for radiation therapy and/or surgical removal of the tumour. After treatment, hormone imbalance is likely to persist and preparations of hormones are needed.
Causes and risk factors: the cause is not known but hereditary factors may be involved.

piles *see* HAEMORRHOIDS

placenta praevia
Description: attachment of the placenta in the bottom part of the uterus (womb) so that it may partly or completely cover the cervix. It occurs in about 1 in every 200 pregnancies.
Persons affected: pregnant women.
Organ or part of body involved: placenta (the temporary organ that develops during pregnancy and attaches the embryo to the uterus. It consists of both maternal and embryonic tissues and allows oxygen and nutrients to pass from the mother's blood to that of the developing baby. It secretes hormones that regulate the pregnancy and is expelled after the birth of the baby as the afterbirth.)
Symptoms and indications: there is a sudden onset of bleeding late in the pregnancy, which, although painless, may become severe. Bright red blood is passed. A pregnant woman with bleeding of this nature requires emergency admittance to hospital.
Treatment: placenta praevia resembles ABRUPTIO PLACENTA and normally, an abdominal ultrasound scan is necessary to confirm the diagnosis. If the bleeding is not severe but only minor, and the pregnancy is not near to term, the patient is usually kept in bed for observation. If the bleeding is severe, the mother will require blood transfusions and the baby is delivered, usually by Caesarian section. Occasionally, vaginal delivery may be possible.
Causes and risk factors: the cause is not known but the risk increases in women who have had several pregnancies, have FIBROIDS in the uterus or other abnormalities e.g. scarring that prevents normal attachment, and are in an older age group. The bleeding occurs because the placenta partially or completely detaches from the uterus, and may be triggered by changes as the pregnancy nears full term, such as dilation of the cervix, which occurs just before labour begins. There is a risk to the life of the mother due to the blood loss if admittance to hospital is delayed. The baby may not survive if very premature at the time of delivery.

pleurisy or pleuritis
Description: inflammation of the pleura, the serous membrane (one that lines a body cavity) that covers the lungs (visceral) and the inside of the chest wall (parietal). The membranes normally have a smooth surface that is moistened to allow them to slide over each other.
Persons most commonly affected: all age groups and both sexes.
Organ or part of body involved: pleura.

Symptoms and indications: generally, a chest pain that starts suddenly and varies in severity from relatively mild to intense. The pain is of a stabbing nature and is worse with movement, breathing, and coughing. Hence, breathing is shallow and rapid and, eventually, a characteristic sound called pleural frictional rub may develop, which can be heard with a stethoscope. The sound may be of a crackling, rasping or grating nature. Fluid may collect between the two layers, called pleural effusion, and this tends to deaden the pain but may decrease lung volume through pressure so that breathing is even more laboured. Sticky fibrous material may be discharged onto the surface of the pleura, which can cause adhesions, although this does not occur in all forms of pleurisy. A person with symptoms of pleurisy should seek medical advice.

Treatment: depends upon the underlying cause of the pleurisy, and is likely to require admittance to hospital. It involves the use of various drugs, including analgesics, antibiotics and bronchodilators. Strapping of the whole chest with elastic bandages and the use of heat may be needed to ease pain. Measures to ease the coughing up of bronchial secretions (such as the use of humidifiers) may be advised. In some cases, drawing off or aspiration of pleural effusion is required via a small incision in the chest wall. This relieves distressed breathing by enabling the lung(s) to expand properly once more.

Causes and risk factors: there are a variety of causes of pleurisy including injury, especially fracture of a rib, respiratory tract infections e.g. PNEUMONIA, BRONCHITIS and TUBERCULOSIS, other diseases including SYSTEMIC LUPUS ERYTHEMATOSUS (SLE), RHEUMATOID ARTHRITIS, cancer and asbestos-related disorders. There is a risk of pneumonia, collapse of the lungs and scarring as a result of pleurisy.

pneumoconiosis

Description: a general term for a chronic form of lung disease caused by inhaling dust while working. Most of the cases are coal miner's pneumoconiosis or anthracosis, ASBESTOSIS and SILICOSIS.

Persons most commonly affected: men in middle age or older who have been exposed to dust at work. Can affect adults of both sexes.

Organ or part of body involved: lungs.

Symptoms and indications: in the early stages there may be few or no symptoms; e.g. coal dust can be deposited in the lungs without causing much disruption of lung tissue. However, this situation may change and the patient may develop progressive massive fibrosis in which there is damage to the lungs and disruption of respiratory function. The person may be breathless, have a cough, pains in the chest, and shadows on the lungs revealed by X-rays. A person with symptoms of pneumoconiosis should seek medical advice.

Treatment: preventative measures are mainly aimed at suppression of dust in the workplace and monitoring of workers. If X-rays reveal changes in the lungs that are a cause for concern, the person should no longer work in this environment. Treatment includes the use of various drugs such as bronchodilators and analgesics. Any infections should be promptly treated with antibiotics and the person should rest in bed during attacks, until symptoms subside.

Causes and risk factors: the cause of this disorder is various types of industrial dusts, especially coal dust, but also beryllium (berylliosis), tin, barium and iron oxide. Berylliosis is a rare, severe form that appears to develop in those hypersensitive to the dust. The risk of more serious lung disease and complications is greater in those who smoke. There is a risk of LUNG CANCER, PLEURISY and congestive heart failure.

pneumonia

Description: a severe inflammation and infection of the lungs caused by many different kinds of bacteria, viruses and fungi. Most cases are caused by bacteria. It results in the filling of the air sacs (alveoli) of the lungs with fluid and pus so that they become solid and air can no longer enter.

Persons most commonly affected: all age groups and both sexes.

Organ or part of body involved: lungs, bronchi, bronchioles (the major and minor air passages supplying the lungs).

Symptoms and indications: symptoms vary in intensity depending upon how much of the lung is affected. They include chills and shivering, high fever, sweating, breathlessness, chest pain, coughing and there may be cyanosis. (In cyanosis, there is a blue appearance of the skin due to insufficient oxygen within the blood and tissues.) A sputum is produced that is often rust-coloured or may be thicker and contain pus. Breathing is laboured, shallow and painful. The patient may become drowsy and confused if cyanosis occurs and convulsions can occur in children. A person with symptoms of pneumonia requires immediate medical attention.

Treatment: may require admittance to hospital for antibiotics, which may need to be given intravenously in the first instance. The patient may require oxygen and analgesics to relieve pain, and measures such as tepid sponging to reduce fever. Fluids may need to be given intravenously. Amantadine and acyclovir may be given for viral pneumonia. Recovery from pneumonia depends upon the severity of the illness, and whether it occurs in a person who was previously

well, or as a complication of existing illness. The elderly and very young and those with previous illness are most at risk, and it remains a major cause of death.
Causes and risk factors: pneumonia is usually caused by a bacterial infection and numerous different kinds may be responsible. Commonly, *Streptococcus pneumoniae*, *Staphylococcus aureus*, *Chlamydia pneumoniae* or *Mycoplasma pneumoniae* are the causal organisms. The elderly and very young, persons with a depressed immune system e.g. transplant patients and those who have been treated for cancer, AIDS patients, those with ALCOHOLISM and people with respiratory disorders, such as obstructive airways disease (ASTHMA), are most at risk from pneumonia. The infection is usually caught by inhalation of airborne deposits containing the bacteria.

pneumothorax
Description: air in the pleural cavity between the two layers of the pleura (the double serous membrane that covers the lungs and the inside of the chest wall), which exerts pressure and causes the lung to collapse.
Persons most commonly affected: all age groups and both sexes (depending upon the cause).
Organ or part of body involved: lungs and pleura.
Symptoms and indications: symptoms vary greatly depending upon the nature and extent of the pneumothorax and whether underlying lung disease is present. They include a sharp pain in the chest that comes on suddenly and may travel to the shoulder and abdomen, breathlessness and a dry, barking cough. If severe lung disease is present there may be collapse and shock with respiratory and circulatory failure. A person with symptoms of pneumothorax should seek medical advice.
Treatment: depends upon the nature and degree of severity of the pneumothorax. A patient with a simple, small pneumothorax and who has no existing lung disease requires no special treatment other than to rest until symptoms subside. The air is reabsorbed naturally and the affected part of the lung re-expands. If a larger area of lung is involved, this may take some time and the person requires monitoring to ensure that there is no leak of fluid (pleural effusion) or development of fibrous deposits. For a more severe or complicated pneumothorax, where there has been an injury or the person has existing lung disease, or is elderly and generally at greater risk, admittance to hospital is needed. The person may require a chest tube and various drugs including pain relief. In some emergency cases, the air may need to be drawn off rapidly by means of a needle

or catheter into the chest wall, in order to save life. A person who has more than one pneumothorax on the same side may eventually require surgery.

Causes and risk factors: causes include a penetrating external wound or internal injury e.g. a lung punctured by a fractured rib. Also, rupture of one or more small air sacs inside the lung due to diseases such as EMPHYSEMA, ASTHMA, TUBERCULOSIS, CYSTIC FIBROSIS, inflammation and infection e.g. abscess or FISTULA in the lung. A simple pneumothorax may occur for no apparent reason or be associated, in some people, with taking part in high-altitude flight or deep diving.

polyarteritis nodosa or periarteritis nodosa

Description: a disease in which there is inflammation and death of sections of medium-sized arteries, with the development of small ANEURYSMS and nodules in their muscular walls. The tissues supplied by these arteries suffer from a decreased blood supply (ischaemia). This is a disorder of collagen (a collagen vascular disease), an important protein substance that is the major constituent of all connective tissue.

Persons most commonly affected: all age groups and both sexes, especially adults aged between 40 and 50 years but more common in men.

Organ or part of body involved: any part of the body may be involved.

Symptoms and indications: the symptoms are variable and imprecise, and can mimic those of other disorders, because any part of the body or organ can be affected. Commonly, the gastrointestinal tract, heart, kidneys and liver are affected. The most common symptoms include fever, pain in the abdomen, numbness and tingling in the feet and hands due to peripheral nerves being affected, loss of weight, general weakness and malaise, retention of fluid (oedema), high blood pressure (HYPERTENSION), a reduction in the quantity of urine passed and presence of urea in the urine. Also, gastrointestinal upset, bleeding in the gastrointestinal tract and nausea and vomiting, headaches, muscle and joint pains. A person with symptoms of polyarteritis should seek immediate medical advice.

Treatment: depends to some extent upon the area of the body that is affected. However, it may require admittance to hospital and, usually, high doses of corticosteroids (e.g. prednisone) and/or immunosuppressive drugs are needed. Complications and conditions caused by the effects of the disease on particular organs require appropriate treatment. The drugs used in treatment may themselves be responsible for certain side effects, especially when used for an extended period of time.

Causes and risk factors: the cause is not known but it is believed to be a hypersensitivity disorder in susceptible individuals. Bacterial infections such as those caused by staphylococcus or streptococcus, viral infections e.g. HIV, influenza and serum HEPATITIS and the use of some drugs and vaccines may trigger off the disease in some people. There is a risk of death from failure of major organs (especially of the kidneys), if these are affected, or from rupture of an ANEURYSM. Immunosuppressive drugs used in treatment make potentially dangerous infections more likely to occur.

polycystic disease of the kidney or polycystic kidney disease or PKD

Description: one of a group of abnormal disorders of the kidney characterised by the development of cysts in the kidneys. These disorders are inherited and may be either dominant or recessive.

Persons most commonly affected: all age groups and both sexes. Different types of disease may be present at or even before birth, in childhood or in adult life.

Organ or part of body involved: kidneys.

Symptoms and indications: the kidneys enlarge but have a reduced ability to perform their normal functions. Normal tissue is replaced by diseased cysts that are expanded portions of kidney tubules. The cysts may cause low back pain or sharp pain of a colicky nature in the kidneys. Also, there may be blood in the urine, high blood pressure and, in some patients, ANEURYSMS or subarachnoid haemorrhage, which is a dangerous and life-threatening condition. Patients are likely to suffer from frequent urinary tract infections and cysts may also occur in the liver. Persons with symptoms of polycystic kidney disease should seek medical advice.

Treatment: depends upon the severity of the symptoms and is aimed at maintaining kidney function, treating infections and managing high blood pressure. Dialysis or a kidney-transplant operation may eventually be necessary.

Causes and risk factors: the cause of the disorder is usually a mutant gene located on chromosome 16. The disease tends to reduce life expectancy and some affected persons die from ruptured ANEURYSMS, causing brain haemorrhage, or eventually from KIDNEY FAILURE. People with a family history of this disease should seek genetic counselling before having children.

polycythaemia (rubra vera and secondary polycythaemia)
Description: an excessive production of red blood cells in the blood. Primary polycythaemia or polycythaemia rubra vera is a rare disorder in which red blood cells, white blood cells and platelets are all produced in excessive amounts. Secondary polycythaemia arises as a result of some other disorder.
Persons most commonly affected: adults of both sexes but more common in men aged 60 years or over.
Organ or part of body involved: bone marrow and blood.
Symptoms and indications: symptoms include headache, weariness, breathlessness, disturbance of vision, itching, flushed skin, bleeding and enlargement of the spleen. Complications may arise, including symptoms of peptic ulcer, pain in the bones, THROMBOSIS, GOUT and KIDNEY STONES and liver disorder (Budd-Chiari syndrome). Some patients have no symptoms. A person with symptoms of polycythaemia should seek medical advice.
Treatment: may involve admittance to hospital for phlebotomy (the incision of a vein to allow blood to be collected, now usually known as 'venesection'). Also, chemotherapy with CYTOTOXIC drugs and radiotherapy with radioactive phosphate may be required. Treatment is tailored to the individual needs of the patient and one or more methods may be needed, depending upon response. Also, other drugs such as aspirin and preparations to relieve itching may be needed. Primary polycythaemia is not curable, although the symptoms can be relieved. Secondary polycythaemia can be cured if the underlying disorder can be treated.
Causes and risk factors: the cause of primary polycythaemia rubra vera is not known. Secondary polycythaemia may arise as a result of smoking, living at a high altitude for a long period of time, chronic lung disease or tumours in the kidneys, liver, brain or uterus. There is a risk of death from thrombosis, bone marrow abnormality, haemorrhage and development of LEUKAEMIA.

polymyalgia rheumatica and temporal arteritis
Description: pain and stiffness in certain groups of muscles, which may, in some patients, be associated with temporal arteritis (or giant-cell or cranial arteritis), which is an inflammatory disease of large arteries.
Persons most commonly affected: adults of both sexes aged over 50 but is twice as common in women.
Organ or part of body involved: muscles of shoulder and hip girdles and the neck. Temporal arteritis usually involves the carotid and cranial arteries (temporal arteries) and sometimes peripheral and heart arteries.

Symptoms and indications: symptoms of polymyalgia rheumatica include stiffness and pain in the neck, shoulders, back or hips, which is usually worse on rising in the morning or after sitting still and wears off through the day. There is no degeneration or disease of the muscles. There may also be feverishness, weight loss, loss of appetite, fatigue and malaise. In temporal arteritis, there is, additionally, a severe and pounding headache, disturbance of vision, tenderness of the head and weakness of the muscles of the tongue and jaw. Patients with any symptoms of these conditions should seek immediate medical advice.

Treatment: is by means of steroid drugs in the form of prednisone, which may be needed in high doses at the start of treatment. Treatment should begin immediately if temporal arteritis is suspected, to prevent the risk of blindness.

Causes and risk factors: the cause is not known but treatment is usually successful within two years. Long-term use of steroid drugs may produce side effects. Without treatment or if this is delayed, temporal arteritis poses a risk of blindness, STROKE or heart disease.

polymyositis or dermatomyositis

Description: a disease of connective tissue, with inflammation and degeneration of many muscles (polymyositis) and also the skin (dermatomyositis). It leads to weakness and atrophy of muscles, especially those of the limbs, shoulders and hips.

Persons most commonly affected: both sexes and all age groups but twice as common in females as in males. In children, it usually first appears between the ages of 5 to 15 and in adults, between 40 to 60 years.

Organ or part of body involved: muscles, skin, connective tissue.

Symptoms and indications: the symptoms may be slight or more acute and may be preceded by an infection. In children, the symptoms are more likely to appear in an acute form. Symptoms include muscle weakness, especially noticed in the shoulder and hip girdles and also in those of the throat, leading to swallowing difficulty, regurgitation of food and voice changes. The weakness may be severe so that the person is unable to undertake normal activities. There may be a raised, dusky skin rash that is itchy and can occur on the face, neck, trunk and limbs. There may be muscle tenderness and pain and eventually the limbs may become contracted. A person with these symptoms should seek immediate medical advice.

Treatment: is likely to involve admittance to hospital for treatment with corticosteroid drugs, especially prednisone, during the acute stages of the disease. Some patients may require treatment with immunosuppressive drugs if corticosteroid therapy is not effective. Other medication may be needed, including potassium supplements and antacids. Appropriate exercises are likely to be needed to combat muscle contracture.

Causes and risk factors: the cause is not known, but it may be an autoimmune disease (one in which the body fails to recognise the difference between 'self' and 'non-self' and produces antibodies that attack its own tissue). Sometimes, a preceding infection seems to precipitate the disorder. The outlook is extremely variable and difficult to predict but tends to be more favourable in children, in whom there may be a remission or cure. Most patients become confined to a wheelchair and death may occur due to heart and lung disease, inflammation of blood vessels of the bowel, malnutrition and malignancy.

porphyria

Description: a group of rare inherited metabolic disorders in which there is an increased production of porphyrins within the body. (Porphyrins are naturally-occurring chemical compounds found throughout the plant and animal kingdom in many different types of living tissue.)

Persons most commonly affected: all age groups and both sexes, some types being more common in women.

Organ or part of body involved: whole body.

Symptoms and indications: symptoms include abdominal pain, which may be severe, and there may be gastrointestinal upset such as vomiting and nausea, diarrhoea or constipation. There may be high blood pressure (HYPERTENSION), a raised heartbeat rate and feverishness. There is muscle weakness, due to neuropathy of motor nerves and this especially affects the hands, feet, arms and legs. There is a sensitivity to sunlight, blistering and itching of the skin, production of a dark urine due to the presence of excreted porphyrins and mental disturbances, including depression. There may be liver damage in some forms of the disease. A person with symptoms of porphyria should seek medical advice.

Treatment: is usually aimed at preventing attacks. This involves avoidance (as far as possible) of precipitating factors, including certain drugs, alcohol, sunlight and prompt treatment of infections. Also, the person should have a good diet and plenty of fluids, use sun screen products, and wear a hat and protective clothing when going outside. In some patients, transfusions of packed red blood cells, the taking of beta-carotene (to increase tolerance to the sun) and removal of the spleen may be helpful in reducing the severity of symptoms.

Supportive care in hospital may be needed during a severe attack.
Causes and risk factors: the cause is an inherited disorder and is not curable, although symptoms can be relieved and managed. Various drugs including hormones used in oral contraceptives and hormone replacement therapy, alcohol, barbiturates and sunlight may precipitate an attack in a person with porphyria.

postviral fatigue syndrome *see* MYALGIC ENCEPHALOMYELITIS

potter's asthma *see* SILICOSIS

pre-eclampsia of pregnancy
Description: a complication of pregnancy arising after the 20th week and characterised by high blood pressure (HYPERTENSION), fluid retention (oedema) and the presence of a protein (albumin) in the urine.
Persons affected: pregnant women.
Organ or part of body involved: whole body.
Symptoms and indications: the symptoms of pre-eclampsia are a blood pressure of 140 over 90mm of mercury (or greater), or a rise in systolic blood pressure of 30mm or diastolic blood pressure of 15mm of mercury. Also, fluid retention causing swelling, especially of the hands and/or face and the presence of albumin in the urine. The symptom that is most likely to be noticed by the patient is the fluid retention and this, and any other symptoms, should immediately be reported to the doctor. Other symptoms may be detected during routine antenatal check-ups.
Treatment: in very mild cases of pre-eclampsia, the woman may be treated at home, requiring complete bed rest and careful monitoring until blood pressure falls and symptoms improve. If the woman's condition does not respond or in any other than very mild cases, admittance to hospital is necessary. The patient is usually given a salt solution intravenously and also magnesium sulphate. The aim is to stabilise the woman's condition, to lessen the risk of convulsions and bring about a fall in blood pressure, and then to deliver the child. Other drugs may additionally be needed. Once the patient's condition has improved, labour may be induced and the baby delivered normally, or a Caesarian section may be required.
Causes and risk factors: the cause is unknown but is more likely to occur in a first pregnancy and in women with a history of high blood pressure or blood vessel disorders. There is a danger of the development of ECLAMPSIA OF PREGNANCY and also, ABRUPTIO PLACENTAE, both of which are potentially fatal conditions. With prompt treatment, the outlook for mother and child is usually good.

progressive systemic sclerosis (PSS) see SCLERODERMA

prolapsed intervertebral disc or slipped disc

Description: intervertebral discs are thick, fibrous cartilaginous discs that connect and lie between adjacent vertebrae of the backbone. They permit rotational and bending movements of the back and make up approximately 25% of the length of the backbone, acting as shock absorbers and providing cushioning for the brain and spinal cord. Each disc has an outer fibrous layer over a pulpy centre. A slipped or prolapsed disc is caused by the inner layer being pushed through the fibrous layer to impinge upon a neighbouring spinal nerve-causing pain.

Persons most commonly affected: adults of both sexes in middle or older age.

Organ or part of body involved: intervertebral disc, usually either between the last two lumbar vertebrae (lumbago) or the lowest lumbar vertebrae and the five fused sacral vertebrae that form the sacrum (sciatica).

Symptoms and indications: pain in the lower part of the back, which may come on and worsen gradually or, more usually, is sudden and occurs during an activity that involves bending or sudden twisting of the backbone. A person with symptoms of a slipped disc should seek medical advice.

Treatment: depends upon the severity of the condition but involves bed rest on a flat, firm surface, possibly with manipulation and physiotherapy at a later stage. Epidural anaesthesia (an injection of local anaesthetic into the spine) may be required to relieve pain. Occasionally, surgical removal of the disc may be carried out.

Causes and risk factors: a slipped disc is more likely to occur in middle or later adult life and may be related to degenerative changes that take place. However, the condition is not unknown in younger adults. It is sensible to take extra care when carrying out movements or activities that might stress the back.

prolapse of the rectum see RECTAL PROLAPSE

prostate gland cancer

Description: a malignant growth of cells in the prostate gland, which is a fairly common form of cancer in men. The prostate is a gland in the male reproductive system that is located below the bladder, opening into the urethra. Upon ejaculation, it secretes an alkaline fluid into the semen, which aids the movement of sperm.

Persons most commonly affected: men aged 50 years or over.

Organ or part of body involved: prostate gland.
Symptoms and indications: the cancer normally grows very slowly and causes no symptoms in the early stages. Later there may be urinary obstruction due to pressure of the growth on the bladder outlet or ureter (one of a pair of tubes each leading from a kidney to the bladder). If the tumour has spread and there are secondary growths, there may be pain in the bones. Other symptoms include the presence of blood and white blood cells in the urine. A person with any symptoms of prostate cancer should seek immediate medical advice.
Treatment: involves admittance to hospital for possible surgery to remove the prostate gland (prostatectomy) and sometimes, the testes (orchidectomy), and/or radiation therapy. Also, treatment with hormones (oestrogens, especially diethylstilboestrol) is effective in controlling the cancer and relieving the symptoms. The condition can be cured if caught and treated in the early stages. Even at a later stage, symptoms can be relieved and life prolonged with treatment. A regular rectal examination after the age of 40 may detect the cancer at an early stage and is a possible preventative measure.
Causes and risk factors: the cause is not known but does not appear to be connected with ENLARGEMENT of the prostate gland, which commonly occurs in elderly men.

prostate gland enlargement or **prostatic hypertrophy** or **benign prostatic hypertrophy**
Description: benign enlargement of the prostate gland. (The prostate is a gland in the male reproductive system that is located below the bladder, opening into the urethra. Upon ejaculation, it secretes an alkaline fluid into the semen, which aids the movement of the sperm.)
Persons most commonly affected: men aged over 50 years.
Organ or part of body involved: prostate gland.
Symptoms and indications: increased frequency of urination, especially during the night, causing sleep disturbance. There may be a poor flow of urine and inability to empty the bladder completely and accompanying pain. There may be dribbling and some degree of urinary incontinence and a greater likelihood of urinary tract infection. A man with these symptoms should seek immediate medical advice.
Treatment: usually involves admittance to hospital for surgical removal of the prostate gland, normally by the method of transurethral resection. (This is carried out via the urethra, using a cytoscope, an electric current being used to cauterise and remove the gland. No surgical incision is necessary with this method, and

pseudorubella

recovery is normally good with less likelihood of postoperative complications.) Before surgery is carried out, it may be necessary for any infection to be treated and for the bladder to be completely drained using a catheter. Also, catheter drainage is usually needed for the first few days after surgery.

Causes and risk factors: the cause of prostate gland enlargement is not known but may be associated with hormonal changes accompanying ageing.

pseudorubella *see* ROSEOLA INFANTUM

psilosis *see* SPRUE

psittacosis

Description: a bacterial infection of psittacine birds, e.g. parrots, budgerigars, lovebirds, canaries, pigeons and some seabirds, which is contagious and can be transmitted to human beings.

Persons most commonly affected: both sexes and all age groups.

Organ or part of body involved: lungs, respiratory system.

Symptoms and indications: the symptoms include headache, shivering, feverishness, chills, malaise, loss of appetite and weight, cough and breathlessness. The cough may be dry at first but eventually produces a pus-containing sputum. A person with these symptoms who has recently been in contact with birds, should seek immediate medical advice.

Treatment: consists of complete bed rest and taking tetracycline antibiotics for ten days or longer. Other drugs such as codeine for treatment of the cough may be indicated. The patient should be kept in isolation, as inhalation of airborne droplets may cause a spread of the infection. Preventative measures include keeping imported birds in quarantine and treating them (via their feed) with chlortetracycline. People who routinely handle birds should exercise care and be well informed about this disease. The infection can progress to life-threatening PNEUMONIA if not treated, but usually responds well with recovery in two to three weeks.

Causes and risk factors: the cause is a microorganism called *Chlamydia psittaci* that is transmitted to man by inhalation of dust from feathers or droppings or directly via the bite of an infected bird. There is a particular danger from some virulent forms of the disease and the mortality in human beings can be quite considerable, especially if the disease is not caught and treated early enough.

psoriasis

Description: a chronic skin disorder that tends to remain throughout life and is characterised by alternating active and quiescent periods.

Persons most commonly affected: usually beginning in adolescence or early adulthood and continues throughout life affecting people of both sexes.
Organ or part of body involved: skin.
Symptoms and indications: the appearance of raised, red, roughened patches covered by silvery, shiny scales. These usually first appear on the elbows and knees but may affect other areas of the trunk, arms, legs, scalp and back. The nails may also be affected, with thickening, pitting and splitting, which may be confused with a fungal infection. A person with symptoms of psoriasis should seek medical advice.
Treatment: is by means of various creams and ointments containing coal tar, corticosteroids, salicylic acid and anthralin. Sunlight (but not sunburn) is helpful and also synthetic vitamin A may be prescribed. Ultraviolet light (known as PuVA therapy) may be used to treat more extensive or severe psoriasis, under strict medical supervision. In very severe cases, or where there is additional psoriatic arthritis or exfoliative psoriatic dermatitis (*see causes and risk factors*), methotrexate (a potent antimetabolite drug) may be prescribed.

Treatment is usually effective in controlling the symptoms, although the condition itself cannot be cured. Stress or anxiety seems to exacerbate psoriasis and bring on an attack of the symptoms in some people. Hence, this should be avoided if possible and the person may require counselling and advice to learn to adjust his or her life to the condition.
Causes and risk factors: the cause is not known, but there is often a family history of psoriasis. It is much more common among White races of people. The symptoms of thickening and scaling of the skin are caused by changes in the epidermis with the production of a greater number of cells. Usually, psoriasis does not affect the person's overall health. However, in some people it is associated with a severe and disabling form of arthritis. In others, the skin may be much more severely and extensively affected, leading to a profound deterioration in general health, and this condition is known as exfoliative psoriatic dermatitis. Patients with the most severe forms of the disease may require periods of treatment in hospital.

ptosis
Description: drooping of the eyelid.
Persons most commonly affected: both sexes and all age groups.
Organ or part of the body involved: eyelid; one or both eyes may be involved.

Symptoms and indications: eyelid drooping over the eye and poor blinking reflex.
Treatment: depends on cause. Surgery may be required, or treatment of underlying disorder.
Causes and risk factors: may result from damage or weakness of the muscles or nerve supply of the eyelid, or may be because of restriction of the eyelid by scarring, cysts or a tumour. Other conditions that cause ptosis are MYASTHENIA GRAVIS, birth trauma, MUSCULAR DYSTROPHY, brain tumour, DIABETES.

pulmonary embolism

Description: a condition in which the pulmonary artery (leading from the heart to the lung) or a branch of it, becomes blocked by a clot or embolus, which is usually of blood, and rarely a clump of fat cells. The clot usually originates as a phlebothrombosis of a deep vein in the leg or pelvis. The seriousness of the condition is related to the size of the clot. The clot moves through the circulation, ultimately lodging in a part of a pulmonary artery. Large pulmonary emboli can be fatal, while smaller ones may cause tissue death of parts of the lung, breathing difficulties and symptoms of PLEURISY.
Persons most commonly affected: adults of both sexes but can affect people of all ages.
Organ or part of body involved: a pulmonary artery or one of its branches.
Symptoms and indications: there is a sudden and often severe pain in the chest, breathlessness and a cough that may result in the bringing up of blood. There is a rapid heartbeat rate and the person feels anxious and restless. The person may be feverish or faint and there may be shock and death if the clot is large. Often there are symptoms of PULMONARY HYPERTENSION. A person with symptoms of pulmonary embolism requires immediate emergency medical attention.
Treatment: involves admittance to hospital. Anticoagulant drugs such as heparin may be prescribed in less severe cases, or streptokinase to dissolve the clot. In other cases, emergency surgery may be needed to remove the clot. Pulmonary embolism occasionally arises as a complication of surgery, injury, especially bone fractures, pregnancy and childbirth, due to the formation of a clot in a deep vein of the leg or pelvis. Preventative measures for hospital patients include the wearing of elastic stockings and encouraging leg exercises and walking as soon as possible after surgery, and also the use of drugs to thin the blood.
Causes and risk factors: The risk of phlebothrombosis and

pulmonary embolism is greater in those who smoke or are overweight and in older women taking oral contraceptives. Also, it is more likely in those with existing heart and circulatory disorders, in elderly persons aged over 60 years, and in those with SICKLE CELL ANAEMIA and some other diseases (POLYCYTHAEMIA).

pulmonary hypertension

Description: a considerable rise in blood pressure in the pulmonary artery due to increased resistance to the flow of blood, usually caused by diseases of the lung or PULMONARY EMBOLISM. The result is that the right ventricle (one of the larger lower chambers of the heart) has to work much harder to maintain the flow of blood and enlarges.
Persons most commonly affected: all age groups and both sexes.
Organ or part of body involved: heart, a pulmonary artery or its branches.
Symptoms and indications: there is chest pain or discomfort, fainting and light-headedness and, possibly, convulsive episodes and heart failure. A person with these symptoms requires immediate emergency medical attention.
Treatment: depends upon the underlying cause of the pulmonary hypertension. Admittance to hospital for diagnostic tests is followed by an appropriate course of treatment. (*See* PULMONARY EMBOLISM, BRONCHITIS, EMPHYSEMA.)
Causes and risk factors: the cause is usually underlying lung disease, as described above. There is a risk of death from heart failure, depending upon the severity of the condition.

pulmonary oedema

Description: a gathering of fluid in the lungs arising for a variety of reasons, especially as a result of congestive heart failure or MITRAL STENOSIS. It produces severe and life-threatening symptoms.
Persons most commonly affected: adults of both sexes, especially those in middle or older age groups.
Organ or part of body involved: lungs and heart.
Symptoms and indications: great breathing difficulties with shallow, rapid breaths, cyanosis (a lack of oxygen in the blood), anxiety, restlessness, and a feeling of suffocation. Also, there may be sweating, a cough, dry at first but then producing a pink-stained frothy sputum, a weak or pounding pulse and characteristic crackling sounds from the lungs (called rales) that can be heard through a stethoscope. There may be a collection of fluid in the hands and feet, low blood pressure (hypotension), and veins may become engorged and prominent. A person with these symptoms requires emergency medical treatment.

pulmonary valve stenosis

Treatment: admittance to hospital is required for immediate treatment aimed at saving life. This involves the giving of oxygen, and various drugs may be required including narcotics (morphine sulphate), nitroglycerin, diuretics, e.g. frusemide or ethacrynic acid, digitalis and dopamine. The underlying condition responsible for the pulmonary oedema will require appropriate treatment. The outlook is more favourable if treatment begins promptly.

Causes and risk factors: the usual cause is failure of the left ventricle of the heart (one of the lower larger chambers) or MITRAL STENOSIS. Other causes include poisoning with some drugs, such as barbiturates or opiates, fluids and blood given intravenously, KIDNEY FAILURE, STROKE, head injury, inhalation of toxic fumes and near-drowning.

pulmonary valve stenosis

Description: narrowing of the pulmonary valve, which controls the outlet from the right ventricle (one of the large upper chambers of the heart) to the pulmonary artery leading to the lungs. This leads to obstruction and a reduction of normal heart function.

Persons most commonly affected: both sexes and all age groups. The congenital form is likely to become apparent at or shortly after birth.

Organ or part of body involved: heart.

Symptoms and indications: symptoms are those of ANGINA, along with fainting and signs of congestive heart failure. These include breathlessness, fatigue, fluid retention and a cough which may produce a pink and frothy sputum. Part of the heart may become enlarged. A person with symptoms of pulmonary valve stenosis should seek medical advice.

Treatment: unless the symptoms are very mild, treatment usually involves admittance to hospital for surgery to clear the obstruction and widen the valve.

Causes and risk factors: the cause is usually congenital but rarely it arises as a result of RHEUMATIC FEVER.

pyelitis

Description: inflammation and infection of a part of the kidney, the pelvis. (This is the area from which urine drains into the ureter). It is usually the case that the infection is not limited to the pelvis but involves all the kidney, hence a more accurate term is pyelonephritis.

Persons most commonly affected: females of all age groups but can affect males, especially the elderly and those with underlying disorders such as kidney stones.

Organ or part of body involved: kidney.

Symptoms and indications: the symptoms include pain in the loins, high temperature, chills and shivering, loss of appetite and weight and malaise. There may be frequency of urination and the urine is acidic and may contain pus. A person with these symptoms should seek medical advice.

Treatment: is by means of antibiotics, which may need to be given intravenously in hospital in the first instance. The person requires bed rest, and a high intake of fluids. Pain relief may be prescribed and oral antibiotics may be needed for some time to prevent a recurrence of infection. Investigative procedures are likely to be needed to detect any underlying disease or abnormality that may have caused the inflammation. If this is present, it will require further appropriate treatment.

Causes and risk factors: the usual organism responsible (in three quarters of the cases) is the common gut bacterium *E. coli*. There is an increased risk of this condition occurring during pregnancy and in patients who have had investigations of the bladder, using instruments, or urinary catheters. Also, patients being treated with immunosuppressive drugs or corticosteroids are at greater risk of developing this type of infection.

pyloric stenosis

Description: a narrowing of the pylorus (the lower end of the stomach, the opening from which food passes into the duodenum and which is controlled by a ring of muscle, the pyloric sphincter).

Persons most commonly affected: both sexes and all age groups. A congenital form is present at birth and particularly affects baby boys. This usually becomes apparent in the first two to five weeks after birth.

Organ or part of body involved: pylorus (stomach).

Symptoms and indications: there is vomiting and distension of the stomach, the muscular movements (peristalsis) of which may be visible through the abdomen. Without intervention, the person loses weight, becomes dehydrated and blood and body fluids become alkaline (alkalosis), due to acid loss following prolonged vomiting. In the congenital type, the thickened pyloric muscle can be felt externally. A person with these symptoms requires immediate medical attention.

Treatment: requires admittance to hospital for surgery to correct the condition. In babies, the surgical procedure is called pyloromyotomy or Ramstedt's procedure, and involves dividing the thickened muscle. The baby normally makes a good and complete recovery, with no recurrence of symptoms. In adults, surgery relieves the symptoms

but the long-term outlook depends upon the underlying cause of the condition. Further treatment may be needed.
Causes and risk factors: the congenital form of pyloric stenosis is caused by a thickening of the muscle of the pylorus, which eventually closes the outlet to the duodenum. In adults, the cause is usually a peptic (pyloric) ulcer or cancerous growth that is responsible for the narrowing of the channel.

Q

Q fever
Description: an infectious disease of sheep, goats and cattle and some other mammals and birds (which do not exhibit symptoms), that can be passed to man producing a pneumonia-like disease.
Persons most commonly affected: all age groups and both sexes; persons in close contact with animals.
Organ or part of body involved: lungs, respiratory system.
Symptoms and indications: the symptoms usually begin suddenly and include a severe headache, high fever, breathing difficulties, chills, muscle and chest pains, cough and general malaise. A person with these symptoms should seek immediate medical advice. The illness lasts for about two weeks.
Treatment: is by means of antibiotics, especially tetracycline and chloramphenicol, and the person should be kept in isolation, rest in bed and drink plenty of fluids. An effective vaccine is available for those who may be at risk.
Causes and risk factors: the cause of the infection is a microorganism named *Coxiella burnetti*, which is present in the droppings, urine, milk and tissues (especially the placenta) of infected animals. Transmission to humans is usually by means of inhalation of airborne droplets, but also through drinking unpasteurised milk. In slaughterhouses and other industries connected with animals, strict standards of hygiene, and health and safety measures including dust suppression, should be employed.

R

rabies

Description: a very severe and fatal disease affecting the central nervous system, which occurs in dogs, wolves, cats and many other mammals. Human beings are infected through the bite of a rabid animal, usually a dog. The UK is currently free of rabies but it occurs in many countries throughout the world.

Persons most commonly affected: all age groups and both sexes.

Organ or part of body involved: brain and central nervous system.

Symptoms and indications: symptoms may begin from ten days up to a year, following a bite from a rabid animal. Usually, however, they begin after four to eight weeks, starting with depression and irritability. Swallowing and breathing difficulties develop, and feverishness, and there are periods of great mental excitement, increased salivation and muscular spasms of the throat that are very painful. Eventually, even the sight of water causes severe muscular spasms, convulsions and paralysis, with death following in about four days. A person who is bitten by an animal that may be rabid should immediately thoroughly cleanse the wound with soap or detergent and antiseptic to remove all traces of saliva, being especially careful about deep punctures. The wound should be covered with a clean dressing and then medical advice should be sought. The appropriate authorities should also be notified so that the animal can be caught and dealt with.

Treatment: is by means of injections of rabies vaccine, antiserum and immunoglobulin. A person who has previously received rabies vaccine as a preventative measure, and who receives a bite, requires further injections. The incubation period for rabies enables effective treatment to be given. However, if symptoms start, the outcome is normally fatal (in 80% of cases), although some people survive with vigorous supportive treatment.

Causes and risk factors: the cause of rabies is a virus that is present in populations of wild and feral animals in many countries of the world. Rabid animals exhibit one of two forms of behaviour, known as 'mad' or 'furious' rabies and dumb rabies. In the former, the animal may exhibit wild, uncontrolled behaviour, running around and snapping and biting if it is a dog, or losing its normal fear of humans and behaving unusually, in the case of a wild creature. In the other form, which is a more advanced stage of the furious type, the animal is more or less paralysed and drags itself around but may bite if cornered. Preventative treatment with rabies vaccine is advisable for all those living, working or visiting countries where rabies is endemic and who are likely to be in contact with animals. If prompt medical care is available, rabies is uncommon in human beings but remains one of the most feared diseases.

radiation sickness
Description: any illness that is caused by harmful radiation from radioactive substances. It often occurs as a complication of radiotherapy for cancer.
Persons most commonly affected: all age groups and both sexes; cancer patients.
Organ or part of body involved: any part of the body may be involved, depending upon site and degree of exposure to radiation.
Symptoms and indications: the symptoms vary a great deal, depending upon the site and nature of the exposure to radiation. Symptoms due to radiotherapy for cancer are usually relatively short-lived. These include nausea and vomiting, loss of appetite and weight, diarrhoea, a reddened and itchy skin. Also, there may be hair loss, increased likelihood of other infections, bleeding and ANAEMIA. These symptoms should be reported to a doctor.
Treatment: antihistamine drugs and tranquillisers, such as chlorpromazine, are used to alleviate the condition, and also soothing preparations to relieve itching. The person should have plenty of rest and endeavour to eat a nutritious diet and drink plenty of fluids. A liquid diet may be needed for a time, or fluids given intravenously.
Causes and risk factors: the cause is radiation from radioactive substances and high doses (related to accidents in the nuclear power industry or nuclear weapons industries) may prove fatal. There is a risk of the development of cancer, sterility, genetic abnormalities and birth defects in those accidentally exposed to high doses of radiation.

rat bite fever
Description: two types of infection, with similar symptoms, that may be transmitted to man following a bite from a rat, mouse or possibly some other animal e.g. a weasel. Occasionally, drinking unpasteurised milk that is contaminated with the causative microorganisms is responsible for this infection.
Persons most commonly affected: all age groups and both sexes.
Organ or part of body involved: skin, respiratory system, gastrointestinal tract, joints.

Symptoms and indications: the symptoms usually develop about ten days after a rat or mouse bite. They include fever, headache, chills, malaise, vomiting, joint pains and skin rash. A person with these symptoms should seek medical advice and you should always consult a doctor following a bite from a wild animal.

Treatment: is by means of penicillin or erythromycin and the person should rest in bed until the symptoms subside.

Causes and risk factors: the causal organisms are *Streptobacillus moniliformis* or *Spirillum minus*. Persons most at risk are those likely to come into contact with rats, such as workers in sewage-treatment plants, laboratories or those in poor or overcrowded living conditions.

Raynaud's disease and Raynaud's phenomenon

Description: a disorder of the circulation, in which there is a periodic interruption in the blood supply to outlying parts of the body, due to spasm of the small arteries involved.

Persons most commonly affected: women below the age of 40.

Organ or part of body involved: small arteries in the fingers, toes, ears and nose.

Symptoms and indications: pale, numb and deadened fingers or toes, ears or nose. If the disease is prolonged, the skin becomes taut and ulcers appear. There is often cyanosis in the affected parts, i.e. a lack of oxygen causing a bluish colouration of the skin. When the spasm passes, and on warming, normal colour returns to the affected part. Raynaud's disease is defined as being present for two or more years without becoming worse, and in the absence of any evidence of underlying disorder. It is a primary disease. Raynaud's phenomenon produces similar symptoms but is secondary to another disease such as ATHEROSCLEROSIS or SCLERODERMA. It usually develops within two years and there may be thickening of the skin and ulcers.

Treatment: in mild cases of Raynaud's disease, protecting the hands, feet, head and face from the cold and avoiding stress (which both precipitate the onset of symptoms) may be all that is required. The person must stop smoking as this is another precipitating factor, causing blood vessels to contract. Various drugs may be prescribed that are vasodilators or calcium antagonists. Some patients may benefit from surgery to cut sympathetic nerves to the affected parts. This usually relieves symptoms for one or two years and is more effective in those with primary Raynaud's disease. Treatment for the underlying cause of Raynaud's phenomenon is also likely to be needed.

Causes and risk factors: the cause is spasms of the small arteries supplying the affected area, due to sensitivity to cold, or precipitated by stress or smoking. Raynaud's phenomenon is associated with diseases of connective tissue and arteries, myxoedema, Buerger's disease and pulmonary hypertension. Also, the taking of certain drugs such as clonidine, beta blockers and those containing ergot alkaloids, all of which cause constriction of blood vessels and may exacerbate the condition.

rectal abscess or abscess of the rectum or anorectal abscess
Description: an inflamed and infected part of the rectum, the final portion of the large intestine in which faeces are stored prior to elimination via the anus.
Persons most commonly affected: all age groups and both sexes.
Organ or part of body involved: rectum.
Symptoms and indications: a superficial abscess in the lower part of the rectum usually causes swelling, heat, tenderness and pain that may be severe, and can sometimes be felt on examination. A person with symptoms of a rectal abscess should seek medical advice.
Treatment: normally involves admittance to hospital for surgery to drain the abscess. Antibiotics may be prescribed and recovery is normally good.
Causes and risk factors: the cause is usually a number of bacteria producing a mixed infection, and these include streptococcus and staphylococcus, *E. coli* and *Proteus vulgaris*. One complication of the surgical procedure is that a FISTULA may develop in some patients.

rectal prolapse or prolapse of the rectum
Description: a protrusion of a greater or lesser portion of the rectum to the outside through the anus.
Persons most commonly affected: children of both sexes and women aged over 60 years.
Organ or part of body involved: rectum.
Symptoms and indications: these include a discharge of mucus that may be tinged with blood and protrusion of a firm mass, especially following a bowel movement. A person with symptoms of this disorder should seek medical advice.
Treatment: the disorder is sometimes associated with straining; hence, measures to correct constipation, including attention to diet and possible use of laxatives may be needed. In children, strapping the buttocks together after a bowel movement for a period of time and correcting diarrhoea or constipation, are usually all that is needed to correct the prolapse. In adults or children with a more extensive prolapse, some surgery may be needed.

Causes and risk factors: the risk increases with age and loss of muscle tone and previous surgery in the region of the rectum. Exercises to strengthen the pelvic floor muscles may be helpful in preventing the occurrence of this condition.

rectal tumour or **benign growth** and **cancer of the rectum**
Description: a benign growth of cells or a polyp within the rectum, or a proliferation of malignant cells. Cancer of the rectum is a fairly common form of malignancy.
Persons most commonly affected: adults of both sexes in late middle and older age. It is rare in younger people.
Organ or part of body involved: rectum, abdominal lymph glands, liver.
Symptoms and indications: symptoms vary but include bleeding and pain or discomfort.

Cancer – in the early stages there may be few or no symptoms but later there is diarrhoea alternating with constipation, bleeding and watery, blood-stained discharge, fatigue and weakness, loss of weight and lower back pain. The tumour may be felt as a projecting mass. A person with any of these symptoms should seek medical advice.
Treatment: for both benign and malignant tumours, usually involves admittance to hospital for surgery. Patients with cancer may require removal of a considerable portion of the whole of the rectum and part of the colon with the production of a colostomy. This is an operation to produce an artificial opening of the colon through the abdominal wall, which then acts as an anus. Patients who have a colostomy require help and counselling to learn to cope with the situation. Recovery is usually good and the person can expect to lead a near-normal life. In addition to surgery, a cancer patient may require chemotherapy and radiotherapy.
Causes and risk factors: the cause is not known, although it is generally accepted that there is a connection with a diet containing too much refined food and little fibre. This disease is more common in people in western countries, where refined foods are more readily available.

Reiter's syndrome (RS)
Description: a disease that produces symptoms of urethritis, CONJUNCTIVITIS and ARTHRITIS (reactive arthritis, i.e. inflammation of the joints resulting from infection elsewhere).
Persons most commonly affected: males aged 12 to 40 years. It is rare in females and younger children.

Organ or part of body involved: urethra, eyes, joints and, sometimes, the skin.
Symptoms and indications: early symptoms include feverishness, frequent need to pass water, discharge that may contain pus, reddened, watering eyes, pains in the joints, and there may be raised, reddened areas on the skin (keratitis). Small painful ulcers may develop on the mucous membranes of the mouth and at the tip of the penis. A person with these symptoms should seek medical advice.
Treatment: is by means of antibiotics such as tetracycline or erythromycin for urethritis, and non-steroidal anti-inflammatory drugs for arthritis. Symptoms of arthritis may continue for some time and physiotherapy and exercises for the affected joints may be needed. With the sexually transmitted form of Reiter's syndrome, the patient's partner should also be given antibiotics.
Causes and risk factors: there are two forms of Reiter's syndrome, one of which is thought to be sexually transmitted and the other as a result of infections in the gastrointestinal tract (dysenteric RS). Women, children and elderly persons are usually affected by the dysenteric form, which is less common. There is evidence of a genetic tendency for this disease, as many of those affected have a particular tissue antigen designated HLA-B27. This is human leucocyte antigen, a genetic marker located at a particular point on chromosome 6. There are known associations between some HLA types and certain diseases.

relapsing fever

Description: a disease caused by spirochaete bacteria of the genus *Borrelia*, which exists in two forms. One type of infection is transmitted to human beings by lice and the other by ticks. The former type is endemic in some sub-tropical and tropical countries, while the latter is more widely spread and occurs in Europe and the USA. It tends to occur in populations affected by war and hunger, where there is malnutrition, overcrowding and a lack of hygiene. Characteristically, there are bouts of fever followed by periods without symptoms related to the development and release of the parasitic microorganisms in the body.
Persons most commonly affected: all age groups and both sexes.
Organ or part of body involved: brain, joints, gastrointestinal tract, skin.
Symptoms and indications: symptoms usually appear about six days after a bite from a tick or louse but may occur at any time between three and ten days following infection. They include severe headache, chills, high fever, pains in muscles and joints, vomiting and nose-

bleeds. Heartbeat rate rises and a raised, reddish rash may appear. Eventually as the disease progresses there may be enlargement of the liver and spleen and jaundice, especially in the louse-transmitted type. The fever and other symptoms usually subside after three to five days and there is a period of several days before they return again. There may be anything from two to ten periods of relapse but eventually the illness subsides as the patient develops immunity. However, there is a risk of death from complications and in people who are already suffering from debility. A person with these symptoms, especially having visited a country where relapsing fever occurs, should seek medical advice.

Treatment: is by means of bed rest and antibiotics, especially tetracycline or erythromycin, which may need to be given intravenously, along with fluids in severe cases. Doxycycline is also effective and treatment needs to be given at the start of the fever or after this has subsided, but not when it is at its height. This is due to the risk of the development of the Jarisch-Herxheimer reaction, a sudden rise in temperature with possible shock and collapse. This is a feature particularly of tick-transmitted relapsing fever (and also LEPTOSPIROSIS and SYPHILIS), which may follow once antibiotic treatment has begun. Its effects can be lessened by giving another drug, acetaminophen, before and after the first doses of antibiotics.

Causes and risk factors: the cause of relapsing fever is species of *Borrelia spirochaete* bacteria. Insecticide chemicals to eliminate lice are highly effective but it is more difficult to control ticks. Ideally, good-fitting, protective clothing should be worn to lessen the likelihood of a tick bite.

renal carbuncle

Description: an abscess that develops in a kidney.

Persons most commonly affected: elderly persons, especially men, but can affect people of other age groups and both sexes. Especially likely in those with a debilitating illness, DIABETES MELLITUS and existing bladder infection.

Organ or part of body involved: kidney.

Symptoms and indications: symptoms include pain, feverishness, malaise, chills and possibly symptoms of septicaemia (blood poisoning). Symptoms may appear suddenly or more gradually. A person with symptoms of a renal carbuncle should seek immediate medical advice.

Treatment: is likely to involve admittance to hospital for surgery to drain the carbuncle of pus, and antibiotics to combat the infection. The person may require further treatment for underlying illness or

renal cell carcinoma

infection. The condition can be cured, although the outcome may depend upon the overall health of the patient.

Causes and risk factors: usually the cause is a bladder infection that spreads upwards to the kidney or it may be caused by a staphylococcal infection elsewhere in the body.

renal cell carcinoma *see* HYPERNEPHROMA

renal tuberculosis
Description: tuberculosis affecting the kidney.
Persons most commonly affected: adults of both sexes, especially men.
Organ or part of body involved: kidney.
Symptoms and indications: there may be few or no symptoms for a considerable period of time. Eventually, there may be symptoms of kidney inflammation and infection (PYELITIS or PYELONEPHRITIS), including fever, chills, pain, shivering, loss of appetite and weight, and malaise. A person with these symptoms should seek medical advice.
Treatment: the diagnosis is likely to be made after other causes of the symptoms have been ruled out. In men, it can usually be confirmed following analysis of urine samples in which the organism, *Mycobacterium tuberculosis* is likely to be present. In women, other tests may be needed. Treatment is by means of anti-tuberculosis drugs e.g. rifampicin.
Causes and risk factors: the cause of renal tuberculosis is the bacterium Mycobacterium tuberculosis. In both men and women there is a risk of the infection spreading to involve reproductive organs.

retinal detachment or **detachment of the retina of the eye**
Description: a hole or tear in the retina, the layer that lines the interior of the eye and contains light-sensitive cells and nerve fibres. The retina consists of two layers and when the tear is produced, the inner one becomes separated from the outer one and retinal detachment occurs. This is caused by fluid (vitreous humour) leaking through the hole, forcing the inner layer to become detached from the outer layer.
Persons most commonly affected: all age groups and both sexes, especially males.
Organ or part of body involved: retina, usually of one eye only.
Symptoms and indications: symptoms include the appearance of floating spots (floaters) before the eye, blurring of vision, flashes of light and loss of sharpness in the centre of the image. The person

may appear to see a veil or curtain in the affected eye. Any person with these symptoms requires immediate emergency medical treatment in order to preserve sight in the affected eye.
Treatment: consists of admittance to hospital for surgery to seal the hole or repair the separation of the retina by means of electric current, which produces heat (diathermy) or cold (cryotherapy) using liquid nitrogen or solid carbon dioxide. At an early stage, laser treatment may be the preferred method. Occasionally it may be necessary to alter the shape of the eye to bring about healing. The condition can usually be cured if treated at an early stage but a delay in treatment may result in permanent partial or complete loss of vision.
Causes and risk factors: the causes are eye injury or a complication of eye surgery (especially the removal of cataracts) and the risk increases in those with short-sightedness (myopia) and DIABETES MELLITUS. Also, older persons are at greater risk, as are those with a history of this condition. Malignant tumours of the eye may also be a cause of retinal detachment.

Reye's syndrome

Description: a rare and serious disease of childhood that seems to follow on from a viral infection such as CHICKEN-POX or INFLUENZA, often becoming apparent during the recovery phase of the illness.
Persons most commonly affected: children of both sexes, rare in adults.
Organ or part of body involved: brain, liver.
Symptoms and indications: the symptoms usually appear during recovery from an upper respiratory tract infection. They include nausea and vomiting, and mental disturbances that may manifest themselves in a number of ways. The child may be confused, forgetful and lethargic or excited and agitated. Eventually, this leads to unresponsiveness, progressing to coma, with fits and, possibly, fixed, dilated pupils, respiratory collapse and death. In many cases, enlargement and damage to the liver occurs and other organs, such as the pancreas, kidneys, spleen, heart and lymph nodes may be affected. A child with these serious symptoms requires immediate emergency medical attention.
Treatment: since the cause is unknown, there is no specific regime of drug treatment. The child requires admittance to hospital for intensive supportive nursing and may need intravenous fluids, assisted ventilation and monitoring and control of all body functions. Various drugs may be needed to maintain the child in a stable condition. The outlook varies according to the severity of the symptoms but is more favourable in those who receive early treatment.

Causes and risk factors: the cause of the disorder is unknown but aspirin may be implicated in the development of Reye's syndrome. This drug is no longer recommended for children under the age of 12 years. The overall mortality rate is about 21% and children who lapse into the deeper stages of coma are most at risk. The outlook for those less severely affected is generally good. About 30% of survivors have residual brain damage, especially those who suffered fits or were in a deeper stage of coma. Others make a full recovery and the condition is not likely to recur.

rheumatic fever
Description: a severe disease, mainly occurring in childhood or adolescence, which is a complication of infections with the Group A streptococcus bacteria. It generally occurs in those who have had a streptococcal infection of the upper respiratory tract and produces a wide range of symptoms.
Persons most commonly affected: children of both sexes between the ages of 4 and 18.
Organ or part of body involved: joints, heart, skin, central nervous system.
Symptoms and indications: the child may develop a fever, pains, loss of appetite and malaise. Usually there are symptoms of ARTHRITIS with joint pain that progresses from joint to joint. Affected joints are swollen, tender, hot and painful and normally, the wrists, elbows, ankles and knees are involved. Other joints may also be affected. Painless nodules may develop beneath the skin over bony protuberances such as the elbows, knees and wrists. In addition, there may be chorea (involuntary, jerking movements of the muscles) and the development of a transient characteristic rash called Erythema marginatum. A serious set of symptoms that often accompanies rheumatic fever is inflammation of the heart (carditis), which can include the muscles, valves and membranes. The condition may cause rheumatic heart disease, in which there is scarring and inflammation of heart structures. In later adult life, there may be a need for surgery to replace damaged heart valves. A child with symptoms of rheumatic fever requires immediate medical attention.
Treatment: depends upon symptoms but rest in bed is needed until the attack subsides. Initially, treatment consists of destroying the streptococci that cause the disease, with antibiotics such as penicillin. For arthritis symptoms, analgesics, non-steroidal anti-inflammatory drugs or corticosteroids may be prescribed. Those with heart symptoms are likely to require admittance to hospital for special care and treatment with aspirin or salicylate drugs,

corticosteroids and other drugs. Following recovery, low doses of antibiotics may need to be continued to prevent any further streptococcal infections. Patients with known damage to heart valves require intensive courses of antibiotics before dental treatment or other surgical procedures.

Causes and risk factors: the cause of rheumatic fever is previous streptococcal infection but there are likely to be factors making some individuals more susceptible than others. In general, children living in poor, overcrowded living conditions with inadequate nutrition are more likely to develop this disorder but this is by no means always the case. The incidence of rheumatic fever is declining in most developed countries.

rheumatoid arthritis

Description: the second most common form of joint disease (after OSTEOARTHRITIS), which usually affects the feet, ankles, fingers and wrists. The condition is diagnosed by means of X-rays, which show a typical pattern of changes around the inflamed joints, known as rheumatoid erosions. At first there is swelling of the joint and inflammation of the synovial membrane (the membranous sac that surrounds the joint), followed by erosion and loss of cartilage and bone. In addition, a blood test reveals the presence of serum rheumatoid factor antibody, which is characteristic of this condition.

Persons most commonly affected: all age groups and both sexes but especially women and more common in those aged 30 to 50.

Organ or part of body involved: joints.

Symptoms and indications: symptoms usually arise slowly and insidiously, but may occasionally be rapid in onset. There is inflammation, tenderness or pain in the affected joints, and stiffness, especially on first getting up in the morning. By the afternoon, the person may feel unusually tired or unwell. Deformities of affected joints are likely to develop. In other people, after an initial active phase, there may be a long period of remission. A person with symptoms of rheumatoid arthritis should seek medical advice.

Treatment: rest in bed during active phases of the disease is essential, and adequate rest and good nutrition are important at all times. Drugs used in treatment include aspirin and salicylates, non-steroidal anti-inflammatory preparations and slow-acting agents including penicillamine, sulphasalazine, gold and hydroxychloroquine. Many patients improve with treatment and the condition varies greatly in its degree of severity. At its worst, it is progressively and severely disabling, whereas others, less seriously affected, are able to enjoy a relatively normal life.

Causes and risk factors: the cause is not known but there appear to be genetic factors involved. Most affected people have a particular antibody – HLA-DR4, but there are likely to be other factors involved, including a family tendency for the disease.

ringworm
Description: an infection caused by various species of fungi, known medically as tinea. It is contagious from person to person, either through direct contact or from an infected surface such as a floor, face flannel, towel, etc.
Persons most commonly affected: adolescents and adults of both sexes but more common in males.
Organ or part of body involved: feet – tinea pedis or athlete's foot; groin – tinea cruris or dhobi itch; scalp – tinea capitis, tinea favosa favus or honeycomb ringworm; body – tinea corporis; chest and trunk – tinea versicolor; nails – tinea unguium; beard – tinea barbae.
Symptoms and indications: typically, slightly raised, itchy patches on the skin with a ring-like appearance. Blisters and scabs often occur. Ringworm affecting the nails causes a greenish or grey discolouration, with thickening, the nails becoming brittle and somewhat deformed. A person with symptoms of ringworm should seek medical advice.
Treatment: the usual treatment for ringworm, which is, in general, highly effective, is the antibiotic drug griseofulvin, taken by mouth. In addition, various other antifungal creams or ointments may be prescribed. Careful attention to hygiene, wearing clothing and footwear made of natural rather than synthetic materials and keeping the skin dry are important measures. Warm, moist, sweaty conditions favour the growth of ringworm fungus. Ringworm can usually be successfully treated in a few weeks but may recur. Ringworm of the nails is more difficult to treat and it may take longer to cure.
Causes and risk factors: the cause is various types of fungus, which are fairly prevalent. ATHLETE'S FOOT is a very common type of infection.

Rocky Mountain spotted fever
Description: a serious acute infection transmitted to man by the bite of a tick and prevalent in many states of the USA. It is absent from the UK.
Persons most commonly affected: all age groups and both sexes.
Organ or part of body involved: central nervous system, skin, gastrointestinal tract, muscles – whole body symptoms.
Symptoms and indications: the symptoms appear between 3 and 12

days after the bite of an infected tick. They include fever, severe headache, vomiting and nausea, muscular stiffness and pain, chills and the appearance of a characteristic red rash that eventually spreads over much of the body. This may eventually darken and ulcerate. The person shows symptoms of mental confusion, agitation, DELIRIUM leading to coma and possibly death. A person with symptoms of this disease requires immediate, urgent medical treatment.
Treatment: is by means of antibiotics such as chloramphenicol or tetracycline, which should begin as soon as possible once symptoms appear. The disease is usually curable if caught and treated early but may be fatal if treatment is delayed. Preventative measures include the wearing of protective clothing in areas where the disease is endemic and the use of tick-repellent chemicals such as deet (diethyltoluamide).
Causes and risk factors: the cause of the infection is a microorganism called *Rickettsia rickettsii,* transmitted by the bite of ticks that are parasitic on many wild animals as well as man. There are similar feverish infections transmitted by ticks in European countries (*see* TYPHOID FEVER).

rodent ulcer

Description: a slow-growing malignant ulcer generally occurring on the face.
Persons most commonly affected: middle-aged and elderly persons of both sexes.
Organ or part of body involved: the face, especially the edges of the nostrils, eyes and lips.
Symptoms and indications: the symptoms and appearance of rodent ulcers vary greatly and they can be confused with other skin conditions such as dermatitis or PSORIASIS. Usually, it appears as a shiny papule that gradually enlarges and often alternately bleeds and forms a scab. A person with symptoms of a rodent ulcer should seek medical advice.
Treatment: involves admittance to a specialist unit for biopsy and tests. Usually, some form of surgical procedure is required and occasionally, radiotherapy. Recovery is normally good, although occasionally there may be a recurrence.
Causes and risk factors: the cause is not known but fair-skinned European people living in a hot climate may be more at risk. Rodent ulcers do not normally cause secondary growths elsewhere but can destroy underlying healthy tissue, which, in rare cases, may be sufficiently serious to cause death.

rosacea

Description: a disease of the skin of the face characterised by a red, flushed appearance and engorgement.
Persons most commonly affected: adults of both sexes aged over 30 years but more common in women.
Organ or part of body involved: face.
Symptoms and indications: in the early stages there is a red, raised rash (erythema) that comes and goes, usually appearing upon exposure to the sun or after eating a meal. This causes a hot, burning or tingling sensation. Eventually, this becomes permanent and there may be pimples and pustules (the condition known as acne rosacea). In some cases, the sebaceous glands become involved and greatly enlarge, especially in the region of the nose. The skin becomes thickened and uneven and the nose is very red, large and prominent. This condition is called rhinophyma. A person with symptoms of rosacea should seek medical advice at an early stage, in order to prevent the development of rhinophyma.
Treatment: is by means of antibiotic drugs, especially tetracycline, taken by mouth, or isotretinoin, in less responsive cases. Also, topical ointments or creams containing the antibiotic metronidazole may be prescribed. Occasionally, surgery may be needed to correct rhinophyma. Antibiotic treatment is usually very effective in controlling the condition.
Causes and risk factors: the cause is not known but it tends to affect fair-skinned people. Exposure to the sun, excess alcohol consumption and certain foods may exacerbate the condition, although this is not certain.

roseola infantum or pseudorubella or exanthem subitum

Description: an acute fever and skin rash that is highly contagious and affects babies and young children.
Persons most commonly affected: babies and young children aged six months to three years.
Organ or part of body involved: central nervous system, skin.
Symptoms and indications: the child suddenly develops a high fever of 103° to 105°F or 39.5° to 40.5°C, for which there is no obvious cause. The fever usually lasts about three to five days and convulsions may occur. The child is irritable and unwell. The fever normally reaches a peak and then subsides and this coincides in some, but not all cases, with the development of a red rash, mainly on the chest and abdomen. This normally subsides quite soon and by this time the child is evidently feeling much better. A child who develops a high fever should always be seen by a doctor. The doctor should

be summoned urgently if the child has a convulsion or shows signs of dehydration.

Treatment: consists of measures to reduce fever, including the use of medicines containing paracetamol that are designed for young children, tepid sponging and cooling fans. The child should be encouraged to drink plenty of fluids. In rare cases, admittance to hospital may be required. The child normally recovers well after a few days.

Causes and risk factors: the cause is now thought to be, in many cases, human herpes virus type 6 (HHV-6), although there may be others.

roundworms or ascariasis

Description: an illness caused by infestation with a parasitic type of worm (which resembles an earthworm) called *Ascaris lumbricoides*. It is prevalent in warm climates in overcrowded conditions with poor hygiene and sanitation. The larvae of the worm pass through the lungs and may cause respiratory symptoms. They ascend to the throat and are swallowed, maturing into adult worms in the gastrointestinal tract where they may cause further abdominal symptoms.

Persons most commonly affected: children of both sexes.

Organ or part of body involved: lungs and gastrointestinal tract.

Symptoms and indications: during the passage of the larvae through the lungs, there may be coughing, wheezing and fever. Coughed-up sputum may contain the larvae. In the intestine, particularly if there is a heavy infestation, the adult worms may cause pains in the abdomen, loss of appetite and weight, tiredness and, possibly, diarrhoea and vomiting. Sometimes an adult worm is vomited up or passed in faeces. A person with symptoms of roundworm infestation should seek immediate medical treatment.

Treatment: consists of drugs to kill the worms, either pyrantel pamoate or mebendazole. The latter should not be taken by pregnant women and the doctor should be informed if pregnancy is a possibility. The drugs used in treatment are highly effective.

Causes and risk factors: people, especially children, become infected by playing in dirt contaminated by the eggs of the parasite and putting their hands in their mouths. Hence, roundworms are a problem in conditions of poor sanitation and hygiene. Also, eating vegetables (especially raw) that have been washed in contaminated water, and directly drinking contaminated water are other sources of infection. Anyone visiting an area where such conditions exist should be scrupulous about hygiene, food and drinking water. Domestic animals (dogs and cats) may be infested with roundworms

rubella

and should be wormed regularly. Children should be taught to wash their hands after touching animals, and pets should not be allowed near food for human consumption. There is a risk (rare) of obstruction of the gut by adult worms, if the infestation is heavy, requiring urgent medical treatment.

rubella *see* GERMAN MEASLES

ruptured eardrum
Description: a hole that may develop in the eardrum because of infection or injury. It may also be called perforated eardrum.
Persons most commonly affected: all ages and both sexes.
Organ or part of body involved: ear.
Symptoms and indications: there may be sudden deafness following acute OTITIS MEDIA or injury. Sometimes, there may be sudden relief of the pain of otitis media. There may be a discharge from the ear, and sometimes sufferers complain of tinnitus.
Treatment: a doctor will usually clean the middle ear and prescribe a course of antibiotics. The ear should be protected while showering. In children, a ruptured eardrum usually heals within two weeks; in adults, this may take a little longer.
Causes and risk factors: It can be caused by severe or untreated otitis media. It may also be caused by sudden high pressure applied to the eardrum, either while diving, from a slap on the ear, or by a sudden very loud noise. It may be avoided by wearing ear protectors in a very noisy environment. Otitis media should always be treated and cleared up, and no-one should scuba-dive without training.

S

St Vitus' dance *see* SYDENHAM'S CHOREA

salivary gland enlargement
Description: enlargement of one or more salivary glands due to an infection, salivary duct stone or tumour.
Persons most commonly affected: adults of both sexes.
Organ or part of body involved: salivary glands, ducts, nearby lymph glands.
Symptoms and indications: salivary gland infection: swelling and pain in the affected gland, either sublingual (beneath the tongue), submandibular (beneath the jaw) or parotid (behind the ear). Lymph

glands in the neck may also be swollen and tender and there may be malaise and feverishness. Salivary duct stone: this usually affects the submandibular glands, causing swelling and pain, especially when eating. Lymph glands may be swollen and tender in the neck and there may be malaise and feverishness. Salivary gland tumour: swelling due to mass of tumour growth, which is tender and painful.

A person with enlargement and pain in a salivary gland should seek medical advice.

Treatment: salivary gland infection – treatment is by means of antibiotics and pain-relieving drugs. Salivary duct stone – treatment may involve admittance to hospital for surgical removal of the stone. Antibiotics and pain-relieving drugs may be prescribed. Salivary gland tumour – treatment involves admittance to hospital for surgical removal of the tumour. If the growth is malignant, tumours may require radiotherapy and chemotherapy. The outlook is usually quite good if the tumour is caught at an early stage.

Causes and risk factors: infections are caused by one or other of many different types of bacteria e.g. staphylococcus. Salivary duct tumours may arise as a result of a change in the composition of the saliva. The cause of a salivary gland tumour is unknown. The risk of developing a salivary gland disorder increases with poor nutrition, a lack of vitamins in the diet, inadequate fluid intake leading to dehydration and inattention to oral hygiene. It is important to clean the teeth thoroughly at least twice each day and to visit the dentist regularly.

sandfly fever or phlebotomus fever

Description: a viral infection characterised by fever of short duration, which is transmitted to humans through the bite of a sandfly. It occurs in many warm countries including parts of the Mediterranean.

Persons most commonly affected: all age groups and both sexes.

Organ or part of body involved: central nervous system, whole body symptoms.

Symptoms and indications: the symptoms resemble those of influenza and appear about three to seven days after a bite. They include headache, chills, fever, pains in muscles and joints, flushing and bloodshot eyes. The fever subsides in about three days but the person may be left feeling weak and take some time to fully recover.

Treatment: consists of rest in bed, painkilling drugs and adequate fluid intake until symptoms subside. Preventative measures include the use of insect repellent preparations, protective clothing and sandfly netting.

Causes and risk factors: the cause of the infection is a virus transmitted by the sandfly *Phlebotomus paparasi*.

scabies
Description: a contagious skin infection caused by a mite and characterised by severe itching.
Persons most commonly affected: all age groups and both sexes.
Organ or part of body involved: skin between the fingers, wrists, buttocks, genitals and under the arms, breasts, elbows.
Symptoms and indications: the burrows of the mites are visible on the skin as thin, dark lines, each with a small pimple at one end. These may soon be obscured by scarring due to scratching. There is severe itching, which is particularly marked when the person is in bed. A person with symptoms of scabies should seek immediate medical advice.
Treatment: consists of cream or ointment to kill the mites, which is applied to the whole surface of the body and is left in place for at least 12 hours and preferably longer. It is usually a preparation of 5% permethrin or Lindane gamma-benzene hydrochloride, although for babies or pregnant women other ointments (containing sulphur) may be prescribed. Clothing and bed linen should be carefully washed although, as the mites do not survive for long off the human body, spread is more likely to be due to direct skin contact between people.
Causes and risk factors: the cause is a mite called *Sarcopetes scabei*. The female burrows into the skin, lays eggs and the larvae, which hatch in a few days, cause the itching and are mature mites in about three weeks. Secondary bacterial skin infections may occur due to scratching, which may require further antibiotic treatment. The risk of contracting scabies is greater among those living in poor, overcrowded conditions, where cleanliness and hygiene are more difficult to maintain.

scalds *see* BURNS

scarlet fever or scarlatina
Description: an infectious disease, mainly of childhood, characterised by a bright red skin rash that generally follows and is caused by a preceding throat infection due to streptococcus bacteria. Scarlet fever used to be the major cause of death in young children in Britain but is now rare and less severe, due to the availability of antibiotics.
Persons most commonly affected: children of both sexes aged two to ten.
Organ or part of body involved: throat and surrounding tissues, skin, central nervous system, whole body symptoms.

Symptoms and indications: symptoms appear after an incubation period of about three days. There is a high fever (up to 104°F [40°C]), chills, headache, vomiting, rapid pulse and a very sore throat. The tonsils and lymph glands in the neck are usually swollen and tender. Within 24 hours, a bright red rash appears on the face and spreads to include other parts of the body. The rash fades and disappears after about one week, with peeling of the skin. When it is at its height, the tongue is usually a bright strawberry red, as is the face apart from a pale white area around the mouth. Also characteristic are dark red lines in skin folds and creases. Usually, a child with a streptococcal throat infection receives early antibiotic treatment and scarlet fever does not develop. If symptoms of this illness do appear, the child should be seen by a doctor.

Treatment: consists of bed rest and a course of antibiotics, usually penicillin or erythromycin. The child should be encouraged to drink plenty of fluids. Prompt treatment with antibiotics generally ensures that complications do not arise (*see causes and risk factors*) and recovery is usually complete in about ten days to two weeks.

Causes and risk factors: the cause of scarlet fever is erythrogenic toxin produced by Group A streptococcus bacteria. If left untreated, serious complications can arise, particularly inflammation of the kidneys (GLOMERULONEPHRITIS), heart (ENDOCARDITIS), middle ear and joints (ARTHRITIS or rheumatism).

schistosomiasis or bilharziasis

Description: a very severe disease caused by parasitic blood flukes, which affects many millions of people in tropical countries, especially in the Far and Middle East, South America and Africa.

Persons most commonly affected: all age groups and both sexes.

Organ or part of body involved: urinary tract or gastrointestinal tract, spleen, liver.

Symptoms and indications: depending upon the species, the flukes settle in blood vessels of the rectum or bladder. Intestinal symptoms include diarrhoea, with passing of blood, ANAEMIA, DYSENTERY, enlargement of the spleen and liver and CIRRHOSIS OF THE LIVER. Urinary tract symptoms are those of CYSTITIS, with blood in the urine, bladder stones and an increased likelihood of cancer of the bladder. A person with any of these symptoms should seek immediate medical advice.

Treatment: may involve admittance to hospital and is by means of various drugs, depending upon the type of schistosome parasite. Drugs used include praziquantel, metriphonate and oxamniquine. The parasite is acquired through the skin by contact with infected

water. Preventative measures are therefore extremely important, especially not swimming, bathing or washing in water that may be suspected of containing the parasites.
Causes and risk factors: the cause of the disease is schistosome blood flukes (*Trematoda*) of various species, which complete a part of their life cycle within freshwater snails. The larvae of the parasite burrow through the skin of humans and mature to cause symptoms of the illness. People engaged in planting rice crops or bathing in water containing snails and parasites are especially at risk. The disease affects millions of people and control is by means of education, attempts to eradicate the snail hosts and drug treatment for those affected.

sciatica

Description: pain in the sciatic nerve, which is felt in the back of the thigh, leg and foot.
Persons most commonly affected: adults of both sexes aged under 60.
Organ or part of body involved: sciatic nerve, affecting leg and foot.
Symptoms and indications: the symptoms may develop rapidly, due to an awkward, strained or twisting movement, such as lifting a heavy object. Or, they may begin more gradually, due to an underlying condition causing pressure on the sciatic nerve. Symptoms include stiffness and pain in the back, leg and foot, which can be severe. A person with symptoms of sciatica should seek medical advice.
Treatment: may be in the form of bed rest and painkilling drugs until the symptoms improve. Persistent pain and weakness may require admittance to hospital for corrective surgery depending upon the underlying cause of the condition.
Causes and risk factors: the cause may be inadvertent stressing of the back, due to an awkward movement. However, the commonest cause of sciatica is a PROLAPSED INTERVERTEBRAL DISC pressing on the nerve root, but it may also be due to ANKYLOSING SPONDYLITIS or some other conditions e.g. spinal tumour.

scleritis

Description: deep inflammation of the sclera, the outer white fibrous layer of the eyeball.
Persons most commonly affected: all age groups and both sexes but more common in adults.
Organ or part of body involved: one or both eyes.
Symptoms and indications: pain in the eye, which can be extremely

severe, with purple discolouration of parts of the sclera. A person with symptoms of scleritis should seek immediate medical advice.
Treatment: is usually in the form of a corticosteroid drug, such as prednisone, taken by mouth. However, if scleritis occurs in conjunction with rheumatic disorders or does not respond to corticosteroid treatment, immunosuppressive drugs such as azathioprine or cyclophosphamide may be prescribed by a specialist. In this case, the patient requires careful monitoring, due to the potent effects of these drugs.
Causes and risk factors: the cause is not known but scleritis is sometimes associated with rheumatic conditions such as rheumatoid arthritis. It may also occur in connection with CROHN'S DISEASE. There is a risk of perforation of the eyeball and loss of the eye. If perforation occurs, admittance to hospital for surgery to preserve the eye is necessary. Even if the eye is saved, there is likely to be some loss of vision.

scleroderma or progressive systemic sclerosis or PSS
Description: a condition in which connective tissue gradually and progressively hardens and contracts. The tissue affected may be the skin, heart, kidney, lung, etc, and the condition may be localised or it may spread throughout the body, eventually becoming fatal. If the skin is affected it becomes thickened and rough with patchy pigmentation. There may be stiffening of joints and wasting of muscles.
Persons most commonly affected: adults of both sexes but four times more common in women.
Organ or part of body involved: skin (e.g. of fingers and face), oesophagus, joints, gastrointestinal tract, body organs, particularly heart, lungs and kidneys, blood vessels.
Symptoms and indications: there are a wide range of symptoms depending upon the nature and extent of the disease. There may be RAYNAUD'S DISEASE, which is often an early indication of the disease. Other symptoms include thickening, stiffening, pigmentation and shiny skin, ulcers on the fingers, swallowing difficulty due to effects on the oesophagus, with symptoms of heartburn and indigestion. There may be stiffening and contraction of joints, especially the fingers, wrists, elbows and knees. There may be malaise and loss of weight. If fibrosis of organs occurs, particularly of the lungs, heart or kidneys, a range of serious symptoms may occur, including pulmonary and renal HYPERTENSION, heart and kidney failure. Eventually, most patients have some degree of organ involvement but many years may elapse before symptoms occur as the disease tends to progress in a slow and unpredictable fashion. A person with

any symptoms of scleroderma should seek immediate medical advice.
Treatment: the disease is not considered to be curable but a wide range of drugs are available to control and limit symptoms. These include corticosteroids, penicillamine and nifedipine, preparations to relieve digestive symptoms, analgesics, skin lubricants and drugs to improve heart, lung and kidney function. The person should keep warm and other helpful measures include eating frequent small meals and raising the end of the bed (to prevent reflux of stomach acid).
Causes and risk factors: the cause is not known but it may be an autoimmune disease. (This is one in which the immune system, for some reason, fails to recognise the difference between 'self' and 'non-self' and produces antibodies that attack its own tissues.) Serious, life-threatening symptoms can occur but other patients are less severely affected, hence the outcome is difficult to predict.

secondary polycythaemia *see* POLYCYTHAEMIA

senile macular degeneration
Description: age-related loss of vision due to changes in the retina of the eyes.
Persons most commonly affected: elderly persons aged 65 years and over of both sexes. It is more common in White races of people.
Organ or part of body involved: one or both eyes.
Symptoms and indications: there is a rapid or more slowly worsening loss of sharpness and accuracy of vision in the centre of the visual field. Peripheral and colour vision remain and large objects can be seen but detailed central vision is lost. A person who experiences these symptoms should seek medical advice.
Treatment: there is little effective treatment for this condition. The aim is to preserve and enhance the vision that remains with the use of glasses, etc. Laser treatment may help some patients.
Causes and risk factors: the cause is not known but hereditary factors may be involved. There is, at present, no way of preventing the development of this condition.

septicaemia *see* BLOOD POISONING

shingles or **herpes zoster**
Description: an infection produced by the virus that causes CHICKEN POX in children. The infection affects the central nervous system (dorsal root ganglia), running along the course of a nerve, producing severe pain and small yellowish blisters on the skin.
Persons most commonly affected: adults of all age groups and both sexes, especially those over 50 years.

Organ or part of body involved: sensory nerve of the skin. It affects the course of a nerve on one side only.
Symptoms and indications: early symptoms include chills, headache, slight fever and a general feeling of malaise. Blisters then appear on the skin following the route of a nerve, often in a semicircle around one side of the chest, side and back. There is pain, which may be very severe. The blisters form scabs that drop off and heal in about two weeks but pain may persist for some time (post-herpetic neuralgia). A person with symptoms of shingles should seek medical advice.
Treatment: there is no specific treatment but pain-relieving drugs, along with tranquillisers when the pain is very severe, may be prescribed. Corticosteroids have been used in some cases and antiviral drugs, such as acyclovir, may be prescribed for certain patients, particularly those with a suppressed immune system. Warm compresses and heat may be helpful for pain. Most people make a full recovery and have immunity from future attacks.
Causes and risk factors: the cause of shingles is the *Varicella-zoster* virus, which is also responsible for chicken pox in children. It is thought that the virus may be dormant in the body until some factor causes it to flare up as shingles. Most adults affected by shingles have had chicken pox in their childhood years. Those most at risk of developing shingles are people who are generally somewhat ill or 'run-down', those under stress or who have received treatment with immunosuppressive drugs. People with HODGKIN'S DISEASE are also at greater risk of developing this illness.

shock

Description: acute, circulatory failure due to blood pressure in the arteries falling so low that blood is no longer supplied to all parts of the body. Hence the normal functions of the body can no longer take place and there is a risk of death.
Persons most commonly affected: all age groups and both sexes.
Organ or part of body involved: blood circulatory system and heart.
Symptoms and indications: shock may develop as a result of injury or illness. The signs are a cold, clammy skin, pallor, cyanosis (blue-coloured skin due to a lack of oxygen in the blood), weak, rapid pulse, irregular breathing and dilated pupils. The person may feel anxious or suffer from confusion or lethargy and there is a lack of urination. Blood pressure falls to a low level and may not be detectable by normal methods. A person in shock requires immediate, emergency medical attention.
Treatment: depends upon the underlying cause of the shock. If due

to bleeding or loss of fluid, this must be halted and the person is likely to require blood transfusion and fluids given intravenously. If it is due to severe infection, large doses of antibiotics are likely to be needed. The person may be given drugs to raise blood pressure. General measures include keeping the person warm and calm and lying down with the legs raised. The patient should be accompanied at all times and emergency artificial respiration may be needed if breathing stops.

Causes and risk factors: there are numerous causes of shock, including a reduction in blood volume due to internal or external bleeding, and loss of fluid from burns or illnesses that cause dehydration and fluid/salt imbalance. Also, reduced heart activity as in CORONARY THROMBOSIS, PULMONARY EMBOLISM and heart rhythm disorders, blood poisoning and ANAPHYLACTIC SHOCK. Shock is a serious, life-threatening condition and the outcome depends upon the severity of the cause and response to treatment.

sickle-cell anaemia

Description: a type of inherited haemolytic anaemia that is genetically determined and that affects people of African ancestry. It is caused by a recessive gene, so people can be carriers of the sickle-cell trait without themselves showing any sign of illness.

The anaemia occurs in a child who inherits the gene from both parents. The red blood cells have a characteristic distorted sickle shape and there are periods of crisis when the anaemia is especially severe.

Persons most commonly affected: present at birth in babies of both sexes, with symptoms usually becoming apparent by the age of six months. The illness is present for life.

Organ or part of body involved: bone marrow, blood, spleen, liver, thymus gland, lymph glands.

Symptoms and indications: the child fails to thrive, has frequent infections, and is anaemic, with symptoms of pallor, fatigue, breathlessness and JAUNDICE. There are episodes of joint and bone pain and fever. In children, pains in the feet and hands are characteristic. The child fails to grow properly and there may be chest and abdominal pain and vomiting. Skin ulcers may occur particularly on the ankles and there are nerve disorders and impairment of lungs, heart and kidneys. The bones are distorted and the spleen and heart become enlarged. A child with symptoms of sickle-cell disease requires ongoing medical help.

Treatment: is aimed at the relief of symptoms as there is no cure for the condition. Blood transfusions may be necessary for severe bouts of anaemia and drugs used include painkillers and courses of antibiotics to treat infections. Any infection should be treated promptly and antibiotics and immunisation given to prevent infection e.g. against PNEUMONIA.

Causes and risk factors: the cause of the disease is a recessive gene, resulting in an abnormal type of haemoglobin (the blood pigment in red blood cells that binds to oxygen and carries it to all parts of the body). The abnormal haemoglobin causes distortion of the red blood cells, resulting in anaemia and the other symptoms described above. Improved supportive and antibiotic treatment has improved the outlook for sufferers of this disease. However, the illness shortens life and victims are at greater risk of a STROKE and other complications. People with a family history of sickle-cell disease are advised to seek genetic counselling before having children. Many people are carriers of the defective gene and because this confers increased resistance to MALARIA, the gene persists at a high level.

silicosis or 'potter's asthma'

Description: a type of PNEUMOCONIOSIS caused by the inhalation of silica (quartz) as particles of dust. The silica causes fibrosis of lung tissue and a greatly increased risk of contracting tuberculosis.

Persons most commonly affected: adults of either sex could be affected. In practice, this is an occupational disease of men aged over 40 years who have been long-term workers in certain industries and exposed to silica dust over a prolonged period (20 to 30 years). These industries include sandstone and granite cutting, sandblasting, tin and anthracite mining, metal grinding and pottery manufacture.

Organ or part of body involved: lungs.

Symptoms and indications: symptoms include increasing breathlessness and coughing, chest pains, hoarseness, fatigue and malaise. There is likely to be a loss of appetite and disturbance of sleep. A person with these symptoms should seek medical advice.

Treatment: is aimed at the relief of symptoms and includes the use of drugs such as bronchodilators (inhalers), antibiotics and analgesics.

Causes and risk factors: the cause is inhaled particles of silica, which lodge in the alveoli (minute air sacs) of the lungs and cause the formation of fibrous tissue, resulting in loss of lung elasticity and function. People with silicosis are three times more likely to develop TUBERCULOSIS and are at risk of PULMONARY HYPERTENSION, which may prove fatal. Effective measures can now be taken in most industries to suppress dust. Workers can also wear protective hoods with

sinoatrial node disease

breathing equipment and should be monitored by means of regular health checks and chest X-rays.

sinoatrial node disease *see* SINUS NODE DISEASE

sinusitis
Description: inflammation of a sinus (one of a number of air cavities in the bones of the face and skull). It usually refers to the sinuses in the face that link with the nose. Hence, the cause of the inflammation is often due to a spread of infection from the nose.
Persons most commonly affected: all age groups and both sexes.
Organ or part of body involved: sinuses.
Symptoms and indications: there is usually a preceding upper respiratory tract infection. Symptoms include headache, blocked nose with a greenish infected discharge, a feeling of heaviness and pain inside the head and face and, possibly, disturbance of sleep. Depending upon the location of the affected sinus, there may be eye pain and inflammation. A person with symptoms of sinusitis should seek medical advice.
Treatment: is by means of antibiotics and also decongestants, usually in the form of nasal drops. Painkillers may be taken to relieve headache and pain. Rarely, if the problem is persistent and severe, admittance to hospital for surgery to drain the affected sinus may be necessary. The condition usually improves but may recur.
Causes and risk factors: the cause is usually an upper respiratory tract infection such as a cold, which spreads to the sinus.

sinus node disease or **sinoatrial node disease**
Description: any disorder of the sinus node or sinoatrial node, the natural pacemaker of the heart. This consists of specialised muscle cells in the right atrium (upper smaller chamber) of the heart. These cells generate electrical impulses, contract and initiate contractions in the muscles of the heart and hence are responsible for the heartbeat. Some disorders may be inherited and others may be acquired.
Persons most commonly affected: all age groups and both sexes.
Organ or part of body involved: heart.
Symptoms and indications: depending upon the type of disorder, there may be either a speeding up or a slowing down of heartbeat rhythm. This may not be perceived by the patient or may be felt as palpitations. The person may experience anxiety, fainting or dizziness. Any person who is aware of heartbeat irregularity should seek medical advice.
Treatment: usually, the person is admitted to hospital for monitoring of the heartbeat (Holter 24-hour ECG monitoring). Treatment

methods include the use of a number of different drugs and surgery to install an artificial heart pacemaker.
Causes and risk factors: causes may be congenital or due to disease or disorder of the node. The condition can often be corrected but the outlook may depend upon the extent and nature of any underlying disease.

skin cancer or **squamous cell carcinoma**
Description: a growth of malignant cells in the outer epithelial layer of the skin.
Persons most commonly affected: middle-aged and older adults of both sexes.
Organ or part of body involved: skin, especially a part that has been exposed to the sun.
Symptoms and indications: a small, hardened, red, raised lump develops on the skin, which is neither itchy nor painful but has a crusty, scaling surface. Eventually it ulcerates and spreads to affect the surrounding tissues of the skin. The appearance of the lump can vary considerably, and it may also occur on a part of the skin that has not been exposed to the sun. A person with symptoms of skin cancer should seek immediate medical advice.
Treatment: a biopsy is first performed to confirm the diagnosis. Treatment in hospital is usually by means of surgical removal, curettage or scraping and electrodesiccation or, less commonly, the use of X-ray radiation. This type of skin cancer can normally be successfully, treated especially if caught early.
Causes and risk factors: the cause appears to be an overexposure of the skin to sunlight over many years. There is a possibility that the cancer will spread to other areas if left untreated but the risk is generally considered to be fairly low.

sleeping sickness (African trypanosomiasis) and **Chagas' disease (South American trypanosomiasis)**
Description: a parasitic disease found in tropical Africa, which is spread through the bite of tsetse flies. Chagas' disease is a South American form, which is spread through the bite of bugs called assassin bugs. The organisms responsible are minute parasitic protozoans called trypanosomes.
Persons most commonly affected: all age groups and both sexes.
Organ or part of body involved: small blood vessels, lymph vessels and glands, brain.
Symptoms and indications: a few days after the bite of an infected tsetse fly, the person develops a fever and reddish skin rash. The

fever gradually becomes more severe but there are periods when it subsides and the person is somewhat better. Gradually, the person becomes weakened, and there is ANAEMIA, fluid retention and enlargement of lymph glands, which are swollen and painful. Eventually, the brain is involved, and the person becomes lethargic and apathetic, with an increased tendency to sleep, and suffers headaches and, possibly, convulsions. Eventually, these symptoms can lead to coma and death. In Chagas' disease, inflammation of heart muscle (myocarditis) often occurs and may cause death. The early symptoms may occur for years before the brain becomes affected. Any person who develops symptoms of sleeping sickness should seek medical advice. (*See causes and risk factors.*)

Treatment: is by means of various drugs including eflornithine and suramin. In the later stages of the disease, when the brain is affected, arsenic-containing drugs such as melarsoprol are used but great care is necessary due to the toxicity of the compounds. Preventative measures are the key to the control of sleeping sickness. These include measures to eliminate the habitat of the tsetse flies, insecticides to combat the flies or bugs, avoidance of high-risk areas and wearing protective clothing. Drug treatment for Chagas' disease is not very effective and the outlook is often poor, although some forms of the disease are more severe than others. The African forms of the disease also vary in their severity and drugs are more effective in the early stages.

Causes and risk factors: the cause of the symptoms is the multiplication of the parasites in blood vessels and lymph glands. Eventually, the parasites reach the brain, producing the severe symptoms of sleeping sickness. Anyone travelling to an area where sleeping sickness is known to occur should seek advice on how to avoid the possibility of a bite, and take sensible precautions. Visitors are generally at a low risk of acquiring sleeping sickness.

slipped disc *see* PROLAPSED INTERVERTEBRAL DISC

small intestine tumours

Description: any abnormal growth of cells in a part of the small intestine. The great majority of these growths are benign.

Persons most commonly affected: adults of both sexes.

Organ or part of body involved: small intestine.

Symptoms and indications: there may be few or no symptoms but those that occur include bleeding, with the occurrence of black stools, fatigue, loss of weight and paleness. There may be partial or complete obstruction of the bowel, with symptoms of pains, vomiting and fever. A person with symptoms of a tumour in the small intestine should seek immediate medical advice.

Treatment: depends upon the site and nature of the tumour but usually involves admittance to hospital for destruction of the tumour by heat, electric current, laser beam or surgical removal, or resection of a portion of the small intestine. Treatment of benign tumours is usually successful but malignant ones can spread to other organs.

Causes and risk factors: the cause of these tumours is unknown but the risk of developing them increases with certain diseases e.g. CROHN'S DISEASE.

spinal cord tumour

Description: an abnormal growth of cells that compresses the spinal cord or the nerve roots that arise from it. The tumour may be malignant or nonmalignant. If malignant, it may be either primary (rare) or, quite commonly, be a secondary growth arising from a malignancy elsewhere in the body e.g. cancer of the breast or lung.

Persons most commonly affected: adults of all age groups and both sexes but can occur in children.

Organ or part of body involved: part of the spinal cord and associated nerves.

Symptoms and indications: symptoms include pain in the back, numbness, weakness and wasting of the muscles supplied by nerves affected by the tumour. There may be a loss of sensation in areas of the body below the level of the tumour. The nerve supply to the sphincter muscles that control the bowel and bladder may be affected and there may be incontinence. The symptoms vary considerably in their severity, depending upon the site and nature of the tumour. A person with symptoms of a spinal cord tumour should seek medical advice.

Treatment: depends upon the site and nature of the tumour. It may involve admittance to hospital for surgery to remove the tumour and/or bone to relieve pressure on the spinal cord. Drugs that may be prescribed include pain relief and corticosteroids to reduce swelling.

Causes and risk factors: the cause of primary tumours is unknown but secondary malignant growths arise as a result of a number of different types of cancer.

spondylosis

Description: degeneration of the intervertebral discs (fibrous discs of cartilage that connect adjacent vertebrae) and joints of the spine. It is characterised by pain in the neck and lumbar region, where the movement may become restricted.

Persons most commonly affected: middle-aged and older adults of both sexes.
Organ or part of body involved: intervertebral discs and joints of the spine.
Symptoms and indications: pain in the neck, lower back, leg and, possibly, the arm. There may be muscle weakness and difficulty in movement if the spinal cord becomes compressed. A person with symptoms of spondylosis should seek medical advice.
Treatment: is by means of physiotherapy, including the wearing of a neck collar, support belt in the lumbar region of the spine and traction. Also, pain-relieving drugs, muscle relaxants and anti-inflammatory preparations may be prescribed. Occasionally, admittance to hospital for surgery to relieve pressure on nerves may be needed.
Causes and risk factors: there is a degeneration of the discs along with the formation of osteophytes (bony projections), so that the space occupied by the discs is reduced. There appears to be a tendency for these changes to occur due to the process of ageing. The symptoms can be relieved, although the degenerative processes cannot be halted.

sporotrichosis

Description: a fungal infection of the skin and lymph nodes, characterised by the presence of abscesses and ulcers.
Persons most commonly affected: adults of both sexes, especially those working with plants and soil.
Organ or part of body involved: skin, superficial lymph channels and nodes. Rarely, it affects the lungs and some deeper tissues, such as the synovial membranes that line the joints.
Symptoms and indications: a small nodule appears under the skin, which can be moved and is not painful. This gradually increases in size and finally becomes pink and ulcerates. After a period of days or weeks, other nodules appear under the skin, following the course of a lymph channel, and these usually appear on the hand or arm. Rarely, if the fungus is inhaled, symptoms of PNEUMONIA may result. If the fungus spreads to other tissues within the body, particularly the bones, joints and their membranes and rarely, other organs, more serious life-threatening symptoms can occur. A person with symptoms of sporotrichosis should seek medical advice.
Treatment: is by means of saturated potassium iodide solution that is usually taken diluted in drinks. Some persons may experience an allergic reaction (iodism) with skin rashes, respiratory symptoms (e.g. BRONCHITIS and LARYNGITIS) or CONJUNCTIVITIS. For a person

with the rare systemic form of the infection, admittance to hospital for treatment with antifungal drugs such as amphotericin B, given intravenously as needed.
Causes and risk factors: the cause is a fungus named *Sporothrix schenckii*, which is found especially associated with sphagnum moss, mulches, barberry bushes and rose bushes. Those most at risk are gardeners and horticultural and farm workers.

sprue or psilosis
Description: this is essentially a composite deficiency disease due to poor absorption of food substances. Primarily, it is a metabolic disorder in which the person is unable to absorb fats, carbohydrates, minerals and vitamins. It was once considered to be a disease of tropical climates (tropical sprue) but versions of it (nontropical sprue and COELIAC DISEASE) have been recognised in temperate countries.
Persons most commonly affected: all age groups and both sexes. Tropical sprue is more common in adults, especially women, and is usually seen in Europeans after a prolonged period of residence in a tropical country.
Organ or part of body involved: gastrointestinal tract, blood, tongue – whole body symptoms.
Symptoms and indications: symptoms include a loss of appetite and weight, diarrhoea and the production of frothy, pale, fatty stools, red, inflamed sore tongue, swallowing difficulty and the development of severe ANAEMIA. A person with symptoms of sprue should seek medical advice.
Treatment: for tropical sprue, consists of bed rest and a high-protein diet, as the person is able to tolerate protein more readily than other food substances. Vitamin supplements, especially vitamin B complex and A and D, are usually required, along with folic acid, to combat anaemia. Nontropical sprue is treated by eating a strict gluten-free diet and also with vitamin, mineral and folic acid supplements, if these are needed.
Causes and risk factors: the cause of these diseases is an inability to absorb certain food substances from the small intestine. In the case of COELIAC DISEASE and nontropical sprue, there is an intolerance to gluten, a wheat protein, which causes the symptoms. In adults, symptoms may be triggered by some other illness or surgery. Tropical sprue is an acquired disease resulting in an inability to absorb many different food substances. It is thought that it may be triggered by gastrointestinal infection, food toxins, vitamin or mineral deficiency or infestation by parasites. There is a risk of death for those severely affected by these diseases, especially if the condi-

tion is not recognised early enough. Some patients fail to respond to treatment or develop life-threatening complications.

squamous cell carcinoma *see* SKIN CANCER

Still's disease or **juvenile rheumatoid arthritis**
Description: a chronic ARTHRITIS affecting children, which may involve several joints in a symmetric fashion.
Persons most commonly affected: children of both sexes under the age of 16 years. Usual age is between two and five years.
Organ or part of body involved: joints and sometimes the blood, glands, eyes, membranes.
Symptoms and indications: symptoms may occur gradually or develop rapidly. They include pain and inflammation in both small and large joints. Often this begins in the fingers and then spreads to other joints in a characteristic symmetrical fashion, usually the wrists, elbows, knees and ankles. Sometimes only one joint is involved. Accompanying the arthritis there may be fever, a characteristic skin rash, eye inflammation, blood changes (an increase in the number of white blood cells), and an enlargement of the spleen and other glands. If the spine is involved there may be a stiff neck and there is muscle wastage, retardation of growth and a receded chin. Some children show the symptoms of rash and fever, etc, before any arthritis develops. A child with symptoms of Still's disease should be seen by a doctor.
Treatment: includes bed rest and the use of certain drugs such as aspirin and, possibly, other non-steroidal anti-inflammatory agents. Gold salts may also be prescribed and, in general, treatment methods are the same as for adults. The outlook in children is usually much better than in adults, and three quarters of those affected experience a total remission of symptoms. However, there is a tendency for relapses to occur and the condition may persist for some years.
Causes and risk factors: the cause is not known but some children go on to develop ANKYLOSING SPONDYLITIS.

stomach cancer
Description: a proliferation of malignant cells in the stomach.
Persons most commonly affected: adults of both sexes from age 40 onwards but more common in men. In general, more common in people with blood group A.
Organ or part of body involved: stomach.
Symptoms and indications: early symptoms are those of indigestion, with discomfort or pain, nausea and vomiting, wind and a feeling of fullness. In the later stages there is poor appetite, loss of weight,

pain in the upper part of the abdomen, passage of black stools due to the presence of blood, and vomiting of blood. Sometimes a hard mass can be felt in the upper part of the abdomen. A person with symptoms of stomach cancer should seek medical advice.
Treatment: is by means of surgery to remove the tumour whenever this is possible and, possibly, chemotherapy and radiotherapy. The outlook varies considerably but treatment can relieve symptoms.
Causes and risk factors: the cause is not known but there is a greater risk with increasing age, excess consumption of alcohol, a family history of the disease and blood group A. In the later stages of gastric cancer there may be secondary growths in other organs with enlargement of the liver, retention of fluid (ascites), JAUNDICE, nodules in the skin and bone fractures.

stomach ulcer or gastric ulcer or peptic ulcer
Description: a broken inflamed portion of the lining or mucosal membrane of the stomach. The ulcer is usually small (about 15 to 25mm across) and is round or oval in shape. In most cases, the ulcer is situated near the point where the stomach opens into the duodenum (the first part of the small intestine) on the lower posterior wall. One or more ulcers may be present.
Persons most commonly affected: adults of both sexes in middle or older age, especially men.
Organ or part of body involved: stomach.
Symptoms and indications: symptoms may be quite vague or more definite and vary in their severity. They include pain felt either at the front or in the back, which may be more severe before a meal. Also, there may be nausea and a feeling of bloatedness after meals. Sometimes, instead of pain there is discomfort felt as a feeling of emptiness or hunger or of an aching nature. A person with symptoms of gastric ulcer should seek medical advice.
Treatment: diagnostic techniques include endoscopy, analysis of gastric secretions and X-ray studies using barium. Treatment is by means of a number of different drugs including antacids, carbenoxolone and histamine H2 receptor antagonists e.g. cimetidine, famotidine, rantidine and nisatidine. Most gastric ulcers respond fairly well to treatment, although there is a tendency for healing and relapse to occur. The person should eat a light diet and irritant foods or drinks should be avoided. These include spicy foods containing pepper, fatty foods, coffee and alcohol. The person should avoid smoking and stress. Complications can arise in the form of blockage of the stomach outlet (pylorus), due to the formation of scar tissue, perforation through to an adjacent space or organ (a medical emer-

gency) and haemorrhage (indicated by the vomiting of blood and passing black, tarry faeces containing blood). In the event of these arising, admittance to hospital for surgery to remove the ulcer and a part of the stomach may prove to be necessary. A person with symptoms of a gastric ulcer should seek medical advice.
Causes and risk factors: the exact cause is not known but is believed to be linked with changes in the mucous-membrane lining of the stomach, mucus secretion, and acid and pepsin (an enzyme) production. Some drugs, particularly aspirin and other non-steroidal anti-inflammatory drugs and corticosteroids, encourage the formation of an ulcer. The risk of developing a stomach ulcer increases with age whereas a duodenal ulcer may occur in younger adults.

stroke or apoplexy
Description: the physical effects, involving some form of paralysis, that result from damage to the brain due to an interruption in its blood supply. The effect in the brain is secondary and the cause lies in the heart or blood vessels and may be a thrombosis, embolus or haemorrhage. The severity of a stroke varies greatly from a temporary weakness in a limb, or tingling, to paralysis, coma and death.
Persons most commonly affected: elderly adults of both sexes although younger people may occasionally be affected.
Organ or part of body involved: brain.
Symptoms and indications: symptoms vary according to the nature and severity of damage to the brain and may be gradual or sudden in their onset. They include loss of control over movement, numbness or tingling on one side of the body, loss of speech, mental confusion and disturbance of vision, headache, loss of consciousness, with noisy breathing. The unconscious person may appear flushed and have a slow pulse rate, and the pupils of the eyes are unequally contracted. A person with symptoms of a stroke requires emergency medical treatment in hospital.
Treatment: is in the form of intensive nursing aimed at maintaining the person in as stable a state as possible. Some drugs might be given depending upon the nature of the stroke and the patient's condition. These include drugs to lower blood pressure, anticoagulants or heparin and nimodipine. Physiotherapy and exercises of paralysed limbs, etc, are usually begun as soon as possible. A severe stroke often proves fatal. Patients who survive are likely to suffer physical and possibly mental disability and require a great deal of continuing help, support and encouragement.
Causes and risk factors: the cause of stroke is usually ATHEROSCLE-

ROSIS, or hardening and narrowing of the arteries, which occurs with increasing age. This can result in a blockage of a small artery by a blood clot interrupting the blood flow to the brain (THROMBOSIS). Or, there may be an EMBOLISM in which a clot or plug is carried from the heart or an artery elsewhere, via the circulation to lodge in a vessel of the brain and cause blockage. Another cause of stroke is haemorrhage of a blood vessel within the brain, causing an escape of blood into the brain tissue. The blood vessels may already have become diseased and the leakage of blood may be due to rupture of an ANEURYSM. In a younger person who suffers a stroke, the cause is usually the rupture of an aneurysm (which has occurred due to some congenital weakness) leading to a SUBARACHNOID HAEMORRHAGE.

stye
Description: a bacterial infection and inflammation of the follicle (small sac) at the base of an eyelash, resulting in a painful, pus-filled abscess.
Persons most commonly affected: all age groups and both sexes.
Organ or part of body involved: eyelid of one eye.
Symptoms and indications: early symptoms are a red, shiny swelling on the edge of an eyelid, which is painful and tender. The 'head' of the stye usually develops around the base of the eyelash and more than one stye may develop. A person with symptoms of a stye should seek prompt medical treatment.
Treatment: is by means of hot compresses to encourage the stye to come to a head, removal of the eyelash so that pus can drain out and application of antibiotic eyedrops or ointment containing chloramphenicol. Care should be taken not to rub or touch the eye so as not to spread the infection. The infection usually clears up within about a week although there is a tendency for recurrence.
Causes and risk factors: the usual cause is a local infection with staphylococcus bacteria. Styes sometimes occur in people who are somewhat 'run-down' or with lowered resistance to infection. The person's general state of health may need attention.

subarachnoid haemorrhage
Description: bleeding into the subarachnoid space of the brain. (The subarachnoid space occurs between two of the membranes or meninges that cover the brain, the arachnoid and pia-mater membranes. The space usually contains cerebrospinal fluid.)
Persons most commonly affected: adults of both sexes between the ages of 25 and 50 but can affect people in any age group.

Organ or part of body involved: brain.
Symptoms and indications: symptoms include a sudden, very severe headache, nausea and vomiting, dizziness, fainting and coma. Sometimes the person may suffer fits and heartbeat and breathing rates are erratic. Within 24 hours, the person develops a stiff neck and certain other muscle and reflex responses (called Kernig's sign and Babinski's sign). During the first few days after the haemorrhage, the person continues to suffer from headache and confusion and has an elevated temperature. There may be paralysis on one side of the body (hemiplegia). A person with symptoms of a subarachnoid haemorrhage requires emergency medical treatment in hospital.
Treatment: following admittance to hospital, diagnostic tests and scans are carried out to determine the nature of the haemorrhage. Treatment is usually by means of surgery to stop the bleeding e.g. by clipping an ANEURYSM. The outlook is best in patients who are well enough to undergo surgery within the first 72 hours. A majority of patients survive a first subarachnoid haemorrhage but there is a risk of a second one occurring, especially within the first few weeks. Surgery reduces the risk of subsequent haemorrhage. Patients who recover may be left with residual brain damage. There may be some degree of paralysis or muscular weakness, difficulties with speech or mental confusion. Hence, recovery and rehabilitation are likely to take some time.
Causes and risk factors: the commonest cause of subarachnoid haemorrhage is accidental head injury. Other causes are rupture of an aneurysm, with ATHEROSCLEROSIS and high blood pressure being significant contributory factors. After a subarachnoid haemorrhage there is a risk of raised intracranial pressure and HYDROCEPHALUS.

subconjunctival haemorrhage

Description: bleeding under the conjunctiva (the lining of the eyelid and the white of the eye).
Persons most commonly affected: all ages and both sexes, but it is spontaneous usually only in the middle-aged or elderly.
Organ or part of body involved: conjunctiva.
Symptoms and indications: the white of the eye becomes partially or totally bright red.
Treatment: none. This condition disappears after a few days.
Causes and risk factors: it can result from inflammation or injury, but is usually spontaneous in the elderly, due to the blood vessels becoming fragile.

subdural haemorrhage and haematoma (acute and chronic)

Description: bleeding or haemorrhage that occurs into the space between the outer (dura mater) and middle (arachnoid mater) membranes that surround the brain, causing a collection or clot of blood, a haematoma. An acute subdural haematoma is a common occurrence following a serious head injury and occurs soon after the event. A chronic subdural haematoma may occur some weeks after a seemingly trivial head injury. The following relates to the chronic condition.

Persons most commonly affected: adults of both sexes aged over 50 years but can occur at any age.

Organ or part of body involved: brain.

Symptoms and indications: symptoms may not arise until some weeks after a relatively minor head injury. They include worsening headaches that occur each day, periods of drowsiness and confusion, muscular weakness on one side of the body. In babies, there may be an enlargement of the head if the haematoma is large. A person with symptoms of a subdural haematoma requires immediate emergency medical treatment.

Treatment: involves admittance to hospital where diagnostic tests and scans will first be carried out. Surgery is then needed to remove the clot and relieve the compression of the brain that is responsible for the symptoms. Once pressure is relieved, the brain may slowly recover or there may be some permanent damage. The outlook is best in those patients who receive prompt surgical intervention.

Causes and risk factors: the cause is previous trauma to the head that results in internal bleeding, even though the injury may appear to have been minor. The risk is greatest in older people or in those who abuse alcohol. There is a risk of death or permanent disability but other patients make a good recovery.

suffocation *see* ASPHYXIA

Sydenham's chorea (St Vitus' dance)

Description: a childhood disorder of the nervous system, which is characterised by involuntary, jerky, purposeless movements and which is associated with acute rheumatism. The disorder is self-limiting and symptoms disappear over a period of time leaving no residual ill effects. However, about one third of affected children develop rheumatism elsewhere in the body and this usually involves the heart.

Persons most commonly affected: children aged over five years, especially girls.

Organ or part of body involved: brain, central nervous system, muscles.

Symptoms and indications: the symptoms are jerky, involuntary movements that can involve any muscles but especially the face, shoulders and hips. The child contorts the face and intentional movements are poorly coordinated. The symptoms tend to start slightly and gradually increase, and usually last between three and eight months. Sometimes, the flailing movements of the limbs are so excessive that the child needs to be sedated. The movements do not occur when the child is asleep. The symptoms of chorea may not appear until up to six months after a rheumatic infection such as RHEUMATIC FEVER. About one-third of children also develop rheumatism, which commonly affects the heart and may cause problems in later life. If a child shows symptoms of chorea, medical advice should be sought.

Treatment: consists of rest and possibly giving mild sedatives if the uncontrolled movements are particularly violent. Reassurance for the child, family, school, etc, is especially important. The child should continue to lead a normal life as the symptoms subside over a period of time without any physical or intellectual impairment. If the child has rheumatic symptoms or if the heart is affected, the treatment is as for rheumatic fever.

Causes and risk factors: the cause is thought to be the same streptococcal bacteria responsible for rheumatic disorders but causing an autoimmune response involving the central nervous system. In temperate countries it is more common in the summer and early autumn months. This correlates with the peak incidence of rheumatic fever, in the spring and first part of the summer.

syphilis (acquired and congenital)

Description: acquired syphilis is a venereal disease caused by a bacterium that produces symptoms in three stages. If left untreated, the final stages may not appear for months or even years and the disease causes widespread damage throughout the body. Congenital syphilis is a much rarer form that is contracted by a developing foetus from the mother via the placenta. Symptoms begin to show a few weeks after birth.

Persons most commonly affected: congenital syphilis – newborn babies of both sexes; acquired form – persons of either sex who have had sexual contact with an infected person.

Organ or part of body involved: reproductive organs, central nervous system, skin and other organs.

Symptoms and indications: first, or primary stage, – bacteria enter the body through the mucous membranes of the genital organs, rectum or mouth. After a few days or weeks, a small ulcer develops at the site of infection. This may be inflamed, or painless and relatively insignificant, but is highly infectious, and is called the primary sore or chancre. Within a short time, the lymph nodes (at first those near the sore and then all over the body), enlarge and harden and this stage lasts for several weeks. The ulcer eventually heals and the swelling subsides. Secondary stage – secondary symptoms appear about two months after infection and include fever, pains, loss of appetite and a red rash that is usually noticed on the chest. The bacteria are found in enormous numbers in the spots of this rash and so this stage is also highly contagious. Third, or tertiary, stage (noninfectious) – the final stage may not appear until many months or years after infection, and symptoms are more likely to occur in untreated or inadequately treated people. In this stage numerous tumour-like masses, called gummas, form and may occur in the skin or within the muscles, bones, brain, spinal cord, heart, liver, stomach, etc. The serious damage that can be caused to tissues and organs may result in blindness, paralysis, tabes dorsalis (a disease of the nerves characterised by weakness of muscles, stabbing pains, unsteadiness in walking, incontinence, loss of vision) and mental disability. Also, there may be heart and artery disease and ANEURYSM. In congenital syphilis, the child is highly infectious and a few weeks after birth, develops second-stage symptoms of the disease.

Any person who suspects that he or she may have contracted syphilis should seek immediate medical advice.

Treatment: is preceded by diagnostic tests on blood serum or fluid from the sore. Treatment should begin as soon as possible after the infection has been acquired, and is necessary both for the person and his or her sexual partners. Courses of antibiotics are needed, mainly penicillin, unless the person is known to be allergic to this. The condition can usually be cured in a few weeks. The person should refrain from sexual intercourse until the infection has cleared, and should receive periodic check-ups for some time afterwards. Preventative measures include the use of condoms, and penicillin is the treatment for all stages of the disease.

Causes and risk factors: the cause of syphilis is the bacterium *Treponema pallidum*. Modern antibiotic treatment has greatly improved the outlook for people with syphilis but it remains a serious and life-threatening disease.

systemic lupus erythematosus (SLE)

Description: an inflammatory disease of connective tissues, believed to be an autoimmune disorder. It is generally a chronic disorder,

characterised by active and quiescent periods that may last for years.
Persons most commonly affected: younger women aged between 20 and 50 years (90%), although can affect males and other age groups.
Organ or part of body involved: connective tissue – whole body is affected.
Symptoms and indications: symptoms vary considerably with some people being more severely affected than others. They may arise abruptly or more gradually and include malaise, fever, arthritic and joint pains and a rash, especially on the face, neck, chest or arms. The rash is of a particular 'butterfly' pattern and there may be a reddening and mottling of the skin on the fingers, palms and hands. Mouth ulcers can develop and there can be increased sensitivity to light. The spleen and other organs may become enlarged. The kidneys may be affected with protein in the urine and inflammation that can prove fatal. Other serious symptoms of PULMONARY HYPERTENSION, inflammation of the pericardium (the membrane surrounding the heart) and PLEURISY can occur. Also, changes in the blood, haemolytic ANAEMIA and mental disorders can occur. A person with symptoms of this disorder should seek medical advice.
Treatment: it may take some time and a series of tests for diagnosis of systemic lupus erythematosus to be made. Treatment depends upon the severity and the nature of the disorder and is aimed at relief of symptoms. Various drugs may be prescribed, including non-steroidal anti-inflammatory agents, aspirin, antimalarial preparations, corticosteroids and immunosuppressives. Infections that arise should be promptly treated with antibiotics. This disorder cannot be cured but effective relief of symptoms can be achieved and the outlook for sufferers is improving.
Causes and risk factors: systemic lupus erythematosus is believed to be an autoimmune disorder, i.e. one in which the body fails to recognise the difference between 'self' and 'non-self'. The immune system attacks its own tissues, in this case connective tissue throughout the body.

T

tapeworms
Description: symptoms of illness caused by infestation with parasitic tapeworms. Several species of tapeworm can affect man and

some produce few symptoms whereas others may be responsible for serious illness.

Persons most commonly affected: all age groups and both sexes.

Organ or part of body involved: depends upon the type of tapeworm involved – gastrointestinal tract, muscles, brain, eyes, liver, lungs.

Symptoms and indications: (and route of infection) *Taenia saginata* – the beef tapeworm (many countries including Europe). People are infected by eating undercooked beef containing the larval stages of the parasite. The worm develops into an adult inside the intestine of the infected person. Many people experience few or no symptoms. Those that can occur include pains, hunger, weight loss, gastrointestinal upset and passing segments of the worm in the stools.

Taenia solium – the pork tapeworm (many countries including Europe). People are infected by eating undercooked pork containing the larval stages (cysts) of the parasite. The larvae of this tapeworm tend to migrate and form cysts in various body tissues. Cysts may form in organs such as the brain, causing serious symptoms resembling those of a BRAIN TUMOUR.

Echinococcus granulosus – dog tapeworm (sheep-rearing countries where dogs are used; Australia, New Zealand, South Africa, Middle East, Europe, USA). The disease produced is called hydatid disease. Human beings, often children, are infected by swallowing the eggs of the tapeworm, which are present in the faeces of dogs. An infected dog may pass the eggs to a person by licking or a child may pick up the eggs on the fingers while playing on ground that is contaminated. Inside the body, the parasite larvae are carried in the blood circulation and lodge in the liver, kidneys, lungs, brain or other organs. They form cysts, called hydatids, that gradually become larger and cause symptoms due to the pressure they exert. Symptoms vary according to the organ or tissue affected. There may be chest pain, cough and coughing up of blood if the lungs are affected, JAUNDICE and abdominal pain, if it is the liver, blindness and EPILEPSY if the brain. The cysts may rupture causing serious allergic responses including rash, fever or anaphylaxis.

Diphyllobothriasis – fish tapeworm (Europe, USA, Canada, Africa, Japan). People are infected by eating raw or undercooked fish. Symptoms are usually absent or mild but include gastrointestinal upset and, occasionally, severe ANAEMIA. Eggs can be seen in the stools.

Any person who has symptoms of tapeworm infestation should seek medical advice.

Treatment: in most cases is by means of drugs to kill and expel the parasite including niclosamide and praziquantel. For hydatid disease, treatment involves admittance to hospital for surgical removal of the cysts, if this is possible. Drugs, including mebendazole and albendazole, are also used in treatment, and relieve symptoms. Most tapeworm infestations can be successfully dealt with but others may cause lasting tissue and organ damage that can prove fatal. Preventative measures include vigilance when travelling abroad, in eating only meat or fish that has been verified as having been thoroughly cooked. Domestic animals and pets should be wormed regularly and strict standards of hygiene observed, especially to protect young children.

Causes and risk factors: the cause of symptoms are various types of tapeworm, as described above. Tapeworms pose a threat to human health in many countries of the world. (*See also* TOXOCARIASIS).

tendinitis

Description: inflammation of a tendon, which is a tough and inelastic white cord, composed of bundles of collagen fibres, that attaches a muscle to a bone. A tendon concentrates the pull of the muscle onto one point on the bone, and the length and thickness varies considerably. The fibres of a tendon pass into, and become continuous with, those of the bone it serves. Many tendons are enclosed in membrane (synovial membrane) – lined sheaths containing synovial fluid that reduces friction during movement.

Persons most commonly affected: young people and adults of both sexes.

Organ or part of body involved: tendons, joints. Tennis elbow is tendinitis of the tendon on the outer part of the elbow.

Symptoms and indications: pain and restriction of movement around a joint with heat and swelling. A person with symptoms of tendinitis should seek medical advice.

Treatment: consists of rest and, possibly, splinting of an affected joint, steroid injections and the taking of painkillers or non-steroidal anti-inflammatory drugs. The use of heat or ice packs may be helpful to relieve pain and inflammation. Preventative measures include avoiding stressing a tendon or joint, especially building up gradually when taking up a new sporting activity.

Causes and risk factors: the cause is often excessive or unaccustomed exercise, which places the tendon under stress. However, it may also result from an infection or as a complication of a rheumatic or connective tissue disorder. Care should be taken when engaged in sporting or other physical activities to avoid exposing a tendon or joint to unaccustomed or excessive stress.

testicular cancer

Description: a proliferation of malignant cells in a testicle. There are several different types of malignancy and some are more virulent than others.
Persons most commonly affected: adolescent youths and young men under the age of 30 years.
Organ or part of body involved: testicle.
Symptoms and indications: a firm mass or lump in the scrotum that gradually increases in size and is only rarely painful. Any person who finds such a lump should seek immediate medical advice.
Treatment: following diagnostic tests, treatment is by means of surgery to remove the affected testicle and, possibly, chemotherapy and radiotherapy. The outlook depends upon the type of malignancy and how soon it is detected and treated. Many forms of testicular cancer can be successfully treated, especially if detected early but this is the most common form of cancer in young men.
Causes and risk factors: the cause is unknown but young men with an undescended testicle (cryptorchidism) in infancy are at a greater risk of developing this malignancy. This appears to remain true, even when the testicle has been brought down by surgical operation at a young age. Preventative measures (as with breast cancer in women) involves self-examination of the testicles each month. If one testicle has to be removed, the remaining one is sufficient to maintain fertility and normal sexual function.

tetanus or lockjaw

Description: a very serious and sometimes fatal disease caused by bacteria that enter through a wound.
Persons most commonly affected: all age groups and both sexes.
Organ or part of body involved: motor nerves, spinal cord, muscles.
Symptoms and indications: symptoms usually appear about two or three weeks after the person has received a wound, often after this has healed. In the early stages, there is usually stiffening and rigidity of muscles near the site of the wound. Later, there is rigidity and spasm of muscles in other parts of the body, which cause extreme agony. Characteristically, the muscles of the face and jaw are affected. The person is unable to open the mouth and finds it very difficult to swallow. The spasms in the muscles of the face give a characteristic appearance, exposing the teeth, called risus sardonicus. The muscular seizures occur at the slightest stimulus and cause extreme agony. The muscles involved in breathing and respiration may be so severely affected that the person dies from ASPHYXIA and exhaustion. Frequently, there is accompanying high fever and profuse

sweating. The person experiences great anxiety, as the symptoms are painful and frightening.

A person with symptoms of tetanus requires immediate emergency medical treatment. Also, a person who receives a wound, especially while outdoors, or who has a wound contaminated with soil or manure, and who is unsure about his or her state of immunity, should seek medical advice. A person who has a wound requiring medical attention is usually given tetanus antitoxin as a precaution unless it is certain that immunisation is up to date.

Treatment: involves admittance to hospital and rest in bed in a quiet and darkened room. Tetanus antitoxin is given by means of injection, and muscle relaxants and sedatives may also be needed. Other antibiotics may be prescribed. The outcome depends upon the severity of the symptoms, the patient's age and state of immunity and how soon treatment begins. Tetanus can be successfully cured in most cases and the incidence of the disease and numbers of deaths have been greatly reduced by immunisation. Preventative measures, including routine immunisation of children, is by means of a course of three antitetanus injections with a booster every ten years.

Causes and risk factors: the cause is a bacterium with a characteristic shape called *Clostridium tetani*. It is found in soil, especially that which has been treated with manure, but also may occur in other circumstances. People engaged in any outdoor sporting activity, farming, gardening, forestry, etc, should take care to keep tetanus immunisations up to date.

thalassaemia or Cooley's anaemia

Description: an inherited form of severe ANAEMIA that affects people in Mediterranean, Middle Eastern and Far Eastern countries. There is an abnormality in the haemoglobin (the red blood pigment that carries oxygen) and it is especially common in Italy and Greece. Two forms of the disease occur, thalassaemia major, in which the defective gene is inherited from both parents, and which produces symptoms, and thalassaemia minor, in which the person has only one defective gene and is a carrier, but usually does not show any symptoms.

Persons most commonly affected: all age groups and both sexes.

Organ or part of body involved: blood.

Symptoms and indications: symptoms include malaise, fatigue, pallor, anaemia, blood in the urine, JAUNDICE, and there may be enlargement of the spleen. Ulcers may develop on the legs. A person with symptoms of thalassaemia should seek medical advice.

Treatment: is aimed at relief of symptoms as there is no known cure.

This takes the form of blood transfusions when symptoms are particularly severe and also the giving of analgesic drugs for the relief of pain. The disorders shorten life expectancy.

Causes and risk factors: the cause is an inherited genetic abnormality affecting the haemoglobin. Persons with a family history of thalassaemia or who may be at risk should seek genetic counselling before having children.

threadworms or **pinworms** or **seatworms** also called **enterobiasis** or **oxyuriasis**

Description: a common intestinal infestation by parasitic nematode worms, which affects people, especially children, throughout the world.

Persons most commonly affected: young children of both sexes but any age group can be affected.

Organ or part of body involved: large intestine, skin around the anus.

Symptoms and indications: there may be no symptoms but when they do occur the commonest indication is itching around the anus, especially at night. The child may scratch extensively and cause the skin to become irritated and inflamed. In girls, the worms may enter the vulva causing irritation and a discharge. Occasionally, the child may experience abdominal pains and a loss of appetite. Rarely, it is possible that the worms are responsible for APPENDICITIS. A parent who is concerned that a child may have threadworms should seek medical advice.

Treatment: is by means of drugs such as mebendazole and pyrantel pamoate. The whole family should be treated at the same time but, since the eggs of the worm can survive for about three weeks in the home environment, re-infestation is common.

Causes and risk factors: the cause is tiny nematode worms, only a few millimetres long. Female worms in an infested person migrate to the rectum and lay their eggs in the skin around the anus. If the child scratches, the eggs are transferred to the fingers and deposited on toys, etc, or find their way onto clothing, bedding, the toilet seat or other objects. The minute eggs are easily transferred to a new host and swallowed, and mature into adult worms in the large intestine. Eggs may float in the air and be inhaled and swallowed, and they remain viable for about three weeks outside the body of a host. It is very rare for these worms to cause harm and it is probable that many people have the infestation without realising that this is the case.

It is thought that the body somehow rids itself of the worms after a period of time, even without treatment, or they die out for reasons that are not known. It is advisable to maintain a high standard of hygiene, to encourage children to wash their hands and not to allow children to put their fingers in their mouths.

thrombocytopaenia

Description: a condition in which the quantity of platelets (disc-shaped cells involved in blood clotting) in the blood is reduced. Due to this, there is an increased tendency for bruising and bleeding to occur as the blood is less likely to clot. Thrombocytopaenia may be a symptom of an underlying disease or arise from a different cause.
Persons most commonly affected: all age groups and both sexes.
Organ or part of body involved: blood.
Symptoms and indications: irrespective of the cause, thrombocytopaenia generally produces a pattern of unexplained bleeding. There tends to be the appearance of petechiae, which are minute reddish or purple spots that appear like a rash. These are due to minute haemorrhages within the skin and often appear on the legs below knee level. Also, bleeding in the mouth, nosebleeds, vaginal bleeding and heavy bleeding following surgery may occur. Unexpected areas of bruising occur following very slight trauma, and gastrointestinal and urinary tract bleeding indicated by black stools and blood in the urine. The spleen may become enlarged if the bleeding is prolonged, symptoms of ANAEMIA may occur, such as pallor and fatigue. A person with symptoms of thrombocytopaenia should seek medical advice.
Treatment: depends upon the primary condition or disorder (*see causes and risk factors*), which must first be established. This is likely to require admittance to hospital for various diagnostic tests and the person may need transfusions of blood platelets given intravenously. The outcome depends upon the underlying cause but can be successfully treated in many cases.
Causes and risk factors: thrombocytopaenia may arise as a result of a failure in the production of platelets or from disorders that cause their destruction or increase their utilisation or dilution in the blood. Causes include SYSTEMIC LUPUS ERYTHEMATOSUS, CIRRHOSIS OF THE LIVER and enlarged spleen, excess consumption of alcohol, certain drugs, especially heparin but also antidiabetic drugs taken by mouth, quinidine, rifampicin, gold salts and some others. Also, surgery and blood transfusions, BLOOD POISONING, LEUKAEMIA, some forms of ANAEMIA, malignancy, some obstetric conditions and HIV infection.

thromboangitis obliterans *see* BUERGER'S DISEASE

thromboembolism

Description: the situation in which a blood clot (thrombus) forms in one part of the circulation, usually a vein in the leg (phlebothrombosis), and a portion breaks off and becomes lodged elsewhere, causing a total blockage (EMBOLISM). The embolism often involves the pulmonary artery (to the lung) or one of its branches, and this is known as a PULMONARY EMBOLISM.

Persons most commonly affected: adults of all age groups and both sexes.

Organ or part of body involved: arteries anywhere in the body.

Symptoms and indications: the symptoms depend upon the site of the embolism. In a limb or extremity, symptoms include numbness and tingling, pain and weakness and a weak pulse. In the brain there are symptoms of STROKE that vary in severity. In the kidneys, there are symptoms of KIDNEY FAILURE and high blood pressure. If the gastrointestinal tract is involved, there is severe pain, nausea and vomiting, and SHOCK may occur. (*See also* PULMONARY EMBOLISM.) A person with the symptoms of thromboembolism requires emergency medical treatment.

Treatment: involves admittance to hospital and, possibly, surgery to remove the clot or bypass a damaged artery. Drugs that may be prescribed include anticoagulants, aspirin and vasodilators to widen blood vessels. Many patients are prescribed anticoagulant drugs before and after planned surgery to lessen the risk of thromboembolism. The condition may prove fatal, depending upon the part of the body that is affected but in other cases it can be cured.

Causes and risk factors: the cause is a blood clot or part of a blood clot that forms in a vein and travels in the circulation to lodge in an artery. The risk increases with conditions such as HYPERTENSION (high blood pressure), ATHEROSCLEROSIS, increased age, DIABETES MELLITUS, surgery, injury to blood vessels, pregnancy, smoking, disorders of the circulatory system and a previous history of thromboembolism.

thrombophlebitis (superficial)

Description: inflammation of the wall of a vein, along with clot formation in the affected section of the vessel. It is very rare for these clots to break away and travel in the circulation to cause THROMBOEMBOLISM. *Compare* THROMBOSIS.

Persons most commonly affected: adults of both sexes, especially women.

Organ or part of body involved: superficial veins.

Symptoms and indications: the affected vein becomes hard and cord-

thrombosis

like with reddening heat and tenderness or localised pain. The person may become feverish. A person with symptoms of thrombophlebitis should seek medical advice.
Treatment: may involve surgical removal of the clot and the wearing of a firm elastic stocking. The person should move the legs as much as possible, especially when resting, and avoid crossing the legs or ankles. It may be helpful to rest with the legs raised. Non-steroidal anti-inflammatory drugs may be prescribed. Recovery is usually complete in about two weeks.
Causes and risk factors: causes include injury or trauma to the vein in which the lining membrane is damaged, an increased tendency for the blood to clot and a decrease in the rate of blood flow. The risk increases with VARICOSE VEINS, smoking and the use of oral contraceptives. A person who develops superficial thrombophlebitis should refrain from smoking and should not use contraceptive pills.

thrombosis (deep vein)
Description: the process of clotting within a vein so that the vessel becomes partially or completely blocked by the clot or thrombus. There is a risk of the clot breaking away and travelling to the lung to cause a PULMONARY EMBOLISM.
Persons most commonly affected: adults of both sexes.
Organ or part of body involved: veins, especially the deep veins of the calves (lower legs).
Symptoms and indications: symptoms include pain, swelling, tenderness, warmth, redness and the superficial veins may become enlarged and prominent. However, this condition can occur with few or no symptoms, as the lower legs are served by three main veins and thrombosis in one does not affect the functioning of the others. The person usually experiences pain on walking or standing still, which disappears when resting with the leg raised. A person with symptoms of deep vein thrombosis requires immediate medical treatment.
Treatment: the person usually needs to be admitted to hospital for tests, including venography (or phlebography), which produces X-ray images of veins using injected radio-opaque dye. Treatment is by means of anticoagulant drugs, usually heparin, given intravenously, followed by coumarin taken by mouth. The condition can usually be successfully treated, provided that pulmonary embolism does not occur. A person who has had this condition may be advised to wear elasticated stockings, to rest with the feet and lower legs raised, and to avoid sitting with the feet or legs crossed.
Causes and risk factors: the cause of deep vein thrombosis is probably a combination of factors, including damage to the lining of the

vein, a pooling of blood due to a decrease in the rate of flow and an increase in the clotting tendency. Risks increase with prolonged bed rest, as occurs after serious illness, injuries or surgery, immediately following childbirth, smoking, taking oral contraceptives and long journeys (especially by air), when a person is sitting for an extended period of time. A person who has to be confined to bed should try to move the legs as much as possible. People who are to undergo planned surgery are frequently given small doses of anticoagulants to lessen the risk of thrombosis.

thrush *see* CANDIDIASIS

thyroid gland tumour
Description: a benign or malignant growth of cells in the thyroid gland. The early stages of these tumours tend to produce similar symptoms.
Persons most commonly affected: all age groups and both sexes. There are various types of growth and some are more common in certain age groups than in others. Malignant forms are more common in females.
Organ or part of body involved: thyroid gland.
Symptoms and indications: generally, the person reports to his or her doctor with a painless lump or swelling in the neck. Some forms are painful and there may be difficulty in swallowing and symptoms of either hypo- or hyperthyroidism. A person with symptoms of a thyroid gland tumour should seek medical advice.
Treatment: usually requires admittance to hospital for specialist surgery to remove the lump and/or a part or the whole of the thyroid gland (thyroidectomy). Some malignant forms require removal of nearby lymph nodes and also treatment with radioactive iodine. The person may require antithyroid drugs or thyroid hormone replacements, depending upon the type of tumour and nature of the treatment. Most thyroid tumours, even malignant ones, can be successfully treated if detected early enough – one form (more common in elderly persons) is highly malignant and tends to have a fatal outcome.
Causes and risk factors: the cause is unknown but the risk increases with exposure to radiation of the chest, neck and head during childhood. In the past, radiation therapy was used to treat some fairly minor childhood complaints, such as tonsillitis, as well as more serious illnesses e.g. HODGKIN'S DISEASE. The thyroid gland was irradiated during this treatment. It is now known that this form of treatment, even though very small doses of radiation were involved,

tonsillitis

increased the risk of later development of a thyroid tumour. In the majority of cases, these tumours are benign.

tonsillitis
Description: inflammation of the tonsils caused by bacterial or viral infection. The term tonsils usually refers to two small masses of lymphoid tissue situated on either side at the back of the mouth (the palatine tonsils). However, another pair, situated below the tongue, are the lingual tonsils, while the adenoids are the pharyngeal tonsils, located at the back of the nose. All are part of the body's protective mechanism against infection and are larger during childhood.
Persons most commonly affected: children of both sexes after infancy and before puberty, but can affect other age groups.
Organ or part of body involved: tonsils, pharynx (throat).
Symptoms and indications: symptoms include a severe sore throat that makes swallowing very painful, accompanied by fever and earache, especially in children. The tonsils are usually swollen and white in appearance, due to infected material exuded from them, and lymph glands in the neck are enlarged. There is malaise and loss of appetite and, rarely, an abscess may develop on a tonsil. A person with symptoms of tonsillitis requires immediate medical treatment.
Treatment: complete bed rest is necessary and the person should drink as much fluid as possible. Tonsillitis is usually a bacterial infection and treatment is by means of antibiotics, especially penicillin or erythromycin, along with analgesics for pain relief. Recovery is usually good and complete within about one week or ten days. In some cases, a child may suffer recurrent bouts of tonsillitis, or the tonsils and adenoids may become permanently enlarged so that breathing is affected. If this occurs, surgery to remove the tonsils and adenoids may become necessary.
Causes and risk factors: tonsillitis is usually caused by streptococcal bacteria, although it can be viral in origin. In the past, tonsillitis often preceded RHEUMATIC FEVER or inflammation of the kidneys. Due to the advent of antibiotic drugs (and improvements in living conditions), this is now much less common in western countries. If an abscess develops on a tonsil, admittance to hospital for surgery is likely to be necessary.

tooth abscess
Description: a bacterial infection causing an abscess around the root of a tooth where it is embedded in the bone of the jaw.
Persons most commonly affected: all age groups and both sexes.

Organ or part of body involved: root of tooth and surrounding tissues of mouth and face.

Symptoms and indications: early symptoms include mild pain or toothache and sensitivity to hot and cold. Later the pain becomes severe, there is swelling at the base of the tooth and the face may become red and puffy on the affected side. There may be fever and malaise and the pain is usually of a throbbing nature. There is a loss of appetite, as chewing is painful. If the abscess bursts into the mouth, there is a foul taste and bad breath but other symptoms are relieved. A person with symptoms of a tooth abscess should seek immediate dental treatment.

Treatment: involves draining the abscess by means of a small incision into the gum or tooth canal. Often, a small wick or tube is inserted to allow the abscess to drain completely. Alternatively, the tooth may need to be extracted to allow the abscess to drain. Antibiotics and pain-relieving drugs may be prescribed and the person should refrain from eating on that side until healing is complete. Recovery is normally good and complete within a few days. Preventative measures include attention to dental hygiene, especially brushing the teeth thoroughly to help prevent decay. Also, regular dental check-ups are necessary so that any problems, especially signs of decay, can be dealt with at an early stage.

Causes and risk factors: the cause is usually a bacterial infection that spreads from the mouth to the base of a tooth. If the abscess occurs in the upper jaw there is a risk that it may rupture into a sinus, or infected material may spread in the bloodstream, causing infection elsewhere in the body.

torsion of a testis or testicle

Description: twisting or rotation of the spermatic cord and testicle, leading to irreversible damage if not treated promptly.

Persons most commonly affected: young adolescent males between the ages of 12 and 20 but can occur at any age.

Organ or part of body involved: testicle – usually only one is affected.

Symptoms and indications: the symptoms may arise for no apparent cause or as a result of strenuous physical activity. Symptoms include severe pain in the testicle, hardening, swelling and reddening of the scrotum, nausea and vomiting, fever and sweating, raised heartbeat rate. A person with these symptoms requires emergency treatment in hospital.

Treatment: is by means of surgery to correct the torsion and to attach the testicle to the wall of the scrotum to prevent a recurrence. Often, the unaffected testicle is similarly fixed at the same

toxic shock syndrome

time as a precaution. Provided that prompt surgical treatment is carried out, recovery is normally good.
Causes and risk factors: the cause is not known but is sometimes present at birth. If treatment is delayed, the blood supply to the testicle is interrupted, leading to irreversible damage. If this occurs, the testicle and spermatic cord are removed by surgery. The remaining testicle produces sufficient hormones to ensure sexual maturation and fertility.

toxic shock syndrome
Description: a state of acute shock, due to a form of blood poisoning, caused by toxins (poisons) produced by staphylococcal bacteria. The syndrome is generally associated with the use of tampons by women during menstruation, but it may arise for other reasons in males as well as females. It is a rare occurrence, whatever the cause.
Persons most commonly affected: females during menstruation but can affect people of both sexes and all age groups.
Organ or part of body involved: respiratory system, blood, organs.
Symptoms and indications: symptoms include a sudden high fever, diarrhoea, red skin rash, anxiety, headache, fall in blood pressure, mental changes, and confusion and thirst. A person with symptoms of toxic shock syndrome requires emergency medical treatment.
Treatment: involves admittance to hospital for intensive supportive nursing. The person requires high doses of antibiotics (especially penicillin and cephalosporin), fluids and electrolytes all given intravenously until symptoms subside. The condition can be cured if caught and treated early but may prove fatal in some cases.
Causes and risk factors: the cause is toxins released by staphylococcus bacteria into the blood circulation. The syndrome can arise as a result of an infection within the body or from a wound, as well as from the use of tampons. Women should wash their hands before and after the insertion of a tampon and change tampons frequently. It is thought that young women or girls in whom the immune system is not fully developed may be at greater risk, particularly if a tampon is left in place too long.

toxocariasis
Description: a disease caused by a parasitic infestation with the larvae of roundworms that normally infect the domestic dog (*Toxocara canis*) or cat (*Toxocara cati*). The parasites are passed to man by swallowing eggs that are deposited in the faeces of infected pets.
Persons most commonly affected: young children of both sexes but may occur in older persons also.

Organ or part of body involved: various body tissues and organs, including the eyes, liver, lungs, central nervous system, heart.

Symptoms and indications: there are a variety of symptoms, depending upon which tissues are affected and whether allergic reactions take place. They include eye lesions and uveitis (an inflammation of the uveal tract of the eye, the iris, choroid and ciliary body). This usually occurs as the only symptom when the infestation has been with just a few larvae. Also, there may be wheezing, cough, symptoms of PNEUMONIA and lung inflammation, enlargement of the liver and spleen, blood changes, skin rash, muscular pains, vomiting, convulsions and fever. A person with symptoms of toxocariasis should seek medical advice.

Treatment: if the eyes alone are affected, treatment is by means of corticosteroids alone. Drugs that are likely to be prescribed for other manifestations include mebendazole (vermox), prednisone and diethylcarbamazine. The activity of the parasites and course of the disease lasts for about 6 to 18 months, when the larvae die off and do not mature into adults. Hence, the outlook is generally good, although the lesions produced by the larvae may remain. Preventative measures include excluding dogs from children's play areas and regularly de-worming pets. Care should be taken to ensure that small children wash their hands after playing or handling pets, especially before eating.

Causes and risk factors: the cause of the disease, as indicated above, is the larvae of toxocara roundworms. After the eggs have been swallowed, the larvae hatch in the intestine and pass through the wall into the blood circulation. They disperse and lodge in other tissues and organs in the body and may cause considerable damage and allergic reactions. The body responds to the presence of the larvae by producing a form of scar tissue (called granulation tissue). In the eye, this leads to the formation of a small nodule or nodules called granuloma(s). It is thought that about 2% of people in the UK may be affected by this parasite, but many do not exhibit symptoms.

toxoplasmosis

Description: a disease caused by a protozoan organism known as *Toxoplasma*. The disease occurs in two ways, an acquired infection that is generally mild and a much more serious and often fatal congenital form passed from mother to baby during pregnancy.

Persons most commonly affected: all age groups and both sexes. The illness may be severe in AIDS patients or others with a suppressed immune system, and newborn babies.

toxoplasmosis

Organ or part of body involved: lymph nodes and vessels, muscles, central nervous system, eyes, liver, blood.

Symptoms and indications: in the case of acquired toxoplasmosis, often there are no symptoms. When they are present they include malaise, muscular pains, slight fever and enlargement of lymph nodes and glands. Also, liver and blood changes, ANAEMIA and low blood pressure may occur. These symptoms may be present for several weeks or longer and then subside and disappear. A chronic form of toxoplasmosis occurs that produces eye inflammation as its main symptom. Patients with a suppressed immune system (due to some other medical condition or illness) tend to have more severe symptoms, including chills, skin rash, high temperature, lung, heart, kidney or brain inflammation. Similarly, patients with AIDS may exhibit severe symptoms, especially encephalitis (inflammation of the brain), with headache, muscle weakness in one half of the body, tremor, visual and hearing disturbance, confusion and coma.

Congenital toxoplasmosis – symptoms vary from mild to extremely severe and may appear shortly after birth or be delayed until later in childhood. They include eye problems, loss of sight and hearing, mental retardation, HYDROCEPHALUS (water on the brain), convulsions, JAUNDICE, enlarged liver and spleen, inflammation of the lungs and heart and skin rashes. Toxoplasmosis may cause abortion or stillbirth and, in general, is more severe in those infected during the early stages of pregnancy.

A person with symptoms of toxoplasmosis should seek medical advice.

Treatment: for those with symptoms is by means of various drugs, especially sulphonamides and pyrimethamine, folinic acid and corticosteroids. The outlook is good for those with slight symptoms of the acquired disease, but is poor in immunosuppressed and AIDS patients, and in the severe congenital form. Children identified as having congenital toxoplasmosis require ongoing monitoring and treatment. Preventative measures are in the form of education. Pregnant women and those trying to conceive should avoid soil or cat litter contaminated with cat faeces, wash hands after handling raw meat or garden produce and eat only well-cooked meat.

Causes and risk factors: the cause is the protozoan organism *Toxoplasma gondii*, which is common throughout the world, affecting about 8% of human populations. The infection is transmitted by eating undercooked meat or through direct contact with soil contaminated by infected cat faeces. The organism undergoes sexual reproduction in cats, the eggs passing out in faeces. In other animals and birds, it reproduces asexually within the cells of its host. The host's immune system attacks the organism and renders it ineffective within a period of weeks or months. Hence, the disease is usually mild or produces no symptoms requiring blood tests for diagnosis, except in the more serious cases described above.

transient ischaemic attack (TIA)

Description: a temporary decrease in the normal supply of blood to a part of the brain. Usually the artery involved is partially blocked by a small plaque of material due to ATHEROSCLEROSIS, or a blood clot or embolus.

Persons most commonly affected: middle-aged and elderly adults of both sexes but can affect younger people and children with heart and circulatory disease.

Organ or part of body involved: one of the arteries supplying the brain, especially a branch of the carotid artery (in the neck) or the vertebral-basilar system of arteries.

Symptoms and indications: symptoms come on abruptly and last for two minutes to one or two hours (rarely longer). They include muscular weakness and numbness or tingling in the limbs, disturbance of vision or loss of sight in one eye, slurred speech or loss of the ability to speak, giddiness and confusion. The person remains conscious throughout the episode. Attacks tend to recur and vary in frequency from two or three each day to one or two over several years. A person with symptoms of a transient ischaemic attack should seek medical advice.

Treatment: depends, to a certain extent, upon the patient's condition and whether any underlying disorders are discovered or known to be present. The person is likely to be examined for high blood pressure (HYPERTENSION), DIABETES MELLITUS, and heart disease, and a blood sample may be taken to check for raised levels of fats (lipids) and polycythaemia (an abnormal increase in the number of red blood cells). If the attack is an isolated one or a rare occurrence, the person is usually treated with a small daily dose of aspirin. For more frequent attacks, anticoagulants such as heparin may be prescribed, or antiplatelet drugs. Some patients may require surgery to remove atherosclerotic deposits or plaques from a carotid artery. A person who experiences a transient ischaemic attack should have regular medical check-ups and monitoring.

Causes and risk factors: the cause of the condition is a partial temporary blockage of an artery supplying the brain by a fatty deposit, piece of arterial wall or blood clot. The risk increases in those who smoke, who are obese or who have high blood pressure, DIABETES

MELLITUS, high levels of cholesterol or other fats in the blood, ATHEROSCLEROSIS or polycythaemia. There is an increased risk of STROKE in those who have transient ischaemic attacks and treatment is aimed at preventing the occurrence of this serious condition. A stroke is probably more likely to occur in a person who does not receive treatment for a transient ischaemic attack.

trichinosis

Description: a parasitic infestation with larvae of nematode worms that normally live in a number of different mammals including pigs.
Persons most commonly affected: all age groups and both sexes except young babies.
Organ or part of body involved: gastrointestinal tract, blood, lymph vessels and glands, muscles.
Symptoms and indications: symptoms vary greatly in severity, depending upon the overall health of the person and number of parasites that invade the body. Many people experience no, or few, mild symptoms whereas in others they may be severe. The parasites enter the digestive system and, after a few days, the females burrow into the intestinal wall and produce larvae. There may be few gastrointestinal symptoms but if they do occur, they include pains, sickness, diarrhoea and loss of appetite. The larvae of the parasites are then spread throughout the tissues of the body. A characteristic symptom is swelling of the upper eyelids due to fluid retention (oedema), which occurs about 11 days after infection. There may be bleeding into the tissues of the eyes and beneath the tongue, sensitivity to light, muscular pains, high fever and profuse sweating, thirst and painful, irritated skin. The person is generally weak and experiences pain and difficulty in swallowing, chewing and speaking, these muscles often being greatly affected. There is an increase in the number of a certain type of white blood cells (eosinophils) in the blood (an immune response), which reach a peak and then gradually decline. Most symptoms gradually decline and disappear after about three months. The larvae of the parasites die, except in skeletal muscle where they encyst and may remain alive for several years. The person may be affected by muscular pains and fatigue for many months after the infection.

A person with symptoms of trichinosis should seek medical advice.
Treatment: is by means of drugs to kill the parasites, usually mebendazole or thiabendazole. Complete bed rest is necessary and analgesics, and corticosteroids (for those with allergic symptoms or where the heart or central nervous system is involved) may be necessary. Plenty of fluids should be drunk. The outlook is normally good

but is more serious in those who develop severe complications (*see causes and risk factors*). Most affected persons recover completely but some deaths have occurred. People with severe symptoms require admittance to hospital for intensive supportive care. Preventative measures are making sure that all pork meats and products are thoroughly cooked before being eaten.

Causes and risk factors: the cause of the infection is a species of nematode worm, *Trichinella spiralis*, which infests various mammals, including pigs. The larvae of the parasite encyst in muscle tissue and human beings are infected by eating poorly cooked pork, especially sausages. The disease is generally mild but a few people develop serious complications involving the heart, lungs and central nervous system. These include MENINGITIS, encephalitis (inflammation of the brain), myocarditis (inflammation of the heart muscle), pneumonitis (lung inflammation), PLEURISY, disorders of vision and hearing.

tuberculosis (TB)

Description: a group of infections caused by a bacterium (bacillus) of which pulmonary tuberculosis of the lungs (consumption or phthisis) is the best-known form. In the lungs, the infection causes the formation of a primary tubercle that spreads to lymph nodes to form the primary complex. Later, the bacteria may enter the lymph and blood system and spread throughout the body, setting up numerous tubercles in other tissues (miliary tuberculosis). The tubercles of tuberculosis are minute, nodular masses of tissue that gradually change and fuse together and destroy surrounding healthy tissue.

Persons most commonly affected: all age groups and both sexes.

Organ or part of body involved: lungs (usually) but may spread to other tissues and organs.

Symptoms and indications: there may be few or no symptoms in the early stages. X-ray examinations and post-mortem studies have revealed that many people are affected by tuberculosis (showing the presence of old calcified tubercles and scarring in the lungs) but recover without suspecting that they have the disease.

If symptoms develop at an early stage, they resemble those of INFLUENZA or upper respiratory tract infections. Later, more serious symptoms may develop, including fever and copious sweating (especially at night), wasting, with loss of appetite and weight, malaise and tiredness. A severe cough develops with a thick sputum often containing blood, there is chest pain and breathing difficulty and, in some cases, the production of discoloured, red, cloudy urine. A person with symptoms of tuberculosis requires immediate medical treatment.

Treatment: is by means of antituberculous drugs, especially ethambutol, rifampicin, isoniazid (INH) and streptomycin. The person should rest in bed until symptoms subside, and drink plenty of fluids. It is advisable to limit contact with other people as much as possible but it is now thought that the disease is likely to have been spread before diagnosis. An infected person is thought to become noninfectious after about two weeks of drug treatment. Treatment may need to continue for some months with periodic check-ups to make sure that the TB is inactive. Most people make a full and complete recovery but complications can arise, and the disease may prove fatal in those who do not receive treatment. Preventative measures in the UK are the BCG vaccination given to children and X-ray screening to detect carriers.

Causes and risk factors: the cause of the infection is a bacterium, the bacillus *Mycobacterium tuberculosis*. The route of infection, especially in developed countries, is almost always by inhalation of airborne droplets containing the bacteria from an infected person, resulting in the pulmonary form of the disease. The organism may also be acquired by eating contaminated meat or milk, as a form of the disease occurs in cattle. However, bovine tuberculosis is rigorously screened for, and controlled in developed countries, so this route of infection is rare.

A further rare route of infection is via a cut, the bacteria gaining direct access from an infected person or animal. Tuberculosis can affect almost any organ or tissue and serious complications can arise. One of the most severe is tuberculous meningitis, which particularly affects children and the elderly. Other serious complications can occur in the kidneys, peritoneum (PERITONITIS), pericardium (the smooth membrane surrounding the heart) causing inflammation, lymph nodes, bones and joints and Fallopian tubes. Persons most at risk are those with suppressed immunity or who are otherwise ill, and AIDS patients. Also, those living in poor and overcrowded living conditions, suffering from DIABETES MELLITUS, people who are alcoholics and, as with many diseases, young children and the elderly.

In some countries there are worrying signs of the emergence of drug-resistant forms of the disease and, worldwide, the incidence of tuberculosis is increasing. There are about 6000 new cases each year in England and Wales. Hence, there is a continuing need for vigilance and prompt treatment of this disease.

typhoid fever

Description: a severe infectious disease of the gastrointestinal tract that is caused by a bacterium. It is more likely to occur in conditions of poor water sanitation, where there is inadequate disposal of sewage. It is uncommon in developed countries.

Persons most commonly affected: all age groups and both sexes.

Organ or part of body involved: gastrointestinal tract, skin, sometimes the lungs, spleen, tongue, bones, central nervous system.

Symptoms and indications: symptoms vary considerably in their severity depending upon the number of organisms swallowed. Some persons are carriers who do not show signs of the illness and in others, a mild attack may be mistaken for GASTROENTERITIS. Early symptoms include malaise, headache, nosebleeds, joint pains, sore throat, abdominal aches and tenderness. If not treated, there is a rise in temperature, occurring in steps and known as a stepladder temperature. Changes in the appearance of the tongue, thirst, diarrhoea that may contain blood and a characteristic pink rash of 'rose spots' on the abdomen and chest (in some cases). When the fever is at its height, the person is weak and unable to rise and there may be a lowering of heartbeat rate. There may be enlargement of the spleen, disturbance of liver function, ANAEMIA, blood changes and protein in the urine. Usually, the symptoms gradually subside, but in some severe cases, there may be ulceration of the intestinal wall, which can lead to PERITONITIS if an ulcer bursts, or serious haemorrhage from the bowels. Other complications include PNEUMONIA, acute HEPATITIS, CHOLECYSTITIS, MENINGITIS, tissue abscesses, ENDOCARDITIS (inflammation of the endocardium, the fine membrane lining the heart, and heart valves and muscle) and kidney inflammation. These complications may prove fatal in some cases. A person with symptoms of typhoid fever requires medical treatment.

Treatment: may necessitate admittance to hospital if the illness is severe, and is by means of antibiotics and, possibly, fluids, salts and nutrition given intravenously. Antibiotics used include chloramphenicol, ampicillin, ceftriaxone and cefoperazone. Scrupulous attention to hygiene is needed to prevent the spread of infection, including treatment of faeces, and the person may need to be isolated. Clothing and bedding may need to be sterilised. The patient and those involved in nursing care must wash their hands frequently. Recovery is usually good, with prompt treatment, unless complications occur. The person should rest in bed and may take some time to recover completely. Follow-up tests are needed for some time to ensure that the person is clear of the infection and is not a carrier of the organism. A preventative measure against typhoid fever is available in the form of a vaccine that gives temporary immunity. Anyone travelling to an area or country where the disease is known to occur should be vaccinated.

Causes and risk factors: the cause of the illness is the bacterium *Salmonella typhi*. The infection is acquired by swallowing food or water contaminated by the organisms. Water may easily become contaminated where standards of sanitation and sewage disposal are poor. Food may be contaminated directly by an infected person or one who is a carrier. In countries where typhoid fever occurs, raw foods, such as salads, which may have been washed in contaminated water, should be avoided. Food eaten should be thoroughly cooked and eaten immediately, and all drinking water boiled or treated with sterilising tablets. Persons identified as carriers should not handle food and may also require treatment to eradicate the organism.

U

underactive thyroid gland *see* MYXOEDEMA

undulant fever *see* BRUCELLOSIS

urethra, stricture of

Description: a narrowing of the urethra, the narrow tube carrying urine from the bladder to the outside of the body. It is about 3.5cm long in women and 20cm in men. The stricture may be spasmodic, which is a temporary, reversible condition and is not serious or progressive, or chronic, which is more severe.

Persons most commonly affected: both sexes and all age groups.

Organ or part of body involved: urethra.

Symptoms and indications: the symptoms are those of urethritis (*see* NON-SPECIFIC URETHRITIS) including pain or burning feeling on urination, frequent need to urinate even though little is passed, and a discharge. As the urethra becomes progressively more narrow, there may be an occasional complete blockage, causing severe pain due to distension of the bladder from accumulated urine. As this is a progressive condition, there is a tendency for inflammation and infection of the bladder to occur and this may spread to involve the kidneys. A person with these symptoms should seek prompt medical advice.

Treatment: involves admittance to hospital for tests to establish the extent and position of the stricture. An operative procedure is usually required to widen the stricture, which may involve the passage of

special instruments called bougies or surgery. Follow-up procedures are usually required to ensure that the passage does not contract again. Antibiotics may be prescribed to fight off infection.
Causes and risk factors: the cause of the stricture is usually a previous injury or recurrent or chronic inflammation and infection. These lead to the formation of scar tissue that contracts and causes the narrowing of the urethra.

uterine cancer or cancer of the uterus
Description: a growth of malignant cells in the uterus or womb, which is a relatively common form of cancer in women.
Persons most commonly affected: older women past the menopause, especially those aged 50 to 60.
Organ or part of body involved: uterus (or womb).
Symptoms and indications: the main symptom is unusual, abnormal bleeding. In postmenopausal women this occurs after menstruation has ceased and may be preceded by a watery or mucus-containing discharge that may be streaked with blood. In premenopausal women, abnormal bleeding occurs that is not connected with menstruation. A woman with symptoms of abnormal vaginal bleeding should seek medical advice.
Treatment: involves admittance to hospital for surgery to remove the womb (hysterectomy) and also, usually, the ovaries and Fallopian tubes. Also, radiotherapy and treatment with progesterone (a hormone) may be necessary. With prompt treatment, the outlook is quite good for the majority of patients.
Causes and risk factors: the cause is unknown but the risk of developing cancer of the uterus increases with DIABETES MELLITUS, a family history of cancer of the breast or ovaries, menstrual cycles in which an egg is not released and there is no input of progesterone, and oestrogen therapy. Also, those who are overweight or who have high blood pressure (HYPERTENSION) or disorders of hormonal imbalance are at greater risk. There is a risk that the cancer will spread to set up secondary growths elsewhere (metastases), which are likely to be fatal.

V

vaginal cancer or cancer of the vagina
Description: uncontrolled growth of malignant cells in the vagina.
Persons most commonly affected: adult women aged between 45 and

vaginitis

65 but can occur at any age. One form (embryonal rhabdomyosarcomas) can affect babies and girls in childhood.

Organ or part of body involved: vagina; often spreads to rectum and bladder.

Symptoms and indications: symptoms include abnormal vaginal bleeding especially with sexual intercourse (which may be painful), or internal examination by a doctor. There may be a thin, watery discharge and, if the cancer spreads to the bladder or rectum, a frequent need to empty these organs accompanied by pain. A person with symptoms of vaginal cancer should seek medical advice.

Treatment: consists of admittance to hospital for surgery to remove the affected part and, possibly, hysterectomy and removal of lymph nodes in the pelvis. Radiotherapy, both external and internal (by means of implants of radium or caesium) is likely to be needed. The outlook varies, depending upon the extent of the cancer but symptoms can be relieved.

Causes and risk factors: in most cases, the cause is unknown but in children, the cancer is linked to exposure to oestrogen (diethylstilboestrol) taken by the mother during pregnancy. It is thought that exposure to human papilloma virus (HPV) may influence the development of other forms of this cancer. Risks increase in women with family members who developed cancer of the reproductive organs.

vaginitis

Description: inflammation and, frequently, infection of the vagina, often involving the vulva. Usually, the condition is accompanied by a vaginal discharge.

Persons most commonly affected: females of all age groups, depending upon cause.

Organ or part of body involved: vagina and vulva.

Symptoms and indications: symptoms include vaginal discharge that may be thick, discoloured (yellow or greenish) or white and can be foul-smelling. Also, itching of the skin or burning in the region of the vulva, reddening, discomfort and pain. Symptoms may vary in severity, depending upon the cause of the condition. A person with symptoms of vaginitis should seek medical advice.

Treatment: depends upon the cause, which is established by means of a physical examination and discussion, and may involve obtaining a swab so that infective organisms can be cultured. Treatment for inflammation without infection may be by means of soothing creams or anti-inflammatory preparations such as hydrocortisone. Bacterial infections are treated with appropriate antibiotics such as doxycycline erythromycin and metronidazole, which is also used for infections caused by the parasite *Trichomonas*. If the cause is *Candida* (*see* CANDIDIASIS), treatment is by means of miconazole or clotrimazole. In older, postmenopausal women, in whom the vaginitis may be atrophic (due to the thinning of tissues, with or without infection) the treatment is usually hormone replacement therapy with oestrogen. The condition can usually be successfully treated.

Causes and risk factors: include bacterial and fungal infections, infestation with a minute protozoan parasite, *Trichomonas vaginalis*, mechanical or chemical irritation, e.g. by tight clothing, use of deodorants, foam baths, body sprays and detergents, etc, or presence of a foreign body, and atrophic changes due to ageing. CANCER OF THE VAGINA may also be the cause. Various factors may make vaginitis more likely to occur, including general poor health, DIABETES MELLITUS, hot, humid conditions that favour infections, taking oral contraceptives and exposure to human papilloma virus.

varicella see chicken pox

varicose veins
Description: veins that have become stretched, distended and twisted. The superficial veins in the legs are often affected, although it may occur elsewhere.
Persons most commonly affected: adults of all age groups and both sexes.
Organ or part of body involved: veins.
Symptoms and indications: early symptoms include discomfort and aching legs after a prolonged period of standing still, and there may be cramp-like pains. Later, the veins become enlarged and visible as bluish cords beneath the skin. The feet and ankles may swell and the person may be unusually tired. Eczema and ulceration of the skin may occur. A person with symptoms of varicose veins should seek medical advice.
Treatment: in mild cases, the wearing of elasticated stockings provides effective treatment. More serious cases may require surgical removal of the affected vein (phlebectomy). Another form of treatment is sclerotherapy. An irritant substance, usually sodium tetradecyl sulphate, is injected into the vein, which causes fibrosis of the vein lining, with clot formation and scarring, leading to the obliteration of the vein. This treatment is usually very successful, with few side effects or complications. Varicose veins can be treated but new veins may become affected. Treatment is aimed at relief of symptoms and to improve appearance. If ulcers are present, they are treated with compresses and

vasovagal attack

dressings. Preventative measures include taking regular exercise to improve the flow of blood through the veins.

Causes and risk factors: the cause is distension and failure of the valves in the vein so that blood does not drain properly. This may occur due to congenital factors, obesity, pregnancy, THROMBOPHLEBITIS (inflammation of the wall of a vein, with secondary thrombosis in the affected part), and also prolonged standing. Varicose veins that develop during pregnancy usually go down after the birth of the child.

vasovagal attack

Description: intense activity in the vagus (the tenth cranial nerve, which supplies various organs and has motor sensory and secretory functions). This causes a slowing of the heartbeat and a fall in blood pressure, resulting in fainting (syncope).

Persons most commonly affected: all age groups and both sexes.

Organ or part of body involved: vagus nerve, heart, blood circulation, brain.

Symptoms and indications: the episode is preceded by a sudden unpleasant event. Symptoms include weakness, disturbance of vision, sweating, nausea followed by fainting. As there are many causes of fainting, it is usually advisable for a person who has experienced such an attack to be seen by a doctor.

Treatment: depends upon the cause of the fainting and overall condition of the patient. Usually, gently and slowly raising the person to a sitting position, along with reassurance, brings the episode to an end. Further treatment depends upon the nature of the patient's condition.

Causes and risk factors: there are various causes of a vasovagal attack, usually involving severe emotional shock, or sudden intense pain or fear. The attack normally involves a person who otherwise appears healthy. However, fainting may be a symptom of underlying disorders. It is advisable to seek medical advice.

verrucas *see* WARTS

W

warts or **verrucas**

Description: small, solid benign growths on the skin, caused by a virus, which are contagious and may spread rapidly from one person

to another. There are several types: plantar, on the foot; juvenile, in children, and venereal, on the genitals. Warts often disappear spontaneously but can be dealt with in various ways. In adults, flat parts may persist for years.
Persons most commonly affected: all age groups and both sexes.
Organ or part of body involved: skin.
Symptoms and indications: one or more small raised bumps, or they may be fairly flat, that occur on the skin. Colour varies, in adults flat warts may be dark brown. A person affected by warts or who notices any change in a wart should seek medical advice.
Treatment: depends upon the type and site of a wart; some may not require treatment unless they are troublesome or unsightly. Others disappear spontaneously after a period of time. Treatment that may be given includes painting or coating the wart with chemical cauterant solutions, and removal by cryosurgery (freezing), laser beam or electrocautery (burning away with an electrically heated wire or needle).
Causes and risk factors: the cause is a virus that infects the skin, the human papilloma virus. The infection may be acquired directly from contact with another person or from the floor of changing rooms e.g. public swimming pools.

Weil's disease *see* LEPTOSPIROSIS

whooping cough or **pertussis**
Description: an infectious disease of childhood, caused by a bacterium producing a characteristic cough and other respiratory symptoms. Due to immunisation, the incidence and severity of the disease is generally less severe than formerly.
Persons most commonly affected: children of both sexes aged under ten years but can occur in other age groups.
Organ or part of body involved: respiratory tract, lungs.
Symptoms and indications: the mucous membranes lining the air passages are affected and after a one, or two-week incubation period, fever, catarrh and a cough develop. The cough then becomes paroxysmal, with continual bouts lasting up to one minute. At the end of each bout the child draws in the breath with a characteristic whooping sound. Nosebleeds and vomiting may follow a bout of coughing, with diarrhoea and fever. After about two weeks the symptoms start to lessen, although the cough may persist for some time. Subsequent respiratory infections may produce a similar paroxysmal type of cough that is not a recurrence of whooping cough itself. A child with symptoms of whooping cough should receive medical attention.

Treatment: the child should be kept in bed, and isolated from others, while symptoms are at their height, and encouraged to drink plenty of fluids. Salt solutions may be needed if the child has been continually sick. In general, medication such as antibiotics are not recommended except for infants who are seriously ill or patients with complications. Treatment in hospital is necessary for those more seriously affected. Recovery normally takes about six weeks. Prevention is by means of vaccination given in infancy.

Causes and risk factors: the cause of whooping cough is a bacterium, *Bordetella pertussis*, and infection is by inhalation of airborne droplets coughed out by an infected person. Patients are not infectious after the paroxysmal stage. Whooping cough is serious in small children aged less than two years, and in elderly persons, but generally not so in other age groups unless complications arise. Infants may suffer from ASPHYXIA, bronchopneumonia and convulsions. Other serious complications include rupture of blood vessels in the brain (cerebral haemorrhage) or eye, and RETINAL DETACHMENT due to the violent coughing, TUBERCULOSIS and encephalitis (inflammation of the brain). Some children may sustain lung damage, leading to EMPHYSEMA or ASTHMA. Severe complications can result in death or permanent brain damage, but vaccination provides protection and should be given to all children (with rare exceptions).

Wilm's tumour or congenital nephroblastoma

Description: a malignant tumour of the kidney, which is present at birth and is usually diagnosed in children aged under five years. Symptoms may appear later in childhood or, rarely, in adults.

Persons most commonly affected: children of both sexes aged under five years.

Organ or part of body involved: kidney (normally only one).

Symptoms and indications: the usual symptom that is first noticed is an abdominal mass that can be felt through the skin. There may be fever, pain in the abdomen, blood in the urine, loss of appetite and weight, vomiting and nausea. Blood pressure may be high. A child with these symptoms requires immediate medical attention.

Treatment: involves admittance to hospital for tests and scans to confirm the diagnosis and evaluate the extent of the tumour. Treatment is by means of surgical removal of the diseased kidney, chemotherapy with anticancer drugs and, possibly, radiotherapy. The outlook depends upon the nature and extent of the tumour and whether it has spread, and the age of the child. Younger children usually have a more favourable prognosis and in some cases the condition can be cured.

Causes and risk factors: the cause is unknown but there is an association with some other congenital abnormalities. In rarer cases (about 4%) both kidneys may be affected. There is a risk of secondary growths occurring in other organs, which can cause death.

Wolf-Parkinson White syndrome
Description: a tachycardia (increased heartbeat rate) caused by abnormally fast electrical conduction in an accessory pathway. This links the atria and ventricles (the upper and lower chambers) of the heart while bypassing the normal pacemaker system.
Persons most commonly affected: all age groups and both sexes.
Organ or part of body involved: heart.
Symptoms and indications: the condition is a complex one but symptoms include chest pain, dizziness and temporary loss of consciousness. More serious symptoms of ATRIAL FIBRILLATION can occur. A person with any symptoms of heart abnormality requires immediate medical attention.
Treatment: involves admittance to hospital for tests and electrophysiological studies to determine the best course of treatment. Anti-arrhythmic drugs are used with extreme caution and, usually, a surgical procedure to correct the condition is required. This is a skilled procedure but one that produces excellent results.
Causes and risk factors: the cause is an abnormality in the electrical conducting system of the heart, involving accessory pathways.

Y

yaws or pian or framboesia
Description: an infectious bacterial disease of tropical countries, particularly occurring in the West Indies and Africa, and characterised by the appearance of small tumours on the skin. Similar infections occur in South America.
Persons most commonly affected: all age groups and both sexes.
Organ or part of body involved: skin, usually on the legs at first and then hands, feet, face, buttocks. Bones may be affected especially the tibia (leg) and nasal bone.
Symptoms and indications: the bacteria enter through cuts and abrasions on the skin, often the legs. Following an incubation period of two or more weeks, a lesion appears at the site of infection, which usually heals. This is followed by the eruption of more small tumours on the skin, each with a yellow crust of dried serum. During the incubation period the person suffers fever, pain, itching and general

malaise. The tumours may form painful deep ulcers if the condition remains untreated e.g. on the face and soles of the feet. Ultimately, possibly after several years, there may be deep lesions of the skin and bone, especially of the face and leg. A person with symptoms of yaws requires immediate medical treatment.
Treatment: is by means of penicillin, which works dramatically and effectively in this disease and also can be used as a preventative measure.
Causes and risk factors: the cause of this and similar diseases are species of spirochaete bacteria belonging to the genus *Treponema*. They are spread by direct bodily contact with an infected person or via contaminated clothing or bedding, usually in poor, unhygienic conditions. Anyone visiting or working in an area where yaws occurs should receive preventative treatment with benzathine penicillin.

yellow fever

Description: a severe viral infection, occurring in Africa and South America, that is transmitted to humans via the bite of mosquitoes.
Persons most commonly affected: all age groups and both sexes.
Organ or part of body involved: gastrointestinal tract, central nervous system, muscles, liver, kidneys.
Symptoms and indications: symptoms appear in stages and vary greatly in severity.

First stage: symptoms appear rapidly and include high fever, an initial rise in pulse rate and then this becomes slow, flushing of the face, bloodshot eyes and furring of the tongue. Also, vomiting, nausea and constipation, irritability, headache and muscle pains. The amount of urine passed decreases and it contains protein, indicating inflammation of the kidneys. In mild cases, these symptoms gradually subside and the person recovers.

Second stage: symptoms subside and the person feels better. This period of remission usually lasts from a few hours to a few days.

Third stage: characteristically there is the development of JAUNDICE (hence yellow fever), the bringing up of black vomit (containing blood), slow pulse (bradycardia) and fever. The person is extremely weak, urine production may cease and the urine contains protein, and there may be haemorrhages from mucous membranes. The person may suffer DELIRIUM, convulsions and coma, leading to death. The kidneys, liver and gastrointestinal tract are inflamed and undergo degenerative changes. A person with symptoms of yellow fever should seek medical advice.

Treatment: in mild cases, rest in bed and drinking plenty of fluids may be all that is necessary. It is thought that many cases go undiagnosed. In more severe cases, admittance to hospital for supportive nursing treatment is necessary, aimed at reducing the severity of symptoms. Preventative measures are by means of immunisation and control of mosquitoes. Vaccination is effective and gives protection for ten years. A person travelling to an area in which yellow fever occurs should be vaccinated. A person who recovers from an attack of yellow fever acquires natural immunity.

Causes and risk factors: the cause is a virus transmitted by the bite of *Aedes aegypti* mosquitoes, which acquire the organism from an infected person or monkey or ape. Wild primates act as a reservoir for the virus in areas where yellow fever occurs.